A QUEST FOR TRUTH

by

Stephen C. Kincheloe

authorHOUSE™
1663 Liberty Drive, Suite 200
Bloomington, Indiana 47403
(800) 839-8640
www.AuthorHouse.com

This book is a work of non-fiction. Unless otherwise noted, the author and the publisher make no explicit guarantees as to the accuracy of the information contained in this book and in some cases, names of people and places have been altered to protect their privacy.

First published by AuthorHouse 08/15/05

ISBN: 1-4208-3964-0 (sc)
ISBN: 1-4208-3963-2 (dj)

Library of Congress Control Number: 2005902647

Printed in the United States of America
Bloomington, Indiana

This book is printed on acid-free paper.

Cover Photograph taken by Bob Kincheloe.

There are no coincidences in life, only circumstances engineered or orchestrated by God.

Stephen C. Kincheloe

TABLE OF CONTENTS

INTRODUCTION

This book is the story of my own spiritual journey. God inspired me to write this book through the mouthpieces of six friends in the following chronological order: Debra Hand, Kim Heard, Debbie Davis, Lori Sullivan, David Kaseman, Rev. David Weber, and Alice Coker. Of these people, I owe the most to David Kaseman, for his mentorship and encouragement, and David Weber, for his encouragement and being the first to review the manuscript.

I didn't know what I would write a book about when my friends began encouraging me several years ago. But through their encouragement and God's inspiration, it began to crystalize in my brain that I should write a book on my quest for the Truth.

My goal is twofold. 1) to share with you my personal quest and what I have discovered, and 2) to encourage you to seek the Truth on your own volition. This book is for anyone who earnestly seeks the Truth.

My quest really began during my early 40s when a confluence of events unfolded that took the wind out of my sails. The death of a loved one, a 65 percent drop in income, an unsatisfactory part-time job to augment family income, and my wife working two jobs plus raising a family - all led to depression. However, out of the ashes of this depression came a burning desire to seek God. I was looking for comfort. I began reading the Bible for the first time, seeking answers. I attended my first Bible study class in September 1994, studying the book of Genesis. It was during this class that Diane Wells invited me to attend the Walk to Emmaus, a four-day Christian weekend. I was searching for something deeper spiritually.

In 1995, I attended the Walk to Emmaus where I met Jesus Christ for the first time. What followed in the next six months was a series of statistically remote circumstances that pointed inescapably to God's will for me to join Kairos Prison Ministry, an interdenominational ministry for inmates in medium- and maximum-security prisons. In the spring of 1996 I voluntarily entered a maximum-security prison in East Texas much to my astonishment, given that I had harbored a deep prejudice against prisoners for decades. It was here that I witnessed the unmatched power of Jesus Christ in transforming some of the most hardened men imaginable. What I have experienced in prison has had a profound, life-altering impact on my spiritual journey.

I began reading more and more faith-based books, many of which are referenced in this book. After considerable prayer, reading, and observing, I came to the conclusion that for me, Christianity most effectively expresses and encompasses God's will for humanity. The question for each of my readers is: What spiritual path empowers you to see and to know God's Truth?

We rely on ancestral traditions, the faith we were brought up in as a child. We study our own faith, seeking knowledge from religious leaders and reading holy books and other literature related to our faith (embedded theology). We pray to God, asking Him to help us know God more accurately. But I want to encourage you to go beyond relying on what you've been told in your formative years. I want to boldly challenge you to step beyond your comfort zone, wherever that step may lead you. My premise is that people, at some point in their lives, must come to grips with why they're here on this earth. They must come to grips with what they perceive as the Truth. No one can do that for you. Eventually you must go it alone, an endeavor between you and God. Does it take courage to embark on your quest for the Truth? Absolutely! What you may discover could fly in the face of thousands of years of ancestral traditions, rituals, and commandments. But ultimately what is more important: to rely blindly on the faith of your upbringing (embedded theology) or a more deliberative theology in which you are truly guided by all four realms of knowledge: scripture, tradition, experience, and reason. It is up to you, and you only to find out. It is of paramount importance, the most critical quest you'll ever make. Your eternal destiny depends on the results of your search, your decision, and ultimately your commitment to pursue the faith that you believe is the Truth, the faith that has the greatest probability of being the Truth. I can't tell you what the Truth is for your life - nobody can. It's your journey.

Once you've established with confidence what you believe the Truth is, then embrace it. Why? Because all faiths have many good things to offer and all of our faiths have common ground. If we all become the best we can be, with God's help, what a better world this would be. From the admirable commitment and discipline of devoted Muslims to the peaceful-loving Buddhists and Hindus; to the amazing Jewish ethnic group and faith, arguably the most talented ethnic group in history; to the love exemplified by the founder of Christianity, we can all benefit from growth in our respective faiths, and our increasing understanding of each other's faiths by studying other religions in our quest for the Truth. We shouldn't rely blindly on what we've been told all our lives, to the exclusion of knowledge of other faiths. By seeking the Truth through studying other faiths, perhaps from a good book on world religions or taking courses or even reading each faith's holy books and writings, or visiting with members of other faiths, we can all diminish our ignorance and enhance our relationships.

I would like to thank a handful of friends for the time they took to review this manuscript: Rev. David Weber, Dr. Bruce King, Dr. Fred Fifer, Rev. Sandy Copeland, Rev. Wallace Chappell, and Rev. J. Oliver Lee.

I thank God for inspiring me to write this book, Jesus for praying for me and with me, and the Holy Spirit for providing divine guidance, counsel, and encouragement. Last but not least, for the last shall be first, I also want to thank my family, my wife Susan Hagemeier for her encouragement, and my children, Oscar and Hope, for the sacrifices they made while I was writing this book. I would also like to thank my parents, Jim and Ida Lou Kincheloe, who provided a loving home. This book is dedicated to all my Kairos brothers and sisters.

Good luck, think well, and God bless you in your quest for the Truth.

Steve Kincheloe
Dallas, Texas
June 2005

It is not the critic who counts, not the man who points out how the strong man stumbles, or where the doer of deeds could have done better. The credit belongs to the man who is actually in the arena; whose face is marred by dust and sweat and blood; who strives valiantly; who errs and comes short again and again, because there is no effort without error and shortcoming; but who does actually strive to do the deeds; who knows the great enthusiasms, the great devotions; who spends himself in a worthy cause; who, at the best, knows in the end the triumph of high achievement; and, who, at the worst, if he fails, at least fails while daring greatly, so that his place shall never be with those cold and timid souls who know neither victory nor defeat.

Theodore Roosevelt, Speech, the Sorbonne,

Paris, France, April 23, 1910

With a good conscience our only sure reward, with history the final judge of our deeds, let us go forth to lead the land we love, asking His blessing and His help, but knowing that here on earth God's work must truly be our own.

John F. Kennedy, Inaugural Speech

Washington, D.C., January 20, 1961

1

> The men who live in a maximum-security prison are the least of the least.
>
> Hector Negron

GOING TO PRISON

I used to shock my wife years ago when I would make some outrageously judgmental statement. I used to crack jokes about the death penalty. My favorite was: "I don't believe in the electric chair. I believe in electric bleachers." I believed in maximizing sentences with no chance of parole and embraced a build-more-prisons-and-throw-away-the-key attitude. I had totally negative thoughts about prisoners during those rare times when I even thought about them. And here I was going into the arena, a maximum-security prison to share God's love; descending into the valley of the shadow of death, the very belly of the beast that I had railed against for decades; meeting men face to face that I had judged harshly as faceless statistics.

Yes, it was shocking to me when I first perceived God's call to go into Kairos Prison Ministry [see Appendix A in the Addenda for a description of this ministry] because I felt like Moses. My attitude was, "God, you've got to be kidding." I'm the least likely candidate to serve in prison ministry because I am so judgmental; there are many people much better qualified to serve in this ministry. But can you imagine the audacity of telling the Creator of the universe that He picked the wrong man? Still, to this day, I'm amazed at God's call.

It is Thursday, April 11, 1996 at approximately 2:30 P.M. when we leave St. Philip's Episcopal Church in downtown Palestine, Texas, heading southwest toward the Mark W. Michael Unit, a maximum-security prison in Tennessee Colony, approximately 18 miles from the church. Palestine is a small town, approximately 2½ hours southeast of Dallas. There are about 30 men traveling in vans and Suburbans.

After nearly three months of training and preparation, it dawns on me that this is it. I am finally going to prison. I have a nervous feeling in my gut. It isn't the same feeling as the butterflies I used to get before a high school baseball game. No, this is more of an apprehensive feeling deep inside the pit of my stomach. Up until the time I board the van, it is kind of academic to me. I haven't really focused on the abnormality of voluntarily entering a maximum-security prison. The only time I was concerned during training was when we went over the procedures to follow should a riot break out while we were inside the unit. That got my attention and I questioned my involvement.

As we travel to the Michael Unit, I am quiet and pensive, gazing out the window, contemplating the apparent absurdity of it all. I remind myself that I am here because God called me to this ministry and that I had placed my trust in God. I thought of my other free-world brothers and sisters accompanying me on this journey, and how I trusted them. But still I am scared. After all, it isn't normal to voluntarily enter a maximum-security prison. I remember being dumbfounded why God had chosen me for this ministry.

We arrive at the front gate at about 3:15 P.M. where we show our drivers licenses and receive visitor badges. We receive some last-minute instructions. Finally, after about 20 minutes, we are allowed to enter the prison. The thick metal door slides open and we enter a holding pen. The metal door clangs shut, making an unmistakably harsh sound. The metal door at the other side of the holding pen opens and we enter the front recreation yard area. Then the second door closes, locking tightly behind us. We are inside the prison. Now we are prisoners too.

As I gaze around, I see two parallel rows, roughly 30 feet apart, of 15-foot-tall, chain-link fences topped with 2-3 rows of razor-sharp wire and inverted, 5-strand barbed wire surrounding the unit. There are guard towers every 100-200 yards stocked with high-powered rifles, machine guns, handguns, and grenades. There are ground-level motion detectors strategically placed inside the perimeter of the inside fence. After about 100 yards, we enter the visitation building, where prisoners' families and friends can visit. We enter the second gate, where we turn in our drivers licenses and are processed in.

Again, the two heavy metal doors on each end of the holding area open separately to ensure that nobody can pass straight through. The noise of those doors shutting and locking is a very sobering sound. We walk past a small chapel out into an open-air corridor. The walkway is smooth concrete with chain-link fence on both sides and on the top, like an elongated cage at the zoo. There are solid yellow lines near each side, indicating where inmates are to walk in each direction. We walk past the four small cafeterias that are used to feed the 3,300 men in 15-minute shifts. And then we enter a gym where we will spend the next 40 hours over the next four days.

I see inmates playing basketball and handball in fenced-in recreation yards, and others standing around, just like in the movies. I feel extremely vulnerable and humble walking in this environment. My legs are weak and I ask myself again: what I have gotten myself into?

We enter the gym and the first inmate I make eye contact with scares the daylights out of me. He is not a big man but one with very harsh facial features. I immediately avert my gaze and stick by some free-world brothers, making nervous small talk. I look around and see several inmates standing in an oval, arms wrapped around each other's shoulders, heads bowed, looking like a football huddle. It is surreal. I don't know what these guys are doing; for all I know they are plotting to attack us. It isn't until later that I discover that these men are helpers who have been selected to serve the participants during the weekend and that they are praying for us and for the inmates selected to participate.

As I get to know the harsh-faced man, I realize what a gentle spirit he is. His name is Joe Rodriguez.[1] His harsh facial features belie a gentle lamb on the interior. Perhaps his harshness is a scar from the wounds of who he was, his upbringing and the violence that brought him to the Michael Unit. Many of the men who live in a maximum-security prison are there because of terrible crimes.

Joe died within three years from cancer. The last time I saw Joe was in the prison infirmary. A group of free-world brothers visited the prison hospice unit and we entered a room in which Joe was sitting next to a wall. As soon as he saw us, his face lit up, his eyes sparkled, but we could not understand anything he uttered because the cancer had robbed him of speech. We laid hands on Joe and prayed. We all hugged Joe and wished him the best. I found out later that Joe passed away a few months later.

The second inmate I make eye contact with is a man named Rufus Jones. Here is a man that has a glow about him and a beautiful smile. I walk over and introduce myself. Rufus is a musician, whose specialty is the alto and tenor saxophones. He plays his instruments during the weekend with the designated band comprised of prisoners and a few free-world brothers. Rufus and I have become good friends since we served together on that first team. I'll share more about Rufus later.

The 42 participants enter the gym around 4:00 P.M. and their names are announced. Each one is greeted by one of the free-world brothers. The men are then escorted to a section of the gym that has been partitioned with plastic tarps hanging from PVC pipe. We sit in two rows of chairs encircling this area of the gym. Stewards, those men selected to be helpers, begin serving fruit and homemade cookies. The men begin to get acquainted, sharing from a short question list. Each man introduces themselves to the entire assembly, receiving rapt attention and loud applause. This is a strong affirmation for each man, many of whom are not used to having anyone listening to them, much less offering applause.

The leader, Hector "The Rector" Negron, outlines some of the schedule for the weekend. There will be 11 major talks, all building on one another, interspersed with meals, songs, scripture readings, meditations on such topics as forgiveness and acceptance of others, and prayer time.

At about 7:45 P.M., the 42 inmates are dismissed, each with a bag of a dozen homemade cookies to take back to their cells. We stay and partition the basic concrete-block gym into three rooms - the community or conference room, the chapel, and the mess hall.

As we are leaving the prison around 8 P.M., it is dusk. Shadows are lengthening across the prison compound. I look at my fellow brothers in Christ as we walk from the visitation building to the front gate across the front recreation yard. I reflect on the incongruity of it all, the free-world brothers, representing many different cities, churches, denominations, ethnic and racial groups, occupations, educational backgrounds, and socioeconomic strata, voluntarily leaving their families for four days to spend time with some of the least of God's children. It doesn't make any sense, at least by world standards. But I know that each of us has been called in God's own special way to this particular ministry. We are trusting and obeying God. What we are doing this weekend is certainly not normal by world standards, but it is normal by the Kingdom's standards.

As we pull into the church parking lot in Palestine around 8:30 P.M., we are enthusiastically greeted, like sports or military heroes returning from some victorious conquest, by the singing, laughter and joyful banter of the outside team. The outside team, which prays and cooks for us during the weekend, forms a gauntlet on each side of an outside corridor leading to the church, hugging us, giving us exuberant high-fives, and singing Christian songs. We feel ten feet tall. Yet, the big heroes of this weekend are the members of the outside team, who toil virtually all weekend in obscurity, supporting all of us with their love, grace, and prayers.

The outside team for a men's maximum-security prison is normally comprised of 15-20 people, mainly ladies with a few men, reflecting the same denominational, occupational, and racial diversity as the inside team. The outside team cooks five meals for approximately 120 people in the prison (42 pilgrims, 25 stewards, 30-35 free-world team members, and officers, staff, and guests) during the weekend. The outside team also prays for us, including assigned prayer partners among the inmates. Members of St. Philip's Episcopal Church, our home base, prepare a wonderful meal for the entire team. We then have our team meeting, going over some of the highlights of the first afternoon and evening and discussing the game plan for the next day. About 10 P.M. we depart for our motel for an abbreviated night of sleep before rising at 4:45 A.M. for the first full day inside the unit.

It is Friday, April 12. Today is game day. We are pumped up. I'm not quite as nervous as yesterday. I'm eager to enter the prison. We arrive at the church for breakfast and a short meeting before departing for the prison at about 6:15 A.M. We arrive at the prison at 6:45 AM and enter the gym around 7:30 A.M. We have an approximate 12-hour day ahead of us. I've been assigned to the

Table Family of St. John where I'll serve as assistant table leader. I'll bond with six inmates (two blacks, two Latinos, and two whites with no two racial groups among the prisoners sitting next to one another) and two free-world brothers in the next 72 hours. The three free-world brothers at each of the seven tables named after one of the apostles are interspersed between every pair of prisoners. During the next three days, we'll listen to talks and meditations together. We'll make posters together of what talks meant to us. We'll eat meals together. We'll sing together. We'll pray together. Before the weekend is over, we'll even laugh together, form circles during songs either holding hands or with our hands wrapped around each other's shoulders, hug one another, and sometimes even shed tears together.

There are 11 talks, most of which are approximately 20 minutes each, given throughout the weekend. There are community prayers, scripture readings, meditations, breaks, singing, and meals interspersed throughout the day. The talks consist of basic information interspersed with poignant and sometimes painful personal testimony related to the talk. For a brief summary of those talks not discussed herein, please see Appendix B in the Addenda.

During my Kairos weekend John Bunyon and Marvin Schroeder are seated to each side of me. Marvin tells me the reason he signed up for Kairos was because he noticed a profound change in Rufus Jones after Rufus attended an earlier Kairos weekend. Marvin told me that he noticed a glow about Rufus. Marvin approached Rufus one day and stated: "Rufus, I don't know what you got, but whatever it is, I'd like to have some of it." Rufus made sure Marvin had an application by the end of the day.

The Kairos motto is "love, love, listen, listen." We try to concentrate on listening to the men, not only at the table, but throughout the entire weekend and beyond. These men are impressed because nobody listens to them in prison. Marvin told me how he was very close to his grandmother and how sad he felt when she died while he was incarcerated. The men don't get released to attend funerals of loved ones and so miss this important part of the grieving process.

One of the most powerful points during the Kairos weekend is the sharing of handwritten letters with each participant. I reiterated part of Marvin's story about his grandmother in my letter to him. After reading my letter on Saturday afternoon, Marvin stated, "You were really listening to me yesterday."

Listening is hard work, much harder than talking. It takes far more energy to listen. Listening is a form of love to the men in prison. It shows that you care about them as fellow children of God. John tells me that he is serving a 99-year sentence and that he was raised in an orphanage. Other inmates at my table include Charles Rodriguez, Manny Moreno, Earl Hutchinson, and Billy Anvil.

Lunch on Friday is the first meal served by the Kairos team. The meals are one of the highlights of the weekend. Indeed, the cookies and meals are one of the allures of attending this weekend for many of the participants. The outside team works hard to prepare the food. There is usually enough food for everyone to have one meal and all extra food is allocated to the 42 pilgrims. Approximately 25 stewards, Kairos brothers from the prison, serve the meals, clean the tables and do other leg work throughout the weekend. Enough food is prepared that the participants can usually have all they want. A very real problem is men getting sick from simply gorging themselves. Prison food is rather routine and bland. It is amazing to watch these men eat. They are starved for delicious food. Pound-for-pound, in terms of food consumption, I would stack these guys against the Dallas Cowboys offensive line. John Bunyon, after eating three helpings of green beans, remarked, "I haven't come across a stem yet and there's no grit or sand on these beans."

Speaking of green beans, Rev. David Weber likes to share, usually in an emotional voice, the moving story of "Jimmy and the Green Beans" from an earlier Kairos weekend. Jimmy Hogan loved green beans more than any food served during his Kairos weekend. He couldn't get enough, consuming as many servings as he could get. During a subsequent Kairos weekend, Jimmy was selected as a steward. David was also assigned to work with the stewards. During the meal in which green beans were served, Jimmy found himself serving up portions of green beans from the large containers (ice chests) onto the plates of the pilgrims. David stood nearby, fascinated at the sight of Jimmy serving his favorite dish to the new pilgrims. After a while, David moved over to Jimmy and gently whispered, "Jimmy, save a few of these beans for your own meal. You don't need to give them all out." But Jimmy kept dishing out the beans, with a big smile on his face, watching the pilgrims enjoying the green beans he loved so much. As the beans dwindled in the container, David soon realized that Jimmy was not going to get any of his favorite food. It began to dawn on David that he was witnessing a miracle, watching a man deny himself for the joy of giving away green beans that he loved so much. David's emotions got the best of him, as a lump formed in his throat and tears welled up in his eyes. He had to excuse himself to go to the bathroom to hide the tears now streaming down his face, knowing in his heart that Jimmy was now experiencing the deeper joy of giving rather than taking. Jimmy had become a new creation in Christ; the old was gone, the new had come.

I remember Paul Hoffer on Kairos #11 at his first meal staring in stunned disbelief at the food in front of him. Paul, without having eaten a single bite, remarked to no one in particular, "This is the finest meal I've had in the 4½ years I've been in prison." It is common to hear comments like that. We take food like this for granted in the free world. Another common remark is: "I haven't had a banana in seven years." During one of the meals we serve banana splits. I have seen tears trickling down some men's faces when they see their own banana split.

A powerful piece of tangible love during the meals are the placemats drawn by young children, usually with a simple message of God's love. Some of the placemats have the child's handprint outlined on the placemat; I have seen some mighty tough convicts place their large hands over the small imprint of a child's hand with tears welling up in their eyes. Many of the men will take care not to spill any food on the placemats, lovingly folding them up and taking them back to their cells when they are dismissed for the evening. They keep the placemats as sacred documents.

The food is transported from the church 18 miles away from the Michael Unit by two men who are designated "runners." Their job is to help load the food and supplies into a vehicle by a certain time to arrive at the back dock by the designated meal time. Of course, timing is sometimes erratic since they are completely at the mercy of the officers running the prison. But for the most part, the officers are glad that Kairos is involved at their unit. They often benefit from any extra food (especially cookies) that we give them.

The first talk after lunch Friday is entitled *The Church,* usually delivered by a lay person. The purpose of this talk is to present the Church in a positive fashion to counterbalance the often negative perception of church that residents of a penitentiary might have. The participants are informed that the Church is not a building, denomination, or creed. The Church consists of people because God wills community. This talk is known for the question that is repeated several times: "Who is the Church?" And the response is an increasingly resounding: "We are the Church!" Indeed, when we close the monthly Kairos reunions, we always form a large circle around the perimeter of the gym, holding hands and singing the chorus from *Surely the Presence of the Lord* three times (the first two times with our hands down at our sides and the third time with arms raised toward heaven). We then lower our clasped hands and begin to recite the Lord's Prayer in a hushed, reverent cadence with heads bowed. Then someone shatters the reverie with a piercing shout: "Who's the Church?" and the definitive response of "We are the Church!" is an affirmation of the men's sense of belonging.

Surely the Presence of the Lord[2]

Surely the presence of the Lord is in this place

I can feel His mighty power and His grace

I can hear the brush of angels' wings, I see glory on each face

Surely the presence of the Lord is in this place.

Truly as I gaze across the gym during the singing of this song, I see glory on each face. Each man is a precious child of God. The presence of the Holy Spirit is palpable. During the Lord's Prayer, I often get choked up because of how powerful it is to share it with over 100 men - black, white, Hispanics, and even a few Asians - deep inside the prison compound.

After dinner on Friday, the table families present the posters that they have worked on together, describing what the various talks meant to them. After each talk there is time provided for the table families to discuss the meaning of the talk and draw a poster reflecting the principal ideas or themes of the talk. The table leader's job is to encourage participation without any pressure. Sharing the posters with the larger group Friday evening is a fun time for most of the men. After every man introduces himself or gives a poster summary presentation, there is enthusiastic applause. It is interesting to watch the faces of some of the men light up as the applause washes over them. Most of these men have never been applauded before. This is the second time during the weekend that the men receive warm affirmation from the entire group as they receive applause or cheers from the rest of the participants, stewards, and free-world team.

On Friday night the men are given two bags of a dozen cookies each with instructions to share one bag with their friends in their cell block. The men are told to tell their friends that the cookies have been prayed over and blessed. Most of the men are starting to get sick of cookies by this time, and many are still stuffed from dinner. They are dismissed around 7:45 P.M.

When the men from each table family depart on Friday, after the first full day with the free-world brothers, they not only shake hands with their free-world brothers at their table but usually initiate hugs with us as an expression of their overwhelming gratitude. This is a major departure from normal prison behavior. Physical contact, such as a slap on the back or especially a hug, is a sign of aggression and can instigate deadly fighting. Most men don't touch each other in prison unless they want to fight. Most of these men can't remember the last time they received a hug. It is a major event during a Kairos weekend when this barrier is broken. Indeed, the Kairos ministry is known for its affectionate hugging. But as free-world team members we are never to initiate the process. We must be patient and let the Holy Spirit prompt each of the participants to desire this form of love. The unmatched power of love being transmitted through a simple hug is profound. It reminds me of Mother Teresa's philosophy of expressing love in this manner.

> Love is not patronizing and charity isn't about pity, it is about love. Charity and love are the same - with charity you give love, so don't just give money but reach out your hand instead. When I was in London, I went to see the homeless people where our sisters have a soup kitchen. One man, who was living in a cardboard box, held my hand and said, "It's been a long time since I felt the warmth of a human hand."[3]

The team departs for the church around 8 P.M. after preparing the conference room and chapel for Saturday morning's activities. Once again we arrive at the church where we are greeted enthusiastically by the outside team. We have a team meeting, going over highlights of the day and any special prayer concerns for the particularly hard cases. We pray for Gilberto Fernandez, one of the hardest cases to attend a Kairos weekend at the Michael Unit. Some stewards informed my friend David Kaseman that Gilberto was considered one of the seven or eight most dangerous men in the prison, a pistolero (hit man) for a Mexican gang. We also talk about the next day's activities. Our goal is to get back to the hotel quickly so we can complete our letters to the participants. Some of us, especially those sitting at table families and/or who have sponsored residents, must complete our final letters. Each team member commits to writing a letter to each participant (42); these letters are handwritten, not typed using a wordprocessor. It is a major commitment. Generally we are lucky to get to bed by 11-12 P.M. before rising at 4:45 A.M. or so.

It is Saturday, April 13. Each day, I have been told at team meetings, is better than the day before. Each talk builds on the previous talks. The meditations also build on each other, including the all-important series on forgiveness. Today is the day we are encouraged to go to the chapel as a table family to pray together. Again, no pressure is put on anybody to say their prayers out loud. Our first visit to the chapel is Saturday morning. All I can pray about is to ask God to forgive me for my harsh and judgmental attitude toward men like these. I am beginning to have compassion for these men, who for decades were merely faceless statistics that I despised. In some respects my heart is as hard as any of the men I am praying with. It wasn't until I went to prison that my heart was opened. Most of the men in a maximum-security prison come from broken homes; not dysfunctional homes, but flat-out broken homes - homes with only one parent or where there was some type of abuse or abuses inflicted on them as children. Although some kids can overcome terrible environments to be successful in life, the odds are stacked against them. Conversely, there are men in prison who come from good homes but who simply made poor choices. I thank God for allowing me to be born in a loving home and neighborhood. My heart begins to soften and expand with God's love toward these men, straining in some small way to remove the impediments and sludge that has blocked the flow of God's love for so many years. I desire to be a pure conduit or vessel of God's love poured out for some of the least of these children.

Every speaker, laity and clergy alike, generally weaves some personal testimony into their talk. Often the testimonies include deep struggles, sins, anguish, pain, tragedies, failures. By becoming vulnerable ourselves through sharing some of the most difficult and darkest circumstances we have faced in life, often accompanied by voices husky with emotion and eyes filled with tears, we give the participants permission to be vulnerable themselves. This is a major shift for the men behind bars who have built wall upon wall around their hearts to avoid the pain of life's tragedies and adversities. I have listened to many a free-world talk with trembling emotions of my own. I have been moved to tears by the painful testimony of participants at my table family and later during the weekend during open-microphone sessions in which the men can freely choose to share what is on their hearts. After hearing a series of talks laced with personal struggles against sin, a prisoner puts his arm around my shoulder as we are leaving the chapel and remarks, "You guys are just like we are." It was a revelation for the prisoner. No longer were we free-world team members being viewed as super Christians. I reply, "You're exactly right. All of us fall short of the glory of God. We've all done things we are ashamed of, and some of us, by sheer luck, avoided imprisonment because we just didn't get caught." We are all on level ground before God.

After lunch we spend some time in the chapel, singing songs and hearing meditations. During this time, the conference room is being prepared for the men to receive their sackfuls of letters that have been written for them by team members, fellow Kairos brothers, and outside Kairos supporters. Most of the men on a Kairos weekend are well aware of the cookies, fruit, and meals. They may know about a series of talks that will be given during the weekend and about the posters and singing. But the letters are generally a well-kept secret because of their incredible power in shattering the hardest of hearts. The tables in the conference rooms are cleared of all the songbooks, notepads, cookie plates, cups, and pencils. The only thing on the tables are the bags stuffed with letters and nearby Kleenex boxes. When all is ready, we proceed quietly from the chapel into the conference room. Those of us assigned to tables sit down briefly by our brothers before rising to return to the chapel where we sing for about 45 minutes, serenading the men with God's love songs, sung in soft voices, radiating love. A few free-world brothers stay behind with the men who are illiterate or who speak only Spanish to help them read their letters. A common reaction upon approaching the tables is a look of puzzlement about the bags and tissue boxes. But it is often not long after we begin serenading the men that muffled sobs and outright weeping are heard on the other side of the partition separating the chapel from the conference room as the men begin poring over their letters.

The 42 participants are like little children, delighting in the tender, loving embrace of their Heavenly Father. The men, with tears streaming down many of their faces, are opening themselves to God, seeking acceptance, love, and forgiveness. The joy of the realization that 75 people would take time to write them, expressing God's love, is simply overwhelming for the men. There is a powerful desire to be accepted by God and by others.

Of all the agape that we pour out on these men during a Kairos weekend, the letters are the most powerful weapon in softening their hearts. And of the letters, the most powerful are those written and illustrated by young children. I have witnessed time and time again the most hardened convicts reduced to tears by the letters created by little children, illustrated colorfully as only young children can do, often punctuated with blunt but totally honest messages of God's love.

William James wrote of such an experience in *The Varieties of Religious Experience*:

> The stone wall inside of him has fallen, the hardness in his heart has broken down. The rest of us can, I think, imagine this by recalling our state of feeling in those temporary "melting moods" into which either the trials of real life, or the theatre, or a novel sometimes throw us. Especially if we weep! For it is then as if our tears broke through an inveterate inner dam, and let all sorts of ancient peccancies and moral stagnancies drain away, leaving us now washed and soft of heart and open to every nobler leading.[4]

When we return to the conference room, most of the men have not had a chance to read all their letters. They will take them home that night and many will keep their letters, considering them sacred. We usually sing a few songs before taking a break and by this time of the weekend, each table family often forms a circle during the singing. The circle is usually formed by holding hands or wrapping arms around each other's shoulders. Billy Anvil doesn't complete our table family's circle since he continues to hold a letter in one hand while intently poring over it. He looks up one time with a huge smile on his face. We take our break and Billy continues to pore over his letters. David Weber approaches me and whispers in my ear as we gaze across the table at Billy: "You're watching a starving man eat." John Bunyon tells me Sunday morning that he saw Billy at 4 A.M. in a room with a solitary lightbulb reading his letters. I remember wondering when I was writing my 42 one-page letters to men I had never met if these letters would be worth the effort. Billy was God's answer to that concern.

During one of the Saturday afternoon breaks I am leaning up against the guard's office wall in the corner of the gym when Rufus Jones approaches me. Rufus smiles and puts one of his arms around my shoulder. With his other arm sweeping across the gym, he remarks: "Steve, take a look around this gym. This is just like heaven, and won't it be wonderful when it's like this all of the time." Rufus certainly wasn't talking about the physical realities of a maximum-security prison being misconstrued for heaven. What Rufus was talking about is unity, unconditional love, and acceptance. Never in my life have I experienced such unity, love, and acceptance. The men in that gym had widely varying backgrounds and ethnicity. There were blacks, whites, Hispanics. There were some from South and Central America and Mexico. There were mixed races. There were illiterates, high-school dropouts, and college graduates, some with advanced degrees. There were free-world men with professional occupations and blue-collar workers, employees, and entrepreneurs. There were laity and clergy. There were different denominations and non-denominations. There were Protestants and Catholics. There were a few atheists (at least at the beginning of the weekend), and probably every type of criminal imaginable. But none of that mattered anymore. All the distinctions and divisions melt away. Nobody cares what kind of house you live in or what kind of car you drive or how much money you make or what your job title is or how many possessions you have or what kind of clothes you wear [the free-world inside team always wear basic clothes such as jeans and non-insignia embroidered shirts with collars so as to prevent feelings of envy or inferiority among the inmates]. Nobody cares what your academic background is, your political views or your skin color or sexual orientation. None of these things matter. Nobody cares about anything except loving each other as fellow children of God. We are all one; one with each other and one with God. There is unity, joy, peace, love, acceptance. I know Rufus is right.

I begin to understand for the first time that the greatest thing about heaven won't be the beauty of it, but the unconditional love and acceptance among God's people and God's immeasurable, unconditional, and unceasing love for us. And to think I could experience a taste of the Kingdom deep inside a maximum-security prison among the least, the last, and the lost, remains an unfathomable mystery. If heaven can be experienced in a maximum-security prison - Satan's "playground" fomenting unparalleled racial hatred and poison of all sorts - it can be experienced anywhere. Truly the kingdom lies within each of us if we just invite God into our hearts and allow God's love to flow through us to our neighbors.

On Saturday after dinner, we have an open-microphone session in which the men can share briefly about their experience during the weekend. Monte Mason makes the memorable entreaty: "Gentlemen, take off your shoes for we are standing on holy ground." Gilberto Fernandez, considered one of the most dangerous men in the Michael Unit, a hit man for a Mexican gang, actually gets up and shares some thoughts. We watch the Holy Spirit softening this man's heart. Often the toughest cases don't share much at all during a Kairos weekend, but when they do it can be incredibly powerful.

Then the band breaks into some beautiful contemporary Christian songs and the atmosphere is one of warmth and love. The music performed during a Kairos weekend is another powerful tool in God's arsenal in breaking down barriers. Music is a universal language that can be enjoyed no matter what language differences exist. Music can touch a person like no other medium. The Kairos band at the Michael Unit generally consists of residents with an occasional free-world musician joining in. The band may be a combination of two or three guitars, drums, electronic keyboard, saxophone, and trombone.

After a few songs, the band breaks into a spirited and rousing rendition of that famous classic *When the Saints Go Marching In*, with Rufus going all out on his saxophone. For the first time ever at the Michael Unit on the Kairos #8 weekend, in what has subsequently become a cherished tradition, a couple of brothers from one of the tables stand up spontaneously and form a conga line. The idea spreads like wildfire as each table family, as well as stewards and free-world brothers working behind the scenes, join the irrepressible procession. Soon we have approximately 100 men meandering through the tables in a zig-zag fashion, spilling into the chapel and through the mess hall before arriving back in the conference room. The band, infused with the energy of a Titan rocket, pack more emotion into their music-making than ever before, realizing they are an integral part of a very special and unprecedented happening, and refusing to quit until they wear themselves out. Men are laughing, smiling, shouting, dancing and swaying, and slapping high-fives;

there are unrestrained tears of joy. An officer standing on the side of the gym has a look of stunned disbelief, having never witnessed anything remotely close to this in her career. A party has broken out like spontaneous combustion, and this officer no doubt is afraid of a riot erupting given the volatile powder-keg conditions endemic in most penitentiaries. Parties are few and far between in a maximum-security prison and this officer looks genuinely distressed at the boisterous and unabashed exuberance of the revelers. Some of the prisoners even begin shouting encouraging words, motioning for her to join the line but she refuses, trying to maintain some sense of professional detachment.

Psalm 149:1-5 captures the joy of singing and dancing in praising the Lord:

> Praise the Lord.
> Sing to the Lord a new song,
> his praise in the assembly of the saints.
> Let Israel rejoice in their Maker;
> let the people of Zion be glad in their King.
> Let them praise his name with dancing
> and make music to him with tambourine and harp.
> For the Lord takes delight in his people;
> he crowns he humble with salvation.
> Let the saints rejoice in this honor
> and sing for joy on their beds.

I have an epiphany during this dancing, singing, and rejoicing; this is truly God's Special Time. It is an amazing, truly incredible experience to be swept up in such indescribable joy. For a time, however brief, we are all children again in a home made for us, saturated with the goodness of God's love, basking in the glow of God's tender loving embrace. I envision God smiling from the heavenly throne at the sight of God's children having such fun. For a moment, our prison brothers are free, suspended in eternity, totally lost in the moment with no worries or anxieties, our cups overflowing with joy and peace and unity.

As adults we seem to lose that sense of play that is so natural to young children. Gazing across that gym, soaking in the scene of so many men experiencing pure joy, I think of young children at recess. What do you see during recess at a pre-school or elementary school? You don't see kids sitting around discussing what they learned that morning or what tests they have to take that afternoon. You don't see kids debating who has the best designer clothes, the fancier bike, or who lives in the biggest house. Indeed, you don't see kids sitting around much at all. You see kids running, skipping, jumping, sliding, climbing, hopping, playing tag, creating games. The kids are always a blur of motion. The children are totally immersed in the moment, living and loving life to the fullest, not dwelling on the past or worrying about the future. In short, the kids play and they are good at it. We can learn so much from our children if we just observe and listen to them. And so we, at the Michael Unit in that gray gym on that particular Saturday evening, for a bright shining moment at the summit of a mountaintop weekend, are transported back to our childhoods where we can be ourselves again lost in play, not caring what anybody thinks of us, with no worries or anxieties. We are truly free for a glorious interlude in an otherwise hellish institution. George Sheehan captured the essence of this special time in his book *Running & Being*:

> And in those moments there is a light and joy and understanding. For a time, however brief, there is no confusion. I seem to see the way things really are. I am in the Kingdom.[5]

But after play comes work. We can't remain on the mountaintop for long for there is work to be done in the valley. I am nervous, faced with my only talk of the weekend, the fourth and last meditation on forgiveness. When Hector Negron, leader of Kairos #8, assigned this meditation to me early in our training I wondered what I could possibly share with the men that would have any impact on them. Having come from a good home, I agonized for a few days about what I could possibly share with the men that could touch them. After a few days of wrestling with this dilemma and praying for guidance, it dawned on me that the only thing I could share was the most painful thing I had endured for the longest duration in my life; a tragedy that I had buried deep for decades because of shame, embarrassment, and humiliation.

2

> Forgiving is love's revolution against life's unfairness. When we forgive, we ignore the normal laws that strap us to the natural law of getting even and, by the alchemy of love, we release ourselves from our own painful pasts.
>
> Lewis Smedes

HEALING THROUGH FORGIVENESS

We are all imprisoned to varying degrees by our past hurts, especially if we hold someone unforgiven. My release from my past pain started with forgiveness. It was the beginning of healing. The following is what I shared with the men on Saturday evening regarding the deepest hurt of my life:

> "God is love, and our lives are intended to be a journey toward that perfect love. Life is a kind of proving ground in which our ability to love is tested and strengthened. As we move through our lives, God is constantly sending us people to love, but I find myself saying, "No thanks, Lord" to most of them. Yet if I don't want to be blinded by the brightness of God's love when I come to the end of my life, I need to begin learning how to say "yes" to God.
>
> "We are called to be Christ's body, to be a healing, forgiving community, to restore His broken and fragmented body. This means to forgive those who have hurt us and to ask forgiveness from those whom we have hurt, too.
>
> "It can be risky doing this. It requires becoming vulnerable to the other person, and when we become vulnerable we sometimes get hurt. But the person

whose closest friend is Jesus can't get hurt the way a person whose closest friend is himself.

"We need to learn to see people as God intends them to be, not as Satan has them now. God always sees us in the fullness, which is being brought about in us by the action of Jesus, through the Holy Spirit.

"Yesterday, you were told about the "Pearl of Great Price," the hidden treasure in the parable which Jesus told, and so you are. But, so is your enemy and so is my enemy. God loves the person I hate with the same love God has for me. I can't love the person I hate with my own resources, but when I forgive that person and pray for good for him or her and ask God to fill me with divine love and compassion for that person, Jesus can and does make it possible for me to love.

"My biological father, Jim Staples, and my mother, Ida Lou Hagg, were married September 22, 1951 and I was born July 8, 1952. When I was a year old and my mother was eight months pregnant with my brother Paul, my father left us in the summer of 1953, without ever seeing Paul born. My parents got divorced and my mother remarried a couple of years later to James Kincheloe. During the ensuing decades there was no contact whatsoever from Jim Staples: no phone calls, no letters, no birthday or Christmas cards, no presents, no visits, no nothing. As I grew older, I could not understand how anybody could just walk away from a one-year-old baby and a pregnant wife. It made no sense to me. I felt abandoned and rejected. As a teenager, my heart became so hardened with bitterness and acrimony that I vowed that I would never look this man up because I hated him and did not want to give him the satisfaction of rejecting me twice.

"So the years went by and when my brother Paul was 29 years old, in the fall of 1982, he contacted Jim, leaving a phone message for him indicating that they might be related. Jim returned Paul's call and they arranged a visit later in 1982. My mother was upset, still festering resentment and bitterness, and I was grateful to be living 2,000 miles away in Texas. I told Paul that it was his choice to establish contact with Jim, but I wanted nothing to do with him. Every once in awhile Paul and I would talk and he would tell me how Jim really loved us and that he had explained the rationale for his decision not to contact us. My heart remained hardened. About eight years later after Paul had contacted Jim, Susan, Oscar and I visited Oregon on vacation in August 1990. We were at Paul's house one afternoon for a few hours when the phone rang. It was Jim Staples and he wanted to talk to me. My initial reaction was resentment and suspicion - these guys have set me up. But then I decided to talk to him since he had called long distance and I did not want to be rude. It was awkward for the initial few minutes, talking to the man I had hated ever since I could remember, but then it got a little easier. We talked for maybe 5 to 10 minutes and arranged to meet a few days later at a neutral site in Sandy, Oregon, at the western base of the Cascade Mountains.

"We met in the parking lot of a restaurant known as the Frontier House. I remember him walking briskly across the parking lot with a grin on his face. My first comment to Jim was: "Long time, no see." But he was so excited to see me that he ignored the quip. Later we traveled to Timberline Lodge at the base of Mt. Hood, the tallest peak in Oregon, about 60 miles due east of Portland in the Cascades. During this time, Jim handed me a small colorful fuzzy puff ball that the nurses at St. Vincent Hospital in Portland,

Oregon had put on the zipper of my baby jumper suit. He had kept it in his desk drawer for 37 years as a daily reminder of his love for us. He explained why he chose not to contact us. He knew who my mother was marrying, James Kincheloe, because he had dated LaRae Kincheloe, Jim's sister. Jim Staples knew Jim Kincheloe's family background and never had any worries that we would be ill-treated and believed we would be loved and cared for by not only Jim Kincheloe but his parents as well. Jim Staples also knew our mother would be a very good mother to us. Jim told me he longed to see us but once the adoption was final by Jim and Ida Lou Kincheloe, he chose not to contact us out of a fear that it would lead to confusion for Paul and me. So Jim Staples, as much as he longed to see us, chose to deny himself out of love for us, believing his choice was in our best interest. My heart was beginning to soften after three decades of hardening, but I still wrestled with some doubt. Was Jim telling the truth?

"It was a year later in August 1991 when we agreed to visit Jim and Donna (his wife) at their home in Culver, Oregon, with three-year-old Oscar and seven-month-old Hope. We stayed for a couple of days, taking a trip to Mt. Bachelor in the central Oregon Cascades one day and Crater Lake National Park the next day. It was on the road to Crater Lake National Park with me driving Jim's car and Jim riding in the front seat with Susan, Paul and his wife in the back seat, when Jim began explaining why he chose the path he had taken regarding Paul and me. I was concentrating on driving and listening to Jim, again trying to discern if he was being honest. Then, all of a sudden, like a rifle shot piercing the tranquility of a soft mountain meadow high in the Cascades, Jim unleashed a question that stunned me.

"After nearly four decades of no contact, with Jim's heart aching for reconciliation, it had all boiled down to a simple, yet profound, inquiry. Jim turned to me, fixing his gaze on me as I concentrated on the road ahead, and asked, "Will you forgive me?" I quickly looked at him and saw the tenseness in his face. I immediately faced forward, mind racing, in a state of suspended animation. It was no longer five people hurtling down that highway on the eastern side of the Cascades. It was just Jim and me in that front seat as if in a tunnel, separated by a few feet with everything unfolding in slow motion. Here I was spending a couple of days with this man I had hated ever since I could remember, some three decades after I became cognizant of my family background, and now it had all come down to responding to one of the hardest things Jesus asks us to do - forgive those who have personally and unfairly hurt us deeply. I knew Jim had put it all on the line. He had risked great vulnerability. And now my mind raced with how to respond, trying to discern his genuineness, sincerity, and remorsefulness, not knowing fully if he was telling me the truth.

"During this very intense time, the only thing that popped into my mind was the middle of the Lord's Prayer: "Forgive us our trespasses as we forgive those who trespass against us," the one prayer that my grandmother Berniece Hagg had always shared with Paul and me while tucking us in at night when we were little boys. I thought to myself: "How can I not forgive this man when God in Christ has already forgiven me?" And so I turned and faced Jim and remarked: "Yes, I forgive you, Jim." The nervous tension burst like a balloon being popped and joy filled that car. Jim's countenance changed. His tense facial muscles melted into a big grin, radiating brightness. He relaxed as if a heavy burden had been lifted off his shoulders. And the healing began for me. All that poison stored in my heart for most of my life was now oozing away. I know that holding someone unforgiven is like consuming poison, hoping that it harms the other person you hate. The poison, however, only harms yourself. I discovered that forgiveness may not immediately erase all pain from the past, but it is when the healing begins, when God's miracle of forgiveness offers a new freedom and release from being held hostage by the pain of past hurts.

"So after nearly four decades of pain and hatred, poison and resentment, love has grown from the seeds of forgiveness. Our relationship has blossomed into a cherished friendship since that day in the car on the way to Crater Lake National Park. Something that I vowed would never happen, happened because of God's great love and desire for reconciliation and healing. God worked through Paul, whose heart was softer than mine, to eventually reconcile Jim and me. I had a small picture of the situation, hating Jim because I thought he hated us. Jim had a small picture too, staying away from us because he perceived it would be better for us to avoid confusion on who our father was. Jim's motive was love, but I never knew until we had been reconciled. Now as the father of two adopted children myself, my understanding has been reinforced about Jim's decision. But God has the big picture and it was God's will that we come together. It was God's desire that the pain and hatred be shattered and healing flourish through divine love. So I thank God for the miracle of forgiveness and for blessing me with reconciliation and love. One of my favorite Bible verses is from Ephesians 4:32:

> Be kind and compassionate to one another, forgiving each other, just as in Christ God forgave you.

Jim and I have been reconciled since 1991 just as we are reconciled to God through Christ Jesus. And it all started when God used Paul to initiate contact with Jim. God orchestrated the circumstances of that fateful phone call that arrived during those few hours we were visiting Paul. It wasn't until years later that Jim informed me that the phone call that day was not pre-arranged by him or Paul. Jim told me that he was in the habit of calling Paul about once a month and that just happened to be the time he called. So there is no doubt that the brief phone call from Jim during a rare short-term visit to Oregon, with an interlude of a few hours spent at Paul's house, was a miracle and a profound example of God's providential grace.

Prior to our visit in August 1990, the last time Jim had seen me was as an infant on the courthouse steps in Forest Grove, Oregon, following the divorce. In October 1955 Jim received the adoption papers for us from Jim Kincheloe and he didn't respond for two months, praying about making the right decision. Jim felt deep anguish; he felt all alone and it was so painful and personal that he didn't talk about it. Jim decided that the best thing he could do to promote unity in the family that Paul and I would be raised in was to stay out of the picture. He finally signed the adoption papers after two months of hell and prayed that if there was a God that someday Paul or I would contact him. Jim told me there was a popular song in the early 1950s that had the following line: "How much is that doggie in the window?" Jim hated that song because it reminded him of letting Paul and me go.

I ended my forgiveness meditation with the following comments:

> "I just want to ask you to pause for a moment, think about God's great love for us, and ask God again to give us the names of any person whom we hold unforgiven so that we may add their names to our own. . .

> "Please join me as I offer up my names. We will have a few minutes of silence after this prayer in which you can say what you wish to God as you offer up the names on your list.
>
> "Merciful and Almighty God, here are my names. . .the names which I believe you have brought to my mind. Lord, you know how I feel about these people, and some of that feeling is certainly not expressive of your love. I forgive them and pray for good for them, Father, and I ask you to forgive me for my unforgiveness of them. Fill me with your love and compassion for them. Remove any anger or resentment which I might have in my heart and heal our relationship. I ask this, Father, in Jesus' name. Amen."

The final act in Kairos on Saturday evening before the participants are dismissed, is known as the "Offering of Lists." This solemn ceremony is one of the most powerful during a Kairos weekend. Clergy lead us in offering up our lists of those people we hold unforgiven. This is a powerfully moving time for the inmates, who realize intuitively that forgiveness of others could entail harsh consequences in the prison environment. Many of the inmates pray before depositing their lists into the bucket or large metal bowl.

After everyone has a chance to deposit their lists, the clergy person speaks briefly about God's forgiveness, maybe says a few words about the use of the scapegoat in ancient Hebrew tradition and then asks God to forgive all present. After a time of prayer, the clergy person steps forward, removes one list from the bucket and lights it, and with it ignites the other lists in the bucket [this procedure is no longer allowed due to fire hazard]. This is a time when healing begins as some of these men unload more baggage than a fully-loaded Boeing 747. Many of these men are forgiving people they've held unforgiven for decades.

The pilgrims are then dismissed to return to their cells, but this evening they are given three bags of a dozen cookies: one for the themselves, one for their friends, and one for their worst or one of their worst enemies in the prison, to be given as an act of seeking forgiveness, reconciliation, and healing.

The team departs from the prison again around 8 P.M. for a team meeting and a deeply moving communion service back at our home church. The communion service is particularly special, coming when it does during our Kairos weekend and considering that ministers and priests from different denominations share in leading the service.

3

> Moses encountered God on Mount Sinai. Jesus encountered God, Moses, and Elijah on a mountain where he was transfigured. Kairos participants - free-world brothers and sisters and prisoners alike - encounter God during their mountaintop experience. As Hector Negron put it, "Nobody can go through a Kairos weekend and deny that they have been in the presence of Almighty God. Nobody can deny it."
>
> Steve Kincheloe

THE PINNACLE

It is Sunday, April 14, our final day of this glorious weekend. The residents are experiencing bittersweet emotions, knowing that this day will be the greatest of the weekend, yet dreading the hour when it is time to descend the mountain back into the valley of the shadow of death which is the harsh, hostile, and hellish environment of a volatile maximum-security penitentiary. We are all tired from the intensity of the weekend and lack of sleep. Yet we are excited to have one final crack at Satan on his home field in striving valiantly to win as many of these 42 men as we can for Jesus Christ. Our goal at the end of a Kairos weekend is for a final score of JESUS - 42, Satan - 0.

The first lay talk of the day is entitled *The Journey.* This talk reinforces earlier talks and introduces some new ideas. This talk discusses how choices affect our journey in life, not just physically but spiritually. The talk emphasizes the inward journey that we are all on, the fact that we enjoy being on the mountain but that God calls us to spend most of our time in the valley. The speaker discusses the challenges ahead including returning to the same environment in which old friends have not changed. They still live in the way of the world - based on power, possession, prestige, threats, competition, and falsehood. The key to overcoming this challenge, the speaker asserts, is to turn the leadership of our lives over to Jesus. Through a growing relationship with Jesus lived out in prayer, study, and fellowship with other disciples, we learn more about ourselves. The men learn about servanthood and are reminded again that they are the Church. We share The Servant Song with the men, both in singing and in reading at two different points in the talk.

The Servant Song

Won't you let me be your servant - Let me be as Christ to you

Pray that I may have the grace to let you be my servant, too.

We are pilgrims on a journey - we are travelers on the road

We are here to help each other, walk the mile and bear the load.

I will hold the Christlight for you in the night time of your fear

I will hold my hand out to you, speak the peace you long to hear.

I will weep when you are weeping - When you laugh I'll laugh with you

I will share your joy and sorrow, till we've seen this journey through.

When we sing to God in heaven, we shall find such harmony

Born of all we've known together, of Christ's love and agony.

Won't you let me be your servant - Let me be as Christ to you

Pray that I may have the grace to let you be my servant, too.[6]

The Journey talk concludes with an invitation for the Kairos brothers to meet weekly in a prayer-share group where they will share in confidentiality with small accountability groups their struggles, concerns, and joys. The men are encouraged to accept each other wherever they are in their journey. Silence is always permissible in these prayer/share meetings since the Kairos motto is "listen, listen, love, love." The men are informed that people, not ideas, are the top priority in Kairos.

The second lay talk on Sunday morning is *Lifelines*. This talk models for the residents a line drawing the physical or secular highs and lows of our life and another line depicting the spiritual highs and lows in relation to the Church, the body of Christ. Mechanically the horizontal space on the paper is segmented into five- or ten-year increments indicating the age of the presenter at a given point or into actual calendar years. A solid line may be used to illustrate one's "natural" life and a dotted line for one's spiritual life. A horizontal line is drawn through the center of the space indicating a neutral plane; positive or favorable events in our life are drawn above the neutral line and negative or unfavorable events are depicted below the neutral line. After the speaker demonstrates his lifeline, the table families are encouraged to draw their lifelines. Then we split into pairs, sharing what we feel comfortable sharing about our lives. Sharing our stories with one another is a way to begin building a caring community. Each story is personal and each person is precious. Many people live very isolated lives in a maximum-security prison, abandoned by family and friends in the free world and under pressure to maintain a macho facade in the prison for survival reasons. Sharing within a group, especially one that has spent three days together on the mountaintop in song, prayer, meditation, food, and fellowship, is an effective way to experience the power of God's love.

Following our final specially-cooked meal during lunch we return to the conference room where we hear the final lay talk of the Kairos weekend entitled *How to Care for Others through the Gift of Listening*. This talk ties directly into the Kairos motto of "listen, listen, love, love." For the gift of listening is a powerful affirmation of love for another human being. This talk discusses the benefits of being a good listener for those listening and for those being listened to. It is far easier to talk than listen because it takes more energy and concentration to be an effective listener. Good listeners become better ambassadors for Christ because they communicate love to others. In studies on small-group or one-on-one listening, the results are remarkable. When a person experiences actually being listened to, they perceive that the listener really cares about them. For the person doing the talking, a good listener will build their self-esteem because someone has taken their life seriously - their thoughts and feelings.

Hardly anybody really listens to prisoners. For the most part, the officers in the prison have to maintain a certain professional code of conduct and have little time or inclination to listen to inmates. Other prisoners often don't care what another prisoner has to say. So when a Kairos volunteer actually listens to a prisoner it is a profound and often unique experience for the prisoner.

Listening helps the speaker clarify his thoughts while offering an outlet for the release of bottled-up feelings. Listening also benefits the listener in a myriad of ways. As a general rule a person doesn't learn much by doing all the talking; the people who learn the most are the ones who listen, pay attention, who hear. As the old saying goes, maybe that is why God gave us two ears and one mouth so we would be better equipped to listen than to talk. The listener realizes that it is a privilege to become trusted enough so that another human being feels comfortable sharing one's inner life. Good listening honors the listener and brings the listener acceptance too. It becomes a gift, a chance to build up another person.

Being listened to diminishes the feelings of isolation, of exclusion. Listening causes the speaker to feel better and offers a sense of belonging, engendering a bond between people. Listening is a form of agape love. It can't be faked, it is hard work. The listener must focus on what is being said, body language, the tone of voice. The listener must diligently concentrate to avoid day dreaming or getting too far ahead of the speaker or being tempted to formulate responses which all lead to gaps in what the listener is hearing.

The residents are instructed in the keys to good listening, including surrendering ourselves to the other person, praying for them, and praying to be a conduit of caring (agape) love for them. A good listener is non-judgmental, which does not necessarily imply that they agree with the speaker's views or actions. To understand without judging is to love.

The talk stresses some of the mechanics of being a good listener, such as good body posture, openness, non-judgmental attitude, good eye contact, occasional affirmative comments (i.e., "I understand. . ." "I am with you. . .", etc.), accurate discernment of the speaker's content and feeling levels, and occasional feedback to ensure you're on the same track with the speaker.

M. Scott Peck, M.D., in his best-selling book *The Road Less Traveled and Beyond: Spiritual Growth in an Age of Anxiety*, offers an insightful analysis of listening well in a subsection of his book entitled "Thinking and Listening":

> Many people think that listening is a passive interaction. It is just the opposite. Listening well is an active exercise of our attention and, by necessity, is hard work. It is because they do not realize this or because they are not willing to do the work that most people do not listen well. When we extend ourselves by attempting to listen and communicate well, we take an extra step or walk an extra mile. We do so in opposition to the inertia of laziness or the resistance of fear. It always requires hard work.
>
> Listening well also requires total concentration upon another and is a manifestation of love in the broadest sense of the word. An essential part of listening well is the discipline of bracketing, the temporary giving up or setting aside of your own prejudices, frames of reference, and desires in order to experience as far as possible another's world from the inside, stepping inside his or her shoes. This unification of speaker and listener is actually an extension and enlargement of ourselves, and new knowledge is always gained from it. Moreover, since listening well involves bracketing, it also involves a temporary total

> acceptance of the other. Sensing this acceptance, the speaker will feel less and less vulnerable and more and more inclined to open up the inner recesses of his or her mind to the listener. As this happens, speaker and listener begin to understand each other better and better. True communication is under way and the duet dance of love has begun. The energy required for the discipline of bracketing and the focusing of total attention on another is so great that it can be accomplished only by love, which I define as the will to extend oneself for mutual growth. . . .
>
> I have found that the knowledge that one is being truly listened to is frequently, in and of itself, remarkably therapeutic. In approximately a quarter of the patients I saw, whether they were adults or children, considerable and even dramatic improvement was shown during the first few months of psychotherapy, before any of the roots of problems had been uncovered or significant interpretations had been made. There are several reasons for this phenomenon, but chief among them, I believe, was the patient's sense that he or she was being truly listened to, often for the first time in years - and for some, perhaps for the first time ever.[7]

The participants at each table family break into groups of three with a free-world brother and two residents comprising a group. The free-world brother is the observer, and each resident engages in the role of the speaker and listener during two sets of practice sessions, applying some of the principles discussed during the talk.

During Sunday afternoon the residents and other team members go into an adjacent gym where they engage in a few significant activities. The table families split off into different areas of the gym and begin praying for one another in a tight circle formation. Each member of the family goes behind the other members in order, saying a short prayer for them. This is an intensely moving experience for everyone involved.

Another major event is the birthday cake that is brought in with every pilgrim's name inscribed on the top of the cake, symbolic of God's assertion in Isaiah 49:15-16: "Can a mother forget the baby at her breast and have no compassion on the child she has borne? Though she may forget, I will not forget you! See, I have engraved you on the palms of my hands."

When the cake is first brought in with lighted candles, the free-world team gathers around the pilgrims, singing "Happy Birthday." The birthday cake is another of those well-kept secrets for the candidates and the participants are generally staring at us in stunned disbelief as the beauty of the moment begins to sink in. Again, emotions spread over the faces of the men as they are hit with another form of agape love. Many of these men never had a birthday party. We hand out birthday cards to every pilgrim, signed by every person on the Kairos team. The men spend considerable time poring over the birthday cake until they see their name and their faces light up when they do.

At Kairos #14, a pilgrim named Spencer Moore got up at the closing ceremony and disclosed in a voice choked with emotion that the birthday cake made an indelible impression on him. Spencer came from a poor family that could only afford two birthday parties a year for the children born during both halves of the year. When he was only five or six years old he remembers looking for his name on the cake but it was omitted. He asked his mom about it and she curtly told him that there wasn't room for his name. He was crushed, it made him feel like he didn't exist. Over three decades later the scar of that ugly wound remained embedded in his heart. And the healing began when Spencer saw his name on the Kairos birthday cake. So the Kairos birthday cake with each man's name written in the icing, the "Happy Birthday" song, and individual birthday cards for each participant are additional weapons in our arsenal in melting the walls around these men's hearts.

The final ceremony prior to "The Closing" is where the rector hands out a cross attached to a lanyard to each pilgrim. This is a meaningful event for each participant who has completed the course. As each table family approaches the front of the gym, the rector places the cross around each pilgrim's neck and remarks: "Christ is counting on you." The pilgrim responds: "And I am counting on Christ."

The pinnacle of a Kairos weekend is known as "The Closing." This is a celebration of spending four days in the presence of Almighty God. Indeed, Hector Negron, our rector, told me early in my training: "Nobody can go through a Kairos weekend and deny that they have been in the presence of Almighty God. Nobody can deny it." The closing ceremony, which lasts a couple of hours in the latter half of Sunday afternoon, is a ringing affirmation of that statement.

The closing ceremony is the only time the outside Kairos team is allowed in the prison as well as about 50 other free-world guests. The outside team, those true and hardworking servants who toil in obscurity all weekend, perform many tasks. They count and bag thousands of cookies baked by free-world volunteers who prayed that the cookies would touch the hearts of the inmates. They cook excellent quality meals, clean dishes and containers, load the runners' vehicle for the twice-daily trips to the prison, purchase odds and ends at the local grocery store when supplies run short, pray for all of us (pilgrims, stewards and inside team members, prison chaplain, warden, officers, and the general prison population), cheer for us in the morning when we depart and in the evening when we return, and hungrily ask every evening how the pilgrims, and especially their prayer partners, are doing. The outside team is introduced at a strategic time during the ceremony. This is a special time within God's Special Time to see the outside team, people that I consider the greatest servants of the weekend because of their work in the background without the joy of witnessing first hand the miracle of God's love transforming some of the least of God's children, showered with a prolonged and exuberant ovation from men who haven't eaten so well since they have been incarcerated. The smiles, the grins, the enthusiastic applause, the waves, the tears in the pilgrims' eyes all convey a powerful "thank you" to the outside Kairos team who are profoundly humbled and filled with love, joy, and peace. There is not a part of a Kairos team that I admire more than the outside team, those dedicated, selfless, and humble servants supporting us all so well, epitomizing grace under pressure and poise under often stressful circumstances.

I am so impressed by the people who serve us on the outside team that I was inspired to write the following note one year to my fellow soldiers in the war against Satan.

OUTSIDE TEAM

> Any war always has at least two fronts: the front lines, where the fighting is done, and the home front, which provides the weapons, the supplies, the transportation, the intelligence, the political and moral support. The home front rarely gets equal credit, but World War II required such a massive buildup in such a short time, the home-front effort was as impressive as the fighting in Europe or the Pacific.
>
> Tom Brokaw, *The Greatest Generation* (New York: Random House, 1998), 87.

"We are engaged in a spiritual war against the evil forces of this universe.

For our struggle is not against flesh and blood, but against the rulers, against the authorities, against the powers of this dark world and against the spiritual forces of evil in the heavenly realms.

Ephesians 6:12

The outside Kairos team, along with all the Christian soldiers who contributed agape, constitute the home front. The soldiers of Kairos serving on the home front are an impressive bunch. God bless you all for your selfless dedication and commitment to win these 42 men for Christ while strengthening the faith of those serving on the front line, free-world soldiers

> and stewards alike. You soldiers on the home front are my heroes. Onward Christian Soldiers!"

On Sunday afternoon the pilgrims are given an opportunity to respond to three questions during the "The Closing."

1. In what spiritual condition did you arrive at Kairos?
2. What did you find here?
3. What are you taking away with you?

Often the testimony is more general or touches on some specific events during the weekend that really touched their hearts. There is an overwhelming temptation for the men to thank individuals or everyone in attendance. Yet, they are specifically instructed, prior to the closing ceremony and again prior to the open invitation, not to thank anybody involved in putting on this Kairos except God, Christ, and/or the Holy Spirit. Witnessing the love of Christ in action and being blessed beyond our wildest dreams is the only reward the Kairos team needs.

The most memorable testimony I heard on the Kairos #8 weekend during the closing ceremony was delivered by Gilberto Fernandez, the man we had all lifted up in prayer during the weekend, asking God to soften his heart. Gilberto Fernandez, hit man for a Mexican gang, feared by many, calmly approached the podium and began to speak. He motioned to Frederico Gonzalez in the far corner of the gym to come join him. Gonzalez was sitting with about 200 other Kairos brothers who had attended earlier weekends and he got up and walked to the front of the gym, standing next to Fernandez. Because of Fernandez's reputation, a hush fell over the packed gym in anticipation of what might unfold. Then Fernandez calmly informed us that after Frederico Gonzalez had attended Kairos #7 six months earlier, he was assigned a contract to hit Gonzalez for leaving their gang and becoming a Christian. Fernandez held off until he had a chance to attend his own Kairos weekend. He was curious about what would cause a man to risk his life. Fernandez told us bluntly that prior to this Kairos weekend he had fully intended to take Gonzalez out when the circumstances were right, including after this Kairos weekend. He also said another primary reason he signed up for Kairos was for the cookies, fruit and meals. Fernandez remarked, "I didn't come here to meet Christ or anybody else, but

I met Jesus Christ this weekend and I am here to tell you that I have accepted Jesus Christ as my Lord and Savior." At that point, Fernandez turned toward Gonzalez and the two men embraced. In an instant you could hear about 300 metal chairs being shoved back across that barren concrete floor with a boisterous eruption of unrestrained cheers, shouts and piercing whistles punctuating a prolonged, thunderous, and standing ovation that sent chills up and down my spine. At this time I was no longer held fast at the summit of the mountain but had escaped beyond the gravity of earth, soaring on wings of eagles, transcending the brokenness of earth, touching the smiling face of God in the heavenly realms. I'll never forget that moment when I was suspended in eternity in the palm of God's hand, witnessing first hand the sheer awesomeness of God's love overpowering Satan's hate in one of God's precious children. I envisioned the angels and saints in heaven celebrating God's victory over Satan in the life of Gilberto Fernandez by vigorously performing the spectacular moves and athletic feats exhibited in a veritable gymnastics meet, three-ring circus, and Olympic Games all rolled into one.

Jesus Christ said He came to earth to fulfill Scripture [Law of Moses, Prophets, and Psalms], including proclaiming freedom for the prisoners and releasing the oppressed [Luke 4:18-19 which in turn was based on Isaiah 61:1-2]. Gilberto Fernandez, held hostage by Satan for most of his life, was rescued by Jesus in a daring SWAT [Savior World All Time] team attack. Gilberto Fernandez, by renouncing his gang membership when he embraced Christ and Frederico Gonzalez, now understood why a person would risk death to know Christ. Gilberto Fernandez was now putting himself at great risk but he resolutely remarked, "When I'm out in the prison, I'm going to watch my front and Jesus Christ is going to watch my back." A month later, Gilberto Fernandez was baptized and told David Kaseman: "If Jesus Christ can get me, He can get anybody." Virtually every time I attended the monthly reunions, Gilberto Fernandez was there. Sometimes I would run into Gilberto during a Kairos weekend when I was assigned to deliver cookies into the far corners of the unit. Invariably Gilberto and I would exchange hugs and often I saw him armed with his Bible.

I attended a Kairos closing ceremony one time at the Beto Unit, also located in Tennessee Colony. A pilgrim got up and said, "I know this Kairos weekend has been anointed by God because not this many people could do this many things right for this length of time."

As we were getting ready to be dismissed from the gym Sunday evening after spending 72 hours on the summit, Bob Williamson hurriedly crossed the gym, giving me a hug and thanking me for my forgiveness testimony the night before. Bob was on the first Kairos weekend at the Michael Unit in October 1992. He told me that many captains and lieutenants were there and I remember initially thinking he was referring to officers in the unit. However, Bob quickly disabused me of that notion, informing me that these were top gang leaders. He said the tension was incredible all through Friday. He said it was like a scene from one of Clint Eastwood's spaghetti westerns in which the good, the bad and the ugly all stared at each other with everyone waiting nervously for someone to make the first move. But he said as Saturday unfolded, especially after the letters on Saturday afternoon, the tension broke and men were hugging and shedding tears, who, a few days earlier, had the circumstances been right, would have killed each other with no qualms whatsoever.

Bob told me that he had hated his mother for most of his life because she had abandoned him in a garbage dumpster when he was three months old. Think of that, the person who is supposed to love you more than anyone else, ditches you in a pile of trash. A lady who lived nearby found Bob. Bob lived a tough life, eventually joining a motorcycle gang and the Ku Klux Klan. He told me the last time he had seen his mother was approximately 25 years earlier in a prison visitation room where he unleashed a stream of malevolent, vitriolic, and vituperative venom toward her, screaming at her to go to that infamous place where snowballs don't have a high probability of surviving in their frozen state. And then Bob told me that he was scheduled to meet with his mother and brother (a border patrol agent) in a non-contact visit in about a month, around Mother's Day. He said he was praying for forgiveness, reconciliation, and healing. I told Bob I would pray for him and his family. In June, at the monthly reunion, I asked Bob how the meeting went with his mother and brother. Bob said it was very awkward for several minutes as they communicated by phone through the thick glass wall. But then Bob was inspired to pray and they all bowed their heads. Bob said the prayer worked because everything went well after that. Bob was now in the process of healing after decades of poisonous hate. He wrote me a letter dated June 6, 1996 describing this momentous occasion of reconciliation with his mother.

> We had a very good visit together. I have learned a lot and I have been lied to a lot by a lot of people. My mother does care about me. She told me that at the time she left she was on drugs. Also she left me with someone who knows her and me very well. And that she was across the street when the lady got me and took me in the store. So at the time she just could not take care of me. And then after she got off drugs and got to know the Lord Jesus, she started to look for me. But no one would tell her where I was at or anything.
>
> Yes, she paid a price that no mother should ever have to pay. You could see it in her face. She really has beat up on herself. Even in the visit she would keep saying, "It was my fault, son." And I would have to tell her it was my fault because I'm here and it was no one's fault but mine . . . Yes, we forgave each other. We both know that we will never have a mother-and-son relationship. But we will have a friendly one and it will grow, that's for sure. We will not forget the past but we forgive the things that happened in the past. We will build a better future. She is coming back in November. We are learning to like each other first . . . Tell everyone the Lord Jesus gave me a very good visit.

Do you believe in miracles? I do. I've witnessed many miracles in maximum-security. As John A. Thompson, Jr., Executive Director of Kairos Prison Ministry, puts it: "Being involved with Kairos is like having a front-row seat at a miracle."

I have seen God's love overpowering Satan's hate. I believe that only through being loved, even loving the lowest of prisoners, is a human being capable of sharing love. As the apostle John put it, "We love because God first loved us." The Lord God blessed me beyond my wildest dreams when he enticed me to join Him in Kairos, in serving Jesus in one of His most distressing disguises, that being the men who are warehoused in a maximum-security penitentiary. I was privileged to be able to witness Gilberto Fernandez break cookies and fruit with us on Thursday evening, who was spiritually dead coming into Friday, rise again in three days to a new life in Christ on Sunday afternoon. It is like planting a seed on Thursday afternoon and watching a flower grow and bloom by Sunday evening. The birth of a human baby is a miracle. Try watching the birth of a Christian in a 72-hour period, especially considering where some of these guys come from and what they have done. Friends, you don't usually get to experience these miraculous transformations in your regular church services, your Sunday School class, your Bible study class, your job, or your recreational pursuits. That's why I thank God on a regular basis for calling me into Kairos Prison Ministry because I have witnessed things that I never dreamed I would experience this side of the resurrection.

4

> Before we choose to follow God's will, a crisis must develop in our lives. This happens because we tend to be unresponsive to God's gentler nudges. He brings us to the place where He asks us to be our utmost for Him and we begin to debate. He then providentially produces a crisis where we have to decide - for or against. That moment becomes a great crossroads in our lives.
>
> Oswald Chambers

LIFELINES

As mentioned in the previous chapter one of the Kairos talks is entitled *Lifelines.* Lifelines allows us to share with each other our secular and spiritual highs and lows. Our life experiences greatly influence our search for the meaning of life. Triumphs, trials, and tragedies mark our path in the quest for Truth. This chapter shares my lifelines.

I was born in Portland, Oregon at St. Vincent Hospital. I had a good childhood with loving parents (Jim and Ida Kincheloe) and grandparents (Oscar and Berniece Hagg and Ray and Ellen Kincheloe). We were raised in a Christian home, although I don't recall going to church every week. The only thorn from my childhood that I discussed in the previous chapter was the feeling of rejection I harbored from my biological father, Jim Staples, who left us when I was a year old. But my adoptive father, Jim Kincheloe, the one who raised me and became a role model for me, was a very devoted father. So I was blessed to have been raised in a loving family. We didn't have material wealth but we always seemed to have enough and we went on some fun family vacations. My grandfather and grandmother on my mom's side, Oscar and Berniece Hagg, also spent a lot of time with us. A highlight every year, beginning when Paul and I were about six and five, was spending homecoming weekend at Oregon State University. Watching the homecoming parade Friday evening, eating barbecue at the OSU Armory Saturday morning, attending the big football game Saturday afternoon (usually in a cold drizzly rain), and eating dinner at grandpa's fraternity with the big college men Saturday evening were all very exciting for us.

My first big pain in life was the death of my grandmother, Berniece, when I was 10. She was only 53. Grandpa came in from the farm and found her in bed, still clutching the nitroglycerin pills in her hand. She had atherosclerosis and died of a heart attack. Paul and I knew she was sick but we didn't know she was that ill. We were stunned when my great aunt, Bonnie Hagg, dropped by to tell us. We cried for days.

Our school years were busy. We played sports. We raised sheep in 4-H, showing them at the county and state fairs. We grew up next to my great uncle Henry Hagg's 200-acre farm, surrounded on two sides by forests and a creek. My great grandparents, David and Augusta Hagg, emigrated from Sweden in the 1880s, purchased the 200 acres and began clearing timber and dynamiting stumps. We used to play in those woods for hours on end, building forts or bridges over the creek. When we got older we hauled hay on my uncle's and grandfather Oscar's farms. Grandpa's 120-acre farm was given to him by Berniece Finigan (maiden name) through their marriage. Several hundred acres on Chehalem Mountain between Newberg and Hillsboro, Oregon were divided up between the four Finigan sisters (Winifred, Claribel, Berniece, and Wanda). The Finigan farm as it was called was also partly cleared of timber in the 1880s by my great grandparents, Lou and Ida (Wohlschlegel) Finigan who had emigrated from Ireland and Germany. So as you can see, I'm definitely a mutt, with ancestors from England (Staples, my birth father, and Kincheloe are both English), Sweden, Ireland, France, and Germany.

Two highlights in high school were serving as senior class president and making the varsity baseball team as the starting left fielder, where I hit .321 and made honorable mention at the end of the season in the Portland Metro League. However, toward the end of May 1970, less than a week from graduation when I was only 17, we got tragic news from Vietnam about my 18-year-old cousin, private first class (Pfc.) Terry Allen Hagg. Terry was like a big brother to me. We did everything together as kids, playing sports, playing army in the woods, wrestling, picking strawberries, and hauling hay in the summer to earn money. We grew up no more than a couple of hundred yards from each other, separated by his grandfather Henry Hagg's farm field. I went into a depression for a few weeks. This was one of the hardest times in my life.

On May 29, 1970, Terry was severely wounded in his right arm, back, and both legs when he stepped on a land mine. Terry had to have both legs amputated and his ileum (the lowest part of the small intestine) had been perforated. On June 3, a year after he sat with 464 other members of Hillsboro, Oregon's high school graduating class, he lay thousands of miles away in DaNang Hospital, both legs gone. Terry never once asked "why," or sought sympathy. He wrote a letter, describing his ordeal.

> Dear Family:
>
> The 29th of May around 1 p.m. we started to move to a position 2,000 meters away. This doesn't seem far, but the heat was well over 115 and the humidity was around 90 percent. To add to our troubles we stopped every 50 feet to let the head squad cut through the brush. As you can see, the heat would soon take its toll. One man finally went down (Tex). I was told to help him, and I did [Terry was a medic, trained at Fort Lewis near Tacoma, Washington].
>
> At this time the whole platoon was on the verge of heat exhaustion, so our new lieutenant said find some shade on the next hilltop and we would wait until it got cooler. The new deal was that we would move up one more hill and set up. This had almost everybody in a mutinous state of mind.
>
> Nevertheless, they said a trail was already cut and that Tex and I were supposed to move on up there and wait. There were already people up there, but the trail we took was an intersection of ours, and that's when the booby trap went off.

The next thing I knew I was sitting on the ground, my left leg blown off above my knee. My right leg (lower half) was turned 90 degrees from its normal position.

I knew I couldn't panic or it would be all over, so I put a tourniquet on my left leg and that stopped the major bleeding. By this time a couple of buddies were there, putting on dressings over my other wounds.

In no time flat - about five to seven minutes - I was flown to 18th Surgical hospital, where I had a 5½-hour operation. After waking up I was told that one of my legs was cut off right above my left knee and my right leg was cut off about three inches below the knee.

I also had my abdomen cut open vertically up the middle, where they removed about 12 pieces of metal from my intestines and bowels. I also had a few pieces of flesh blown off at the right elbow and on the right back shoulder, but that's no sweat.

Tomorrow I go to surgery and they're going to stitch up all the stitchable wounds, and any wounds where there is just a big piece of flesh missing they are going to skin-graft.

My major problem up to this point has been my stomach. They have a tube down my nose to the stomach to suck out fluid. I've been living on liquids out of bottles they have flowing into me day and night through my veins.

I've noticed today that I'm really losing a lot of weight. I should be put on a diet of clear liquids (such as apple juice) in another day. I think I will be here at the DaNang Hospital another week, then flown to Japan for some more work, then to a nearby military hospital, probably the one at Ft. Lewis [Madigan Hospital], where I will get my fake legs.

Love, Terry

Terry was in a hospital in Saigon for a few weeks and then was transferred to a hospital in Tokyo for several more weeks. He didn't arrive at Madigan Hospital at Fort Lewis until September or October. I remember driving to see him with my brother Paul and grandpa and trying to brace myself for what he would look like. I told myself when I first saw him to conceal any shock on my face but it was a hard thing seeing him, legs gone, looking gaunt. For the next few years Terry would be in and out of the VA hospitals in Portland-Vancouver with leg infections, often having to get a little more of his nubs shaved off. I used to visit him in the VA hospitals and it was always depressing. Terry would have to try to wean himself from morphine after these operations. He used some other drugs from time to time and also drank heavily at times. If you saw the movie *Forrest Gump*, the character Lieutenant Dan, played by Gary Sinise, was a vivid reminder of Terry. Lieutenant Dan was in charge of Forrest Gump's platoon in Vietnam and lost both legs. When Lieutenant Dan got angry and hostile, when he drank, he reminded me of Terry during his worst moments. Fortunately Lieutenant Dan's life turned out well. Terry began writing poetry during his recovery and my favorite one is entitled Near-Miss:

Near-Miss

A loud boom parted time.
Wreckage, smoke, agony, death
Moved seconds as if minutes.
Nine humans lay wounded,
Another was dead.
What filled those moments
Were thoughts of God, death,
And life.
And in those seconds a reason
Was found for life.
For we all have a mission
On earth, whether an athlete,

Or cripple, strong or weak,
There is a reason to live.
The beat of our hearts is
Divine, a power, an explosive
Energy, that keeps us all
Alive, because no matter
How small we as one,
Compared to each other,
The next person you see
Could inspire a more vivid
Reality of life in yourself.

Once I left for college in the fall of 1970 I pretty much abandoned the church except for Christmas Eve and Easter services. I no longer felt the need to attend church because I felt self-sufficient. I joined the same fraternity (Alpha Sigma Phi) that grandpa had belonged to in the early 1920s. My four years at Oregon State University were some of the best of my life, a place where I made some life-long friends.

I planned on going to law school at the University of Oregon after graduation but dropped out after only a couple of weeks because I just felt like a duck out of water. This was a low point in my life because previously I rarely quit anything I started. I was depressed because I had planned on going to law school for at least a year. But with the strong feelings I had against being there made it a waste of time and money to pursue it. I just couldn't see making a career in the legal profession. So I went to work for a bank in Portland for a year. A professor friend of mine from Oregon State, John Bates, encouraged me to apply to a top-10 business school to earn an MBA degree. Since I couldn't afford a private business school I didn't bother applying to them. I only applied to one school: UCLA. At the time (1975) UCLA's Graduate School of Management (now known as the Anderson School) was the top-ranked public business school in the nation (it still retains a first-tier ranking as one of the elite business schools).

My two years at UCLA, where I earned an MBA in corporate finance, were among the best of my life. Again, I met several people who became life-long friends during my UCLA days and in the years immediately following graduation, including what became known as the Wolfpack in our younger and wilder bachelor days. We're a rather eclectic bunch including two Ph.D.s, five attorneys, eight MBAs, two CPAs, and one CFA.

The Wolfpack meets periodically for a three-day weekend, generally in California because that's where most of the boys live. We have been meeting since the early 1980s. In our younger days, before the advent of children, we also used to do a 72-mile relay run every year from Tecate, Mexico to Ensenada, Mexico in Baja California, drinking heavily en route to replace lost carbohydrates. The Wolfpack's signature piece is "The Victory Dance," normally performed at bi-annual Wolfpack reunions and at weddings, which now are few and far between since only one of us remains a bachelor. The Victory Dance is where we all gather around in the center of a room, holding hands in clusters of one or two other guys, and jumping in a veritable frenzy in random movements with legs and free arms flying in crazy directions, shouting unintelligible words in raucous voices. This goes on for a few minutes until we are escorted from the premises by security guards. We also traditionally procure a room somewhere in the hotel where we play Spades until the wee hours of the night, drinking beer. Another tradition is on one night we rent the movie *Animal House*. Of course, our wives and children don't attend these functions; they spend their time at the beach or swimming pool or visiting nearby sites.

We have met over the years in such places as Palm Springs, Lake Tahoe, Yosemite, Santa Barbara, San Diego, Los Angeles, Dallas, and Durango, Colorado. It is somewhat of a mystery why a group of 13 men with so many advanced degrees would act like a bunch of children when we get together. Even my daughter Hope recognizes my immature behavior. For my birthday in 2001, when she was 10, she made a card for me that said, "Daddy, you are over the hill but you sure don't act like it." I took it as a compliment.

It takes energy, sacrifice, and commitment to maintain life-long friendships, especially when you're separated by thousands of miles. Yet, the Wolfpack has truly been one of my life's greatest blessings.

On March 9, 1976, during my first year at UCLA, I returned to the graduate dorm one evening with my date. My friend Moses V.

Chao, a graduate student in biochemistry who earned a Ph.D. and is now a professor of molecular neurobiology at the Skirball Institute of Biomolecular Medicine at New York University, informed me that my mother had called. Moses said, "Your cousin Terry took his life." I remember escorting my date back to her place, driving in stunned silence, totally numb. When I returned to the dorm, Moses and I stayed up until the wee hours of the morning, with Moses mainly listening to me about how many fun times Terry and I had. This was an extremely low point for me.

It wasn't until years later that my cousin, Marilyn Hagg, Terry's younger sister, informed me that Terry had been diagnosed with bone cancer in his legs in late 1975. The doctors informed him that the only option was to remove his legs up to his hips, and even that was no guarantee. Terry faced a very painful type of cancer. Three months later, after enduring many painful operations and recoveries from the constant shaving of his nubs due to infections, 24-year-old Terry decided there would be no more operations.

Some people say that suicide is categorically wrong. I say who are we to judge another person's pain. John Bunyon, who sat at my left at Kairos #8 at the Michael Unit, informed me that he saved his cellmate from committing suicide by explaining to him that committing suicide would be sinful, and since it would be his last act on earth he would not go to heaven. I told John that in my view what Christ accomplished on the cross would cover suicide.

A few years ago I read about a movement to raise funds to erect another Vietnam War Memorial in Washington, D.C., this time honoring men who were severely wounded in Vietnam, including men who later committed suicide. It is my fervent hope that this happens. The men who served in Vietnam are all heroes; they served in our nation's most unpopular war. Men, like Terry Hagg, paid a terrible price and it would be fitting to honor these men.

In 1978 my brother Paul was diagnosed with multiple sclerosis (MS) at the age of 25. When I found out about this, I shed tears and prayed to God. In fact this was the only time I remember praying since high school. But my prayers only lasted a few weeks before tailing off and I resumed my secular life.

In 1979 I was finally able to run my first marathon after seven years of knee pain. Moses Chao was my pit crew. I had this burning desire to run a marathon after watching Frank C. Shorter win the marathon gold medal in the 1972 Olympic Games in Munich, Germany. Shorter's victory was very inspiring to me and to many others; indeed, Shorter's stirring triumph sparked the running boom of the 1970s. This was a real high for me, achieving a dream after seven years of frustration.

In 1981 I traveled to Europe for nine weeks by myself for the first time, covering a lot of ground, going to London, Paris, Copenhagen, Stockholm, Munich, Vienna, Salzburg, Venice, Milan, Pisa, Rome, Lucerne, and the Matterhorn. One of the highlights of this trip was attending a reception for American runners at the U.S. Ambassador's residence in Stockholm where I met Bill Rodgers, Olympian and four-time winner each of the Boston and New York City Marathons. Rodgers told me not to beat him the next day. Well, Rodgers won the race, which started outside and finished inside on the track of the 1912 Olympic Stadium, where General George S. Patton, Jr. placed fifth in the pentathlon and Jim Thorpe won his medals. It was a tremendous thrill for me running in the same race with Olympian Bill Rodgers and finishing inside the 1912 Olympic Stadium.

I have run 20 marathons since 1979, including the Marine Corps (Washington, D.C.), New York City, Chicago, San Francisco, Honolulu, Avenue of the Giants (Northern California redwoods), Vancouver (British Columbia), and Dallas. The marathon truly stretches a human being. George Sheehan, in his book *Running & Being*, describes the challenge of overcoming hardship, suffering, and pain in his quest to conquer the Hill. For me the Hill is the marathon. Substituting "marathon" for "Hill" in Sheehan's quotation below captures the essence of my struggle to conquer the marathon.

> But gradually the marathon demands more and more. I have reached the end of my physiology. The end of what is possible. And now it is beyond what I can stand. The temptation is to say, "Enough." This much is enough. But I will not give in.

> I am fighting God. Fighting the limitations he gave me. Fighting the pain. Fighting the unfairness. Fighting all the evil in me and the world. And I will not give in. I will conquer this marathon, and I will conquer it alone. . . .
>
> And still striving for that impossible summit. I forgive God. I accept the pain. I pass the crest [finish line]. And for the briefest of eternities, I am God's child, brother to Christ, filled with the Holy Ghost.[8]

Following graduation I worked in corporate banking for a few years, eventually growing disenchanted with this career path. I also was experiencing a stagnant social life with the opposite sex. So when a job opportunity arose in Dallas, Texas in 1983 I jumped at the chance. Later that year I met Susan Hagemeier at a large church singles class. At our first encounter we discovered that we both liked to run, grew up in rural areas (she is from a 500-acre farm in Indiana), and had raised sheep and showed them in 4-H clubs at the county and state fairs. Our first date was a six-mile run with pizza afterwards.

I began attending church again, not really to worship God but to accompany Susan who was in the habit of attending church. She never nagged me but led by example. I was still spiritually dead since I had no desire to attend Sunday School, a Bible study class, or even to read the Bible.

We got married on May 25, 1985 on Memorial Day weekend on a hot Dallas day (90 degrees) in a church sanctuary with no air conditioning at 4 P.M. The wedding ceremony is still a memorable one for many of my friends who still kid me about my 5-minute collapse during the middle of our wedding vows. Joe Hunt, a good friend of mine in Dallas, hosted the bachelor party the night before the wedding at his house. It was a wild party, composed of my Dallas friends and the Wolfpack, and I'll simply let it go at that. There was heavy drinking. I recall drinking at least six screwdrivers between 7 P.M. and 2 A.M. but Joe told me it was more than that. I don't drink much and when I do it goes right to my brain because I'm a runner. We got home at 3 A.M.

At 7 A.M. we met several of my wedding party and other friends at the Artfest 10K race (6.2 miles) on Saturday near the Cotton Bowl. Susan also ran. Running 6.2 miles on a hot Dallas morning after several drinks the night before on four hours sleep is not what you would call an optimal training schedule. I went home after the race and tried to take a nap but I was too nervous. I didn't eat or drink much that day because of the effects from the night before. So when my best man, Eric "Hoffer" Edmunds and his wife Debora, picked me up to go to the church we stopped at a 7-Eleven to get a Dr. Pepper since I was quite thirsty. I drank it but it only put a dent in my dehydrated state.

We arrived at the church and went to the anteroom off the front of the sanctuary. Rev. Wally Chappell gave us last-minute instructions. He turned to me, seeing my pale and clammy face, and asked, "Steve, are you all right?" Like most males I said, "Sure, I'm fine" even though I didn't feel too chipper. I was very nervous. Finally the time came to go out in front of the sanctuary and my five groomsmen lined up to my left: Eric "Hoffer" Edmunds, Ron "Dirty Dean" Longfellow, Dave "Claugman" Claugus, Raymond "Townsend" Sidrys, and Moses "Malone" Chao. My knees were shaking so bad I thought people were going to start laughing at my fluttering tuxedo trousers. Not knowing any better, I locked my knees. About the time the wedding vows were beginning I began to sweat so profusely that when Susan turned to face me she almost started laughing (I'm a prodigious sweater with a sweat rate of three pounds in 30 minutes of running). Two good friends of mine, John and Loren Tuszynski, were in the fourth row dead center when Loren turned to John and whispered, "He's going to faint." The sweat was literally pouring down the back of my head. I was so embarrassed, knowing that all of Susan's family had come from Indiana, my family had come from Oregon, my UCLA friends and one Oregon State buddy (Dirty Dean) had come from California and Moses had come from the Big Apple.

I couldn't believe what was happening. I swooned once and Eric grabbed my right arm and said, "Kinch, are you O.K.?" Before I could respond, I was out. Eric and Susan grabbed me, and then Wally calmly said, "O.K. folks we're going to take a little break."

Later I was told that all five groomsmen performed a specific task, kind of reminding me of what Patton told the troops in England on May 31, 1944, a week before D-Day: "Every man has a job to do and he must do it." One guy held my head in his lap, another two got my tuxedo coat off, Moses ran down to the basement, retrieving a glass of water and towel, and another guy wiped my face and head with cool water. Susan simply sat down in the front pew, holding my hand. They told me I was out five minutes.

Of course, when all this began happening, Joe Hunt immediately slumped very low in his seat, not wanting anyone to blame him for this debacle. When I began coming to it was eerily quiet, with some ceiling fans whirring softly above me in the two-story high sanctuary. I thought: "Man, this is my wedding and I'm lying down in front of the church. Holy mackerel!" Well, Susan and my friends helped me to my feet. And we resumed where we had left off. I felt a lot better and cooler, especially with that tuxedo jacket off. When we had finished and faced the crowd, applause erupted and continued until we had exited the sanctuary. Susan and I stood on the front steps just outside the sanctuary in the afternoon heat, greeting everyone as they came out. Of course, I received a lot of interesting comments, but my favorite was Wally Chappell's, the last man out of the sanctuary. Wally hugged me and said, "Steve, I've been officiating weddings for 38 years. I've seen bridesmaids faint, I've seen brides faint, I've seen groomsmen faint, but you're the first groom I've ever seen faint." I said, "Gee, thanks Wally for that enviable distinction."

We adopted our children, which was interesting since I was adopted by Jim Kincheloe when he married mom.

It was Tuesday, November 10, 1987 at approximately 3:30 P.M. when the phone jarred me awake as I gazed in a stupor at a Lotus® spreadsheet I was constructing. I had just gotten a home computer and was spending a few days working out of the house. The caller identified himself as Timothy J. Hubert, attorney at law in Evansville, Indiana.

I vaguely recalled when Tim identified himself that Susan had spoken with an attorney in Evansville for about an hour in late August 1987. I had forgotten his name but Susan had shared with

Tim some basic information on our backgrounds and that we were very interested in adopting a baby. Rev. Gene Young, a close friend of Susan's, had told Susan during her vacation to Indiana to contact Tim, since he had helped place some babies for adoption from his congregation. Susan left a biographical sketch of ourselves with Gene; Gene was supposed to have delivered the document to Tim but had forgotten to do so. Based on that one conversation though, Tim had remembered a sufficient amount of information about us that he felt we would be a good match for a baby that was due December 26. A young teenager (a junior in high school at the time) had come in to see Tim about placing her baby in a private adoption earlier that week. She had decided not to go through a public adoption agency and was determined to place her baby with a couple in a private arrangement. Of course, there are more risks in a private adoption especially for the adoptive couple. The birth mother can change her mind more easily and renege on her promise of giving up the baby. There have been some well-publicized incidents of private adoptions being reversed in recent years in this country. And they are very heart-wrenching for all parties involved. Private adoptions in particular, especially inter-state ones, demand very competent counsel familiar with the intricacies of the law.

After Tim and I ended our conversation, I was in a state of disbelief, thinking that in a month-and-a-half Susan and I could be parents. I was also ecstatic and couldn't wait to share the news with Susan but she wasn't home from work yet. I wanted to tell a lot of friends, but decided to wait until Susan came home to spring the big news on her first. I wanted to share this special event with her in person and I relished the role reversal. Typically, it's the woman who gets to inform the man if she is pregnant. Now I had the honor of informing her that we would soon be parents. Needless to say the rest of my work day was shot since I was too excited to concentrate on work. Finally, Susan got home about 5:30 P.M. and came walking through the door. She came into the sun room where I was seated at the desk, pretending to be focusing on the computer screen. I asked her how her day had gone and then, being unable to contain my excitement, I blurted out: "What would be the greatest Christmas gift you could receive?" Susan replied: "We're going to get a new house?" Slap! "What!" I said, "A new house? Isn't this house good enough for you?" And then Susan read my face and asked, "We're going to have a baby?" I shouted, "YES!". And we did a Wolfpack Victory Dance right on the spot. We went for a run later at White Rock Lake, savoring the beauty of the lake and the sunset, anticipating our first child and how that would impact our lives forever.

That night we got on the phone and called Gene Young with the great news and he was very happy for us. We implored him to get that biographical sketch over to Tim Hubert immediately. Tim knew the family of this young teenager since they went to church together and he wanted her to make the decision on where the baby should go based on her intuition after reading various biographical portraits of prospective parents. Tim believed that we were the best match for this young lady's baby, but ultimately the birth mother would have to make the decision.

Gene delivered the biographical sketch to Tim and the following week Tim informed us that the birth mother had picked us out after coming to his office to study the various biographies that had been submitted. She picked us out because she felt we would be the best parents for her child. We were extremely elated, but also a little cautious to get too excited knowing the risk that this teenager could change her mind at any time. At this point, Susan and I began to bond with this unborn baby. It seemed that almost every week, we talked to Gene and/or Tim about any developments, the due date, the birth mother's health, mental status, etc. I told Gene that if anybody deserved to be at that adoption ceremony it would be him because he had been with Susan during the darkest hour of her life in 1980 and he was the one that was instrumental in putting Susan in touch with Tim Hubert. Gene agreed to be there.

In a former marriage gone sour, Susan suffered a miscarriage with her first and only child at six months, lost her reproductive organs because she had a life-threatening infection, and had her house partially burned down by her husband, ruining much of her antique oak furniture. At one point her fever hit 107 degrees and Gene Young told me, "I was with Susan at that time, holding her hand and she was on the brink of death. She could have easily gone." I asked Susan what kept her going, and she said, "The love of God and family and friends." She was so sick the doctors would not allow her to attend the baby's funeral. So try to envision this: You're a 25-year-old woman who has dreamed for years of having children (she ran her own pre-school for four years out of college where she minored in child development). You've been married for six years to a man who freaks out when you first announce your pregnancy, a man who doesn't want the responsibility of raising a child, a man who was discovered during this pregnancy to have breached his marriage vows. And while you're lying gravely ill in a hospital bed after losing your child and reproductive organs, the husband comes in and asks what he can get out of the divorce, not showing any interest in your welfare, and then have your husband set your house on fire. Think of the pain of nearly losing your life, losing your baby, losing your reproductive organs, losing your marriage, and losing part of your house and much of your antique furniture. Imagine the horror of that. The finest steel is tempered in the hottest fire. Susan is one tough lady; few things get to her. When you've been to hell and back, most things in life look pretty tame and trivial by comparison.

Susan's response of what pulled her through that perilous time (God, family and friends) reminds me of what U. S. Air Force Captain Scott O'Grady concluded after he had a spiritual awakening five miles above Bosnia on June 2, 1995 when a Soviet-made antiaircraft missile slammed into his F-16. O'Grady was able to eject 27,000 feet above the earth with his fighter jet screaming along at 350 miles per hour. O'Grady had averted death only to begin a six-day-long crucible on the ground being hunted unyieldingly by Bosnian Serbs. There were times when the enemy was within five feet of O'Grady, who was buried under leaves, trying not to breathe. He relied on his survival training, ingenuity, and profound faith in God to elude seizure and arrange contact with U. S. Marines who, in a bold daylight rescue operation involving two Cobra gunships, two Super Stallion helicopters and back-up cover by F-16 and F-15 fighters, F/A-18 Hornets, and Harriers supported by eight flying tankers to meet fuel needs, plucked him to safety aboard one of the Super Stallions.

> My priorities weren't turned upside down in Bosnia; I'd been reexamining them for quite some time before then. But they sure were slapped into line during that first week in June. By the end of it, I realized only three things mattered in this world.
>
> Number one was faith in God, the source of all goodness.
>
> Number two was the love of family and friends. That love wasn't something apart from faith, nor was it a by-product. It was faith's fullest expression. We spread God's love through our caring toward others.
>
> Number three was good health, the physical foundation for faith and love. . . .Beyond that, everything was negotiable. I liked a saying that went, "Never sweat the small stuff," and almost everything is small stuff.[9]

Now all we had to do was wait for the birth of the baby, finish a home study, and hire an attorney in Dallas.

Even in a private adoption, a home study must be done according to Texas law. The Interstate Compact Administrator for each state, which oversees the interstate adoption procedures, also must approve all interstate adoptions. So we hired an excellent social worker, Janie Golan, to conduct our home study. The purpose of a home study is to assess the quality of the parents and their ability to provide a good family environment for children. Janie spent two or three evenings with us, interviewing us together and separately, observing our routines, and getting to know us and our backgrounds.

We also had to hire an attorney who was familiar not only with Texas adoption law but the requirements of the Interstate Compact Administrator. We contacted Tom Wilson, an attorney who did work for Hope Cottage, a public adoption agency founded in 1917 in Dallas.

Every time we or Janie Golan would talk to Tim Hubert, we asked how the birth mother was doing, what her mental and physical status were. Tim said that she came from a strong Catholic family and that abortion was never an option. He said that her parents had supported her all the way through and that she had not shown any signs of wavering. But Tim cautioned us that one could never predict how a birth mother would react once the baby was born and after she had held the baby in her arms. Tim said there is a tremendous amount of satisfaction in helping adoptive couples and birth mothers successfully complete an adoption. But he said there are many times when he has seriously considered quitting this area of the law due to the heartbreak when a birth mother changes her mind. He said that it tears his heart and soul when an adoption fails. He said it is very hard to see an adoptive couple go through that kind of emotional pain.

Janie suggested that Susan and I write separate letters to the baby prior to its birth. So in early December we wrote our letters; it was a little strange writing a letter to a baby that had not been born and that might not eventually be ours.

Prior to Susan's initial conversation with Tim Hubert in August, we had booked airline reservations to Portland, Oregon for the Christmas holiday. Our vacation plan was to fly to Portland via Denver on Christmas Eve with a return flight on January 3rd.

On December 7 a sonogram revealed that the baby was in a breach position. Tim reported that the birth mother remained firm in her decision to place the baby with us. We told Tim that we did not want to know the gender of the baby until the baby was born. On Tuesday, December 22, 1987 at 8:31 A.M. the baby was born at Welborn Baptist Hospital in Evansville, Indiana. We were notified at 11 A.M. by Tim and he toyed with us for awhile before disclosing what gender the baby was. Tim asked, "What are the names you picked out for the baby?" We replied, "Hope Katherine if it's a girl and Oscar James [named after my grandfather and dad] if it's a boy." Tim responded, "Well, the baby is a healthy 9-pound, 15-ounce, 22-inch-long Oscar James. Susan and I were on the phone together and we were in kind of a state of suspended animation. We had bonded with this baby during the past six weeks and we were praying strongly that the birth mother would not change her mind. A caesarian section was performed due to the breach position of the baby. Tim told us that the birth mother could not sign any documents until the effects of the medication completely wore off. He did not want to risk the birth mother coming back at a later point and claiming that she signed parental release documents while under the influence of medication. Tim said that the earliest a judge could be found to sign off on the initial adoption documentation would be Monday, December 28 due to Christmas falling on Friday and the lingering effects of medication on the birth mother. Due to the C-section delivery, Tim said that Christmas Day would probably be the earliest that the birth mother could sign papers. His plan was to have the birth mother sign the documents sometime that weekend and present the completed forms to the judge on Monday morning.

Tim advised us to continue with our vacation plans to Oregon with a side trip to Evansville on Monday, December 28 if things worked out. We immediately called Gene Young and Susan's parents in Freelandville, Indiana and told them of our tentative plans. We booked a flight to Evansville from Portland via St. Louis on Monday, December 28 with an open return flight to Portland. We couldn't reserve a return flight because the Interstate Compact Administrators in Indiana and Texas had to approve the documentation before we could take the baby out of Indiana. Plus there was always the risk that the birth mother would change her mind.

So it was with excitement and some trepidation that we flew to Portland on Friday, December 24. We had fun at a Christmas Eve dinner and party at my grandfather Oscar Hagg's farm.

My mother is a worrisome type. She was so nervous about the pending adoption and risk that it might not happen, she spent much of the weekend incapacitated in bed. On Saturday and Sunday we tried to contact Tim Hubert but were unsuccessful. We finally reached Gene Young on Sunday and he said that he too had been unable to reach Tim. But Gene assured us that Tim was a very reliable person and a highly capable attorney. Gene said that if something had gone awry Tim would have called us and him. We had trouble sleeping Sunday night. Indeed, Susan never dozed off that night and I slept only a few hours, tossing and turning most of the time. We still did not have any explicit assurance from Gene or Tim that the adoption papers had been signed during the weekend so we basically were going to spend $1,800 on air fare to Evansville via St. Louis on pure faith, not knowing what would happen when we got off the commuter plane in Evansville.

The air fare shocked us but then again Portland-Evansville is not a real popular route for commercial or resort-oriented air traffic! But I knew that if the adoption blew up, the $1,800 air fare would be peanuts compared to the emotional cost that we would incur. I can't comprehend how much the emotional pain would hurt having a birth mother change her mind after you had begun bonding with the baby. Susan and I talked Sunday night about whether we should go or not since we would pay for the tickets at the Portland Airport. Finally I said to Susan, "Let's go for it. It's not in our hands anyway. It's in God's hands." And I truly felt God's presence during this adoption drama, because one thing you understand very early in the adoption process is that you have virtually no control over the outcome. I had this gut feeling that it would work out.

We got up at 4:30 A.M. to catch a 6:35 A.M. flight to St. Louis. My dad volunteered to drive us to the airport. We hugged good-bye and we all hoped that when we returned in a few days that we would be bringing a new baby home. A few hours later we arrived in St. Louis in a snow storm. We barely made the connecting flight to Evansville because airport officials were debating whether to temporarily halt all departing flights. Visibility was pretty poor. We arrived in Evansville around lunch time and I'll never forget getting off on the tarmac and seeing through the windows of the terminal, Gene Young, Susan's parents, Arnold and Gertrude Hagemeier, and Susan's oldest brother, Bob Hagemeier. We both felt that this was a good sign, but then again they might be there to tell us that the birth mother had changed her mind. When we greeted them in the terminal, Gene said that Tim and his wife were at the hospital picking up the baby! We were so greatly relieved that this momentous event was actually going to occur. As it turns out, Tim had gotten the birth mother's signatures that very morning and then had a judge review the documentation and sign his approval. Then Tim had to present the documentation to the hospital in order for them to release the baby to him and his wife. So we had indeed flown to Evansville on pure faith and God blessed us with a beautiful, healthy baby boy.

We drove to Tim's law firm office in downtown Evansville, which was in site of Welborn Baptist Hospital. We waited in the small reception area at the office for at least 30 to 45 minutes, just standing around making small talk, anxiously gazing at the elevator doors that opened directly into the reception area. Then, at about 2:30 P.M., the elevator doors opened and Tim and his wife, holding the baby, strode into the room. Well, we were just kind of dumbstruck, in total awe. It was like being in a dream, in slow motion, almost surreal. All eyes were on the infant as Tim's wife handed the baby to Susan. I was definitely too nervous and did not want to hold the baby unless I was sitting down, given my propensity for fainting at inopportune times. We walked into a board room where we had some privacy from the rest of the law offices. Susan and I sat at one end of the room with our family and friends either standing around or sitting at the table. I had envisioned a lot of emotion in terms of tears, but I don't think anybody cried. There may have been some tears of joy, but our reaction was one of stunned disbelief. It began to dawn on us that this was our baby (although the adoption would not be final for another six months) and that it was our responsibility to care for it and provide a loving home. This was God's gift to us and He was entrusting us to raise him the best way we knew how. Even Susan was somewhat awestruck and she had over a decade of experience as the director or assistant director of a 100-children church daycare center, with babies ranging from six weeks old to after-school children. Why? Because she wouldn't just be responsible for the baby 8-10 hours a day and then release the baby to its parents. This infant was ours 24 hours a day or in current lingo, 24/7, and it is an awesome responsibility.

Tim patiently instructed us what the nurses had told him about how to care for Oscar and what to feed him for the next few weeks; but I couldn't grasp what he was saying because I was just plain stunned. I couldn't concentrate on what he was saying; I just kept saying to myself this is really happening. I was hoping that Susan was paying attention because I didn't have a clue what Tim was talking about. And so I remember the joy of that day quite vividly. It was exhilarating being a daddy, a term that would take some getting used to. And I was so glad to have Susan with me because if anyone deserved to have this joy it was her. I thought of the deep pain and suffering that she had endured earlier in her life and I felt tremendous satisfaction at being involved in this victory celebration of life. I was so happy to have Gene Young there with us and I know he too felt a lot of pleasure seeing God's will at work, seeing Susan enjoying the fruits of God's love seven years after the darkest hour of her life.

In late 1989 we received notification from Hope Cottage that we had been accepted into their six-month adoption program. For six months we attended meetings and classes on parenting and other subjects related to the adoption process, including home studies. We were approved in June 1990 and put on a waiting list with our biographical profiles available to prospective birth mothers. We thought it was a good omen being approved by Hope Cottage because Susan had picked the name "Hope" in high school if she ever had a girl. And we were "hoping," so to speak, to have one boy and one girl.

On Friday afternoon, January 18, 1991, Hope Cottage informed us that Nicki, Hope's birth mother, had selected us to be the baby's parents. A meeting was held at Hope Cottage at 11 A.M. on Monday, January 21 (Susan's birthday) where we visited with Nicki and her mother, Susan, for approximately 1½ hours. The initial information that we obtained on Friday on both the birth mother and birth father was partially incorrect or incomplete; our initial reaction was excitement tempered by certain negative or omitted information. However, as the week progressed, the information was clarified, corrected, or supplied and positive feelings began emerging. The due date was not expected for another two or three weeks when we met Nicki. However, Hope Katherine was in no mood to be delayed when she was born just two days later on Wednesday, January 23 at 3:02 P.M. at Parkland Memorial Hospital, made famous on November 22, 1963 when President John F. Kennedy was rushed there after being gunned down on Elm Street below the former Texas School Book Depository. Hope's speedy entry into the world hastened our decision-making process. We visited Nicki and Hope at Parkland on Saturday morning, January 26 but were strictly prohibited, as the prospective adoptive couple, from touching Hope. A nurse brought her out of the nursery so we could get a close-up look at her.

In a society where abortion is viewed as a form of birth control, in a society where millions of abortions have occurred since the 1973 U.S. Supreme Court decision, in a society where hundreds of thousands of teenagers get pregnant every year and less than 5% make plans for adoption, we salute Nicki and Oscar's birth mother for choosing the adoption option, for their integrity in taking good care of themselves during their pregnancies, enduring the emotional and physical challenges of carrying a baby to term, their respect for the sanctity of human life, and their noble, unselfish, and courageous decision to place their babies with us, the latter being one of the toughest and most painful decisions a woman would ever have to make.

On Monday, January 28, Hope was placed in Susan's arms by Nicki and her mother in a special and highly emotional ceremony at Hope Cottage. We continue to exchange photographs, video tapes, and correspondence with Nicki. We don't know her last name at this point and she doesn't know ours. Oscar's birth mother did not want an open adoption but indicated that she would consider meeting with him after he was 18 if he wanted to establish contact.

From 1983 when I met Susan to 1991 when Hope came along was a great period in my life. It was during this time that I started going to church regularly for the first time in about 13 years, following Susan's example. For about seven years all I did was show up at church most Sundays for an hour. I viewed this as my sacrifice of one hour a week. I participated in no Sunday School classes, no Bible studies, and never read the Bible. If I was spiritually dead for those 13 years out of high school I was now on spiritual life-support, at least enjoying Wally Chappell's sermons.

After I graduated from high school I pretty much ignored God until I met my wife. Things went well for me during most of those years. I had a good education, good income, nice friends, and good health. I didn't think I needed to go to church. I found God an interruption. The only time I remember praying during those 13 years in the spiritual wilderness, as I mentioned earlier, was when I found out Paul had been diagnosed with MS. There were other things I would rather do than spend an hour on Sunday mornings in church. I had built security around my education and credentials, thinking that I would always have a good job.

For 13 years I lived what I thought was a pretty moral life. Yet, years later, I looked back on this time as one of spiritual poverty. For 13 years I had committed the very essence of sin which is defined as "missing the mark" or separation from God. For 13 years I ignored God. No church attendance, no Sunday School classes, no Bible reading. I was spiritually dead. Then I had the audacity to attend church for social reasons, to make friends, not to worship God. And here God blesses me with a wonderful wife when I wasn't even going to church for the right reason to worship Him. That, my friends, remains one of the most profound examples of grace I have ever experienced.

Many of us attend church for the wrong reasons but God will accept you where you're at. If God was proud, He would have turned His back on me a long time ago. But God is not proud; He stoops to conquer. In C. S. Lewis' book *The Problem of Pain*, Lewis talks about how hard it is to turn to God when things are going well. Indeed, how human it is to try virtually everything but God. Lewis says eventually as we fail in our various worldly pursuits, we turn to God, often when we are down and out. Lewis states:

> Everyone has noticed how hard it is to turn our thoughts to God when everything is going well with us. We "have all we want" is a terrible saying when "all" does not include God. We find God an interruption. . .Or as a friend of mine said, "We regard God as an airman regards his parachute; it's there for emergencies but he hopes he'll never have to use it.". . .We are perplexed to see misfortune falling upon decent, inoffensive, worthy people - on capable, hardworking mothers of families or diligent, thrifty little trades-people, on those who have worked so hard, and so honestly, for their modest stock of happiness and now seem to be entering on the enjoyment of it with the fullest right. . .Let me implore the reader to try to believe, if only for the moment, that God, who

> made these deserving people, may really be right when He thinks that their modest prosperity and the happiness of their children are not enough to make them blessed: that all this must fall from them in the end, and that if they have not learned to know Him they will be wretched. And therefore He troubles them, warning them in advance of an insufficiency that one day they will have to discover. The life to themselves and their families stands between them and the recognition of their need; He makes that life less sweet to them.
>
> I call this Divine humility because it is a poor thing to strike our colours to God when the ship is going down under us; a poor thing to come to Him as a last resort, to offer up "our own" when it is no longer worth keeping. If God were proud He would hardly have us on such terms: but He is not proud, He stoops to conquer, He will have us even though we have shown that we prefer everything else to Him, and come to Him because there is "nothing better" now to be had.[10]

From 1993 to 1995, the roughest period of my adult life, I witnessed Divine humility when I turned to God. My brother was deteriorating from the ravages of MS; my grandfather Oscar Hagg was dying; my self-employment income from a career that I enjoyed dropped 65% in 1993 and stayed that low before gradually rising in 1995; I worked a second career in the evenings, missing time with my young children, selling term life insurance for three years which I did not enjoy; and Susan, on top of being a mother, had two part-time jobs, one of which took her into the "hood" delivering papers beginning at 4 A.M. I felt bad that Susan had to work so hard and to take a risk of working such horrible hours in a marginal neighborhood. I worried about her safety, especially when she had to leave the car to deliver the *Wall Street Journal* in office buildings. There were days when I found myself sitting in an easy chair in my living room, with my family out of the house running errands and the shadows lengthening across the room, when I could not get up out of that chair. I felt a heavy and oppressive load on my shoulders. Adversity as God's megaphone came in loud and painfully clear. God had finally gotten my attention. Dr. Charles Stanley, senior pastor of the 15,000-member First Baptist Church in Atlanta, Georgia, author of numerous books, and pastor for the *In Touch* radio and television ministry, writes:

> One of the reasons God allows adversity into our lives is to get our attention. It is easy to get so caught up in our own activities and busy schedules that we lose sight of God. When we focus on our goals, careers, families, and other personal concerns, we neglect to give God the proper priority in our lives. The result is we lose our spiritual sensitivity. . .
>
> Oftentimes it takes more than a sermon to get our attention. Not even heartfelt conviction is enough. Usually it takes a jolt of some kind to bring us around. C. S. Lewis, in his wonderful little book, *The Problem of Pain*, put it this way:
>
>> God whispers to us in our pleasures, speaks in our conscience, but shouts in our pains: it is His megaphone to rouse a deaf world.[11]

It was during this difficult time that I realized I was not in control, that I really didn't have any security. I had tried education (earning a professional designation in commercial real estate valuation), hard work, and material possessions and they did not provide security. One day I told Susan I wanted to read the Bible. I was looking for comfort, especially dealing with the impending death of my grandfather. So I turned to God when my ship was going down, after I had tried many other avenues in life. And yet, God did not turn His back on me but welcomed me with open arms. Despite the stress and anguish in my life during that time there was a huge blessing that came from this crisis: for the first time in my life I turned to God, asking Him to help me. It is a paradox: often out of the suffering and anguish of crushing burdens comes spiritual birth.

Or as Philip Yancey, when describing Jesus' Beatitudes from the Sermon on the Mount, puts it: "Lucky are the unlucky."[12]

Charles Stanley, in his book *How to Handle Adversity,* discusses the concept of adversity being used by God to promote spiritual growth:

> *God uses adversity in the lives of His children.* Adversity, however, is not simply a tool. It is God's most effective tool for the advancement of our spiritual lives. The circumstances and events that we see as setbacks are oftentimes the very things that launch us into periods of intense spiritual growth. Once we begin to understand this, and accept it as a spiritual fact of life, adversity becomes easier to bear.[13]

A month after my grandfather passed away in August 1994, I took my first Bible study class at my church from Dr. Richard L. Dunagin and began attending Sunday School classes for the first time. Susan encouraged me to sign up for Richard's class even though I was apprehensive of being embarrassed because of my ignorance. We spent five months studying Genesis.

In 1995 Richard Dunagin, who is licensed to administer personality and aptitude tests, gave Susan and I some of the best counseling we have ever received. I told Richard that I was really struggling selling term life insurance. I told him that I wanted to confirm if I was in the right field or simply not trying hard enough. He gave me a career aptitude test. A week or so later I turned in the survey to him. A few days later we met and he said, "Steve, you scored very high in technical fields - such as engineering, accounting, and finance. You scored very low in sales. Basically you've been swimming upstream." I responded, "Yeah, and I'm not even a good swimmer going downstream." This test confirmed in my gut that I was a duck out of water, something I suspected all along because one of the reasons I quit corporate banking is that it is primarily a sales job. I had worked the business as best as I could for three years, feeling all the while like I was beating my head against a wall. This test was a huge relief because no longer would I have doubts that I wasn't working hard enough. Shortly after this test, I quit and fortunately income from my own business that I enjoyed began to pick up again. A person has to find his or her strengths and weaknesses and align their efforts with their strengths. Or as one of my favorite movie stars, Clint Eastwood, put it in *Magnum Force*, "A man has got to know his limitations."

In September 1994, shortly after beginning my inaugural Bible study class, Jim Staples, and his wife Donna, visited us from Oregon. Jim could tell I was searching for something deeper. He and Donna invited Susan and I to attend a Cursillo Christian weekend in Oregon the following spring. Cursillo is a forerunner of the Walk to Emmaus and is designed for people seeking spiritual growth. A month later, as I was leaving the Bible study class, Diane Wells asked if I would like to attend the Walk to Emmaus. I asked her if it was similar to a Cursillo weekend. She responded, "Yes." So I told her I would think and pray about it. Nine months later I attended the Walk to Emmaus from June 29 to July 2, 1995.

I was apprehensive about attending the Walk to Emmaus, not knowing exactly what I was getting myself into. I didn't want to become some kind of a Jesus nut or fanatic. I also didn't relish having to give up any of my secular pleasures and activities. So, although I was searching for something deeper, I also didn't want to change or give up too much. There is a reluctance to change for most humans, the fear of uncertainty, the nebulosity of end results. I knew I wanted something more out of life but I was afraid of the sacrifices I might have to make.

The Walk to Emmaus and Cursillo and other similar weekends are the forerunners of Kairos. We enjoy fellowship, singing, eating, and praying together in table families. We hear a series of talks from laity and clergy that build upon one another during the course of the weekend. We are showered with agape love that eventually breaks down the walls we have built around our hearts (just like the prisoners). It is a time of cleansing, renewal, and unloading of baggage and grime that we may have accumulated for much of our lives.

It is impossible to adequately explain the depth of love, emotion, and spiritual power that is unleashed during an Emmaus weekend to one who has not attended such a mountaintop event. You have to be there to fully understand it. You truly have to scale the mountain to know what it is like at the summit. Suffice it to say in a nutshell that my Walk to Emmaus had a similar impact on my life as the encounter of those two dejected pilgrims with the risen Christ on the road to Emmaus 2,000 years ago [Luke: Chapter 24]. My heart burned within me and my eyes were opened to Christ for the first time in my life in the faces, actions, and love of total strangers. No longer was Christ an intellectual exercise, He had taken up residence in my heart.

The Walk to Emmaus was, in many respects, the greatest weekend of my life. I don't think anybody can go through an Emmaus weekend and deny that they have been in the presence of Almighty God or Christ Jesus. I was immeasurably blessed as I experienced God's love flowing through many servants. The Rev. Wally Chappell, who married Susan and I, described the Walk to Emmaus as a weekend of grace bombardment and I would add, love bombardment.

God is at work during the Walk to Emmaus; His reputation is at stake. It is His ministry. I remember feeling overwhelmed and then totally inadequate and undeserving of the efforts of so many strangers in being conduits of God's love. But that's the whole point: none of us deserves God's grace and love but He gives it to us anyway. I became broken bread and poured-out wine during my Emmaus weekend in which the tears flowed, my soul overflowed with the Holy Spirit, my heart warmed under God's loving embrace, and my eyes and heart were opened to the presence of Jesus.

There are not human words grand enough, eloquent enough, lofty enough or majestic enough to describe what happened to me during the Emmaus weekend. It was love in action, not preaching, not sermonizing, not holier-than-thou speeches. I was broken only to be rebuilt into a new creature in Christ. I was no longer the same person on Sunday evening that I was on Thursday evening when I arrived at the retreat center. Although Jesus told Nicodemus that no one can see the kingdom of God unless he is born again, I hesitate to use the expression *born again* since there seems to be a negative connotation in our society associating born-again Christians with holier-than-thou people. I have sometimes viewed the term *born again* as a condescending description from holier-than-thou

Christians who discredit other Christians' faith if they have not had some mountaintop conversion experience. God calls each of us to the gift of faith in different circumstances, some gradual over many years and some in a compressed time frame. However, *born again* best describes what happened to me during the 72-hour Walk to Emmaus. It is the same thing that happens to prisoners during a Kairos weekend. That is why it is a requirement to attend an Emmaus, Cursillo or some similar weekend in order to serve on a Kairos team. You must experience what the prisoners will experience; you can't give away what you don't have. Life would never be the same again for me after the Walk to Emmaus.

William James expresses the joy that can come from a lofty encounter in the religious realm in *The Varieties of Religious Experience*:

> There is a state of mind, known only to religious men, but to no others, in which the will to assert ourselves and hold our own has been displaced by a willingness to close our mouths and be as nothing in the floods and waterspouts of God. In this state of mind, what we most dreaded has become the habitation of our safety, and the hour of our moral death has turned into our spiritual birthday. The time for tension in our soul is over, and that of happy relaxation, of calm deep breathing, of an eternal present, has arrived. Fear is not held in abeyance as it is by mere morality, it is positively expunged and washed away. . .
>
> We shall see how infinitely passionate a thing religion at its highest flights can be. Like love, like wrath, like hope, ambition, jealousy, like every other instinctive eagerness and impulse, it adds to life an enchantment which is not rationally or logically deducible from anything else. This enchantment, coming as a gift when it does come, - a gift of our organism, the physiologists will tell us, a gift of God's grace, the theologians say, - is either there or not there for us, and there are persons who can no more become

> possessed by it than they can fall in love with a given woman by mere word of command. Religious feeling is thus an absolute addition to the Subject's range of life. It gives him a new sphere of power. When the outward battle is lost, and the outer world disowns him, it redeems and vivifies an interior world which otherwise would be an empty waste. . .This sort of happiness in the absolute and everlasting is what we find nowhere but in religion.[14]

It is difficult to adequately describe the feelings I experienced during those three days on the mountaintop. The ineffability of the Walk to Emmaus poses nearly insurmountable barriers in adequately conveying what the experience is like to a non-participant. It is like reading an eloquent account with flowery prose of a great symphonic work from the program notes, trying to imagine what the music sounds like. It can't even be compared to being there in the presence of a world-class orchestra under the direction of a world-class conductor playing a Mozart, Beethoven or Brahms symphony.

Or the difficulty of describing the Cascades in Oregon and Washington based only on pictures or paintings. It can't be compared to a camping trip in the midst of those spectacular volcanic peaks, forests of towering fir trees, and ice-cold water from the melting of the deep snow pack [Timberline Lodge at Mt. Hood has an average snow pack every winter of 22 feet], cascading down swollen boulder-strewn streams. Another example is a recent backpacking trek I made with my son and some Boy Scouts through the Grand Teton National Park, covering 38 miles over five days and scaling two peaks of 10,400 and 10,700 feet with 50-pound packs. The beauty of the Tetons can't be captured in photos. To experience the rugged beauty of this magnificent mountain range you have to probe its canyons, ridges and passes, hearing the wind rushing through the tree tops making a sound like the dull roar of an ocean beach; seeing the patches of sparkling snow, towering waterfalls, cascading brooks, and pristine lakes; a tapestry of multicolored wild flowers in lush meadows; peaceful forests; and a variety of animals including elk, moose, deer and even a black bear along with smaller animals.

I know the ordinary sense of things receded during the Emmaus weekend. For a time, however brief, there was a transcendent joy and exaltation. I was set free, floating on air, soaring on wings of eagles, singing with gusto. There was immense elation, with fears and anxieties evanescing into blissful equanimity, engendering a paradise of inner tranquility. St. Paul talks about the fruit of the Holy Spirit in Galatians 5:22-23: love, joy, peace, patience, kindness, goodness, faithfulness, gentleness, and self-control. Well, the Walk to Emmaus is a veritable fruit orchard with tenderness and charity being shared among total strangers, peace and unity prevailing. It is like being bathed in a warm glow of light, immersed in the infinite embrace of God. There was one point during the weekend in which a special ceremony occurs; I actually felt I was walking off the ground, being wafted upward into heaven.

It is like experiencing the impact of some world-class orchestra playing under a world-class conductor with impeccable precision and high-voltage energy, when all the distinct notes melt into perfect harmony, fading into the farthest reaches of the hall, leaving the listener gripping the edge of his chair, bursting with emotion, wondering in awe at the God who imbued such genius in the composer and craftsmanship in the conductor and orchestra members.

Dave Claugus and I attended such a concert one evening. The Los Angeles Philharmonic under Maestro Carlo Maria Giulini, one of the preeminent conductors of our time, was crammed onto the stage at Royce Hall, one of the original buildings on the UCLA campus and site of many recording sessions because of its fine acoustics. The occasion of this one-time only concert was to commemorate the 50th anniversary of the same exact program performed by the same orchestra led by Otto Klemperer. The mighty LA Philharmonic under Giulini's masterful conducting unleashed its power and precision, like a well-oiled and finely tuned engine with all cylinders and pistons firing in perfect harmony. The program was Mozart's stirring and ethereal 40th Symphony and Brahms' towering and majestic 1st Symphony, the latter of which became Giulini's signature piece during his tenure with the LA Philharmonic. Claugus and I had good seats, dead center in the middle of the main floor. We were on the edge of our seats the whole evening, riveted to the stage.

When the last sounds of Brahms wafted upward into infinity, the packed hall erupted in a thunderous and prolonged standing ovation. We left that concert, emotionally and physically drained.

There have been times, when, after some of my runs, I have felt this incredible peace coursing through me, like I was entering another dimension, a new state of existence. I was definitely in God's kingdom during that weekend, something I will never forget.

It was a real letdown coming off the mountain. But my life had changed for the better. I joined a Christian accountability group of six men; we met weekly. It was a wonderful time in my life, especially after spending three years in the valley. Since the mid-1990s I've had my ups and downs, but more ups than downs. Kind of like the stock market over time, the overall trend in my spiritual life has been upward. Certainly every Kairos team I've served on since 1996 has been a spiritual high, even the two teams I was on that the Kairos weekend got canceled because of gang fights and murders or rumors of gang hits system-wide, causing the prison to be locked down. The fact that we train for two complete weekends prior to going into the prison for a Kairos weekend is a huge blessing. We bond with each other, becoming one unit, the body of Christ when we enter that prison. We become like a big family, sharing prayers, songs, fellowship, food, and fun. Indeed Kairos gatherings, whether in training or in prison, whether at monthly reunions, weekly prayer-share meetings or the big weekend itself, are like a big party.

Tony Campolo, in his book *The Kingdom of God is a Party* tells of Christ's first miracle being performed at a party, a wedding party. Campolo shares the poignant story of how he encountered eight or nine prostitutes in a Honolulu restaurant at 3:30 AM. Campolo had traveled from the East Coast to Honolulu and his body clock was off so he was wandering around in the wee hours of the morning looking for a restaurant to get something to eat and drink. The women were dressed provocatively; they were boisterous, loud, and crude. Campolo felt uncomfortable and was about to exit the restaurant when he overheard the woman sitting next to him at the counter say, "Tomorrow's my birthday. I'm going to be thirty-nine."

> Her "friend" responded in a nasty tone, "So what do you want from me? A birthday party? What do you

> want? Ya want me to get you a cake and sing "Happy Birthday?"
>
> "Come on!" said the woman sitting next to me. "Why do you have to be so mean? I was just telling you, that's all. Why do you have to put me down? I was just telling you it was my birthday. I don't want anything from you. I mean, why should you give me a birthday party? I've never had a birthday party in my whole life. Why should I have one now?"[15]

Many prisoners could identify with that prostitute. I've heard many men tell me the same thing; they've never had a birthday party. That's why the birthday cake we give them Sunday afternoon, while singing "Happy Birthday" to them, and with each man's name inscribed on it, is such an emotional event; many of these men break down in tears when we celebrate their birthdays because nobody ever went to the trouble before.

Campolo was so moved by this encounter that he organized a birthday party for that lady and her friends the very next night when they made their regular stop at the restaurant. The restaurant owner and his wife were excited about the prospect and they baked a cake. Campolo showed up the next night at 2:30 A.M. with crepe-paper decorations and a big sign made out of big pieces of cardboard that read "Happy Birthday, Agnes!" The diner was festooned from one end to the other.

> The woman who did the cooking must have gotten the word out on the street, because by 3:15 every prostitute in Honolulu was in the place. It was wall-to-wall prostitutes. . . .and me!
>
> At 3:30 on the dot, the door of the diner swung open and in came Agnes and her friend. I had everybody ready (after all, I was kind of the M.C. of the affair) and when they came in we all screamed, "Happy Birthday!"
>
> Never have I seen a person so flabbergasted. . . .so stunned. . . .so shaken. Her mouth fell open. Her

legs seemed to buckle a bit. Her friend grabbed her arm to steady her. As she was led to sit on one of the stools along the counter we all sang "Happy Birthday" to her. As we came to the end of our singing with "happy birthday dear Agnes, happy birthday to you," her eyes moistened. Then, when the birthday cake with all the candles on it was carried out, she lost it and just openly cried.

Harry gruffly mumbled, "Blow out the candles, Agnes! Come on! Blow out the candles! If you don't blow out the candles, I'm gonna hafta blow out the candles." And, after an endless few seconds, he did. Then he handed her a knife and told her, "Cut the cake, Agnes. Yo, Agnes, we all want some cake."

Agnes looked down at the cake. Then without taking her eyes off it, she slowly and softly said, "Look, Harry, is it all right with you if I. . . .I mean is it O.K. if I kind of . . . .what I want to ask you is. . . .is it O.K. if I keep the cake a little while. I mean is it all right if we don't eat it right away?"

Harry shrugged and answered, "Sure! It's O.K. If you want to keep the cake, keep the cake. Take it home if you want to."

"Can I?" she asked. Then, looking at me she said, "I live just down the street a couple of doors. I want to take the cake home, O.K.? I'll be right back. Honest!"

She got off the stool, picked up the cake, and, carrying it like it was the Holy Grail, walked slowly toward the door. As we all just stood there motionless, she left.

When the door closed there was a stunned silence in the place. Not knowing what else to do, I broke the silence by saying, "What do you say we pray?"

Looking back on it now it seems more than strange for a sociologist to be leading a prayer meeting with a bunch of prostitutes in a diner in Honolulu at 3:30 in the morning. But then it just felt like the right thing to do. I prayed for Agnes. I prayed for her salvation. I prayed that her life would be changed and that God would be good to her.

When I finished, Harry leaned over the counter and with a trace of hostility in his voice, he said, "Hey! You never told me you were a preacher. What kind of church do you belong to?"

In one of those moments when just the right words came, I answered, "I belong to a church that throws birthday parties for whores at 3:30 in the morning."

Harry waited a moment and then almost sneered as he answered, "No you don't. There's no church like that. If there was, I'd join it. I'd join a church like that!"

Wouldn't we all? Wouldn't we all love to join a church that throws birthday parties for whores at 3:30 in the morning?

Well, that's the kind of church that Jesus came to create! I don't know where we got the other one that's so prim and proper. But anybody who reads the New Testament will discover a Jesus who loved to party with whores and with all kinds of left-out people. The publicans and "sinners" loved Him because He partied with them. The lepers of society found in Him someone who would eat and drink with them. And while the solemnly pious could not relate to what He was about, those lonely people who usually didn't get invited to parties took to Him with excitement.[16]

I belong to a church that throws birthday parties for men (and women) in a maximum-security prison. I belong to a church whose members get up at 4 A.M. on a Saturday each month to drive 100-150 miles one way to a maximum-security prison to be at the front gate at 7:30 A.M. in order to spend half a day with the men in white. And every time we get together, it is a party, with hugging, laughing and singing.

My secular life has experienced some highs as well as some rough times since the mid-1990s. In 1996 I embarked on the pursuit of the CFA® (Chartered Financial Analyst) designation offered by the CFA Institute. The rationale why I would put myself through such a rigorous program was to buy an option on career insurance. Never again did I want to go through the hell of having my income drop 65% for nearly three years running. If my business went in the tank next time I would have more marketability armed with an MBA and a CFA. The CFA charter is considered the preeminent designation in the fields of corporate finance, business valuation, securities analysis, portfolio management, and in the view of many, financial planning, both nationally and internationally. There are three annual six-hour examinations that must be taken sequentially. Because of the low pass rate, many candidates take longer than three years to get the charter. For example, the three years I took the exam (1996-1998), the combined national and international pass rates were 53%, 59%, and 59%, respectively. Thus, if one simply multiplies the ratios sequentially, the probability of one passing all the exams in three consecutive years is about 18%. However, this is only an approximation because every year there are a number of candidates taking the exams multiple times. Thus, the real probability of passing all three exams in three years is less than 18%. I was blessed to be able to accomplish this task.

My mother informed me in January 1997 that she had been diagnosed the previous October with multiple myeloma, an incurable form of leukemia. My dad has had several skin cancer lesions removed in the past few years. My sister Ann had three serious operations involving cervical and uterine cancer. Paul really started deteriorating from the ravages of multiple sclerosis in the mid-1990s. Paul inspired many, including the men at the Michael

Unit whom I shared his courageous testimony with. His positive attitude in the midst of great adversity touched many of my brothers behind the walls. I felt inspired to honor Paul by training to run the Houston Marathon in January 1999, raising funds for the National MS Society. Unfortunately, I had to have emergency gall bladder surgery 10 days before the race, wiping out five months of training. In December 2001, I completed the Dallas White Rock Marathon in Paul's honor, along with my good friend Charles Lightfoot. Less than two months later, on February 1, 2002, Paul died from kidney failure at the age of 48. The following quote by William James is a good description of Paul.

> A life is manly, stoical, moral, or philosophical, we say, in proportion as it is less swayed by paltry personal considerations and more by objective ends that call for energy, even though that energy bring personal loss and pain. This is the good side of war, in so far as it calls for 'volunteers.' And for morality life is a war, and the service of the highest is a sort of cosmic patriotism which also calls for volunteers. Even a sick man, unable to be militant outwardly, can carry on the moral warfare. He can willfully turn his attention away from his own future, in this world or the next. He can train himself to indifference to his present drawbacks and immerse himself in whatever objective interests still remain accessible. He can follow public news, and sympathize with other people's affairs. He can cultivate cheerful manners, and be silent about his miseries. He can contemplate whatever ideal aspects of existence his philosophy is able to present to him, and practice whatever duties, such as patience, resignation, trust, his ethical system requires. He is a high-hearted freeman and no pining slave.[17]

Paul battled the debilitating effects of multiple sclerosis (MS) for 25 years. Some of the most inspirational people I've met are those who struggle with physical disabilities. Somehow these warriors transcend their obstacles, hardships, and sufferings and leave the rest of us in awe.

Paul became a prisoner in his own body. MS is a chronic disease that randomly attacks the central nervous system, with symptoms ranging from slight blurring of vision and speech to complete paralysis. Paul lost the use of his hands and fingers. His legs were so stiff that he couldn't get out of bed on his own power. His only transportation was a motorized wheelchair and he was completely dependent on others. He wasn't able to eat food for four years, getting his only nourishment from a stomach tube that had to be painfully reinserted periodically due to infections. Can you imagine not being able to taste food for four years? He had a catheter that also had to be painfully reinserted periodically and he wore a diaper. He was in and out of the hospital a dozen times preceding his death due to septic/blood poisoning from blockages in his catheter. He often choked as his lungs filled with phlegm. He could barely make an audible sound and his hoarse and gasping speech, when it was audible, was virtually unintelligible because he had lost the use of his tongue and facial muscles. Yet Paul rarely complained. He told me that his reason for living was to inspire others by allowing God's love to shine through him. I shared his testimony with the Kairos prisoners and many of these men were inspired by Paul's courage, tenacity, and cheerfulness. Many of these men prayed for Paul and several wrote him letters.

Paul prayed to be able to get out of bed directly into a wheelchair with no assistance. I complained about having to get up early some mornings. Paul prayed about being able to eat food through his mouth. I complained about some of the food I ate. Paul prayed about being able to go to the bathroom by himself. I complained about having to get up during the night sometimes to go to the bathroom. Paul prayed to be able to walk with a walker. I complained about running injuries. It was no longer I, who was the big brother, setting an example for Paul, teaching him. I was now the student, the younger sibling, observing Paul, trying to emulate his standard of praying more and complaining less, trying to learn from his example of having a positive attitude, gentle humor, grace, courage, and dignity.

I wanted to share a little of my brother with you. He still inspires me with the life he lived. Paul had the heart of an Olympic champion because of the class and caliber of struggle he waged against a relentless foe. Anybody who perseveres in the face of great adversity and hardship, who refuses to yield to the enemy from within, who strives valiantly to overcome the fragility of the human body by embracing the indomitability of the human spirit, is a hero. Paul remains a hero because he refused to quit. I hate what this disease did to my brother.

I saw in Paul a peace that I didn't understand. His acceptance of his condition amazed me. I yearned to know how someone in his condition could be at peace in such adversity. And again my search led me to the Bible for comfort as well as answers.

5

> The call of God is not a reflection of my nature; my personal desires and temperament are of no consideration. As long as I dwell on my own qualities and traits and think about what I am suited for, I will never hear the call of God. But when God brings me into the right relationship with Himself, I will be in the same condition Isaiah was. Isaiah was so attuned to God, because of the great crisis he had just endured, that the call of God penetrated his soul. The majority of us cannot hear anything but ourselves. And we cannot hear anything God says. But to be brought to the place where we can hear the call of God is to be profoundly changed.
>
> If you have received a ministry from the Lord Jesus, you will know that the need is not the same as the call - the need is the opportunity to exercise the call. The call is to be faithful to the ministry you received when you were in true fellowship with Him. This does not imply that there is a whole series of differing ministries marked out for you. It does mean that you must be sensitive to what God has called you to do, and this may sometimes require ignoring demands for service in other areas.
>
> Oswald Chambers

THE CALL

It was during the turmoil of the early to mid-1990s that I realized I was not in control. My education, career, and professional designations did not provide security. I began to search for something that would provide security, comfort, and peace. As the previous chapter concluded, I was despondent over the confluence of setbacks in my life. This crisis in my life was the catalyst in prompting me to seek God for the first time. The pain of those three years led me to read the entire Bible twice. I began attending Sunday School classes and enrolled in Bible study classes. I began reading books, some of which are quoted in this book. I was thirsty and I couldn't quench my thirst; I was hungry to know God. The anguish of this period is what eventually led me to the Walk to Emmaus in the summer of 1995. Nine months later, in April 1996, I found myself voluntarily entering a maximum-security prison to spend time with a group of men that I held more prejudice against than any other group in society. Only God could have engineered something like that because the last thing I would have done in a million years, on my own volition, would be to minister to prisoners. How did I know what He was calling me to do during that nine-month interval?

In the ensuing years I have discovered that my fear of giving up things in the physical or secular world was misplaced. Activities that I found myself abandoning or reducing my time allocation toward were rather trivial when compared to the unmatched joy I received when I accepted God's call into Kairos Prison Ministry. We get so caught up with accumulating things and the busyness of life that we don't realize that the material goods that we acquire and activities that we engage in eventually rust and wither, leaving us empty and unfulfilled. The joy of being centered in God's will, doing what He has called you to do, engenders a joy and a peace and a strength that is unsurpassed. Sharing God's love with the least of His children allows me to experience a slice of heaven on earth, affording me a chance to accumulate treasures in heaven - treasures that won't rust and evaporate like the mist.

So you say, how does a person know when he receives a call from God? I think the answer depends on each individual. For me, it was a series of incredible circumstances over seven months, from my Emmaus weekend to late January 1996, that finally broke my resistance to serving Christ in one of His most distressing disguises, that being the men who reside in a maximum-security prison.

I'll never forget when a man stood up at the back of the conference room at the Emmaus retreat center and started reading excerpts from letters sent to us from prisoners - deeply moving and heartfelt letters. And then we were stunned to discover that these prisoners were praying for us. I was moved by this display of love but my reaction was one of aloofness and detachment. My attitude was: I know it says somewhere in the Bible that we are supposed to visit those in prison but that's not for me God; I'll be glad to do any number of other ministries, let someone else do the prison ministry work. It is often the case that God calls us to ministries that completely dumbfound us and a typical reaction is one of reluctance or resistance. It is so human to want to control what our ministries are, to serve God in our way and in our time and in our controlled environment. But what counts is not our call, but God's call.

There were six table families of eight men each during my Emmaus weekend. Each table had two Emmaus team members - a table leader and an assistant table leader - and six pilgrims. Thus, 36 pilgrims attended my Emmaus Walk; only one other pilgrim, except for another man from my church who was not eligible to sit at the same table as me (to split the pilgrims among tables of non-acquaintances), lived in the Lake Highlands area of Dallas. It turned out that Tim Leslie lived a couple of miles from me. What are the odds of this happening? Two men, who didn't know each other living in the same area, out of 36 pilgrims or one out of eighteen. Thus, there was a 1/18th chance that two men from the Lake Highlands area of Dallas would be at this Emmaus weekend who didn't know each other. The next interesting circumstance is that Tim and I were assigned to the Table of Luke, a one in six chance.

Tim and I were also the only men to have run a marathon out of the 36 pilgrims and we hit it off nicely. At the close of the weekend I suggested we join a weekly accountability group (called a reunion group by the Emmaus community), which the Emmaus movement encourages, since we lived in the same neighborhood. Tim concurred and said his sponsor, David Kaseman, already had an Emmaus reunion group that we could join. Initially we had six men in the group, only one of which, David Kaseman, was involved with Kairos Prison Ministry. To calculate the odds of this circumstance happening, that is, joining a random group of unknown Emmaus "graduates," you would ideally survey the number of reunion groups and the number of groups that had at least one Kairos volunteer. However, this information is unavailable. Therefore, I used the ratio of Kairos volunteers to reunion group members (one in six) as a proxy for this probability.

David Kaseman visited the Michael Unit each month and would always share some of the things he experienced in our reunion group the following week. My attitude during the first four months after my Emmaus weekend was: I'm glad David Kaseman is doing this ministry because I could never do it; my prejudice against prisoners was simply too strong. The idea of even remotely considering the possibility of being a prison minister was so odious to me that I simply could not envision ever doing it.

On October 27 and 28, 1995, about four months after the Emmaus weekend, I attended the first of two Promise Keepers conferences (the other being in the autumn of 1996) at Texas Stadium, home of the Dallas Cowboys. With about 60,000 men in attendance, we heard a number of excellent speakers including James Ryle, a pastor from Colorado. Ryle spoke at the first conference in 1995 but not at the 1996 conference. Thus, the probability of me hearing Ryle's message was a one in two proposition.

It's interesting, when a few years later I was examining the notes I took on Ryle's talk, that the only thing I remembered from his talk was nowhere in my notes! This is because his personal testimony was so gripping that all I could focus on was his message. Ryle delivered an electrifying testimony about a tragedy in his youth that gripped the audience. You could have heard a pin drop when Ryle began dramatically weaving his story, as 60,000 men sat in hushed expectancy. When he was 17 years old he killed a man in a hit-and-run accident. While out on bail, he was advised by some "friends" to begin selling drugs to pay for a good defense attorney. He was caught selling drugs and wound up doing time in a Texas prison, the same one his father helped build as an inmate laborer two or three decades earlier. It was in prison, where Ryle hit rock bottom, that he found Christ. Now here was a gifted preacher, an ordained minister with his own church in the Denver area, the chaplain for the University of Colorado Buffaloes football team (formerly coached by Bill McCartney, founder of Promise Keepers), speaking to hundreds of thousands of men around the country at various Promise Keepers conferences, who at one time was one of the least of the least. The whole time Ryle was presenting his riveting testimony I could only think of one thing - the unmatched power of Jesus Christ to transform a human life. It was during Ryle's testimony that I felt God talking to me through Ryle; it was like I was the only one in that stadium with a tunnel between Ryle and myself and the message was coming in loud and clear. For a time, however brief, it was just Ryle and me in that stadium, with God whispering in that small, soft voice of His: "Go into Kairos."

During this same exact weekend, my friend, David Kaseman, was on the Kairos #7 team at the Michael Unit (October 26-29). What are the odds of Promise Keepers and Kairos #7 occurring during the same weekend? Since there are 52 weekends per year, the odds of both happening on the same weekend would be 1/52. However, realistically, some weekends wouldn't be likely to feature Kairos or Promise Keepers, such as certain holidays. Adjusting for Thanksgiving, Christmas, New Years, Easter, Memorial Day, and Labor Day, the available weekends would be narrowed to 46. Thus, the odds change to 1/46.

Well, the next week at our reunion group I shared about the amazing experience of worshiping God with 60,000 men, the spiritual high of singing wonderful songs like *Amazing Grace; Holy, Holy, Holy*; and *Be Thou My Vision* with so many men, voices and arms raised to heaven, and hearing powerful testimonies from gifted orators. And then it was Kaseman's turn. He slowly began to unveil some of the miracles he had witnessed, eventually getting so emotional that he had to pause a few times. Ed Noble (a fellow pilgrim on my Emmaus weekend) and I were on the edge of our seats, listening intently to Kaseman's testimony, our eyes filling with tears. Ed and I knew in our hearts that we wanted to experience what Kaseman had. When I got home that morning from our breakfast meeting, I excitedly told Susan about all the circumstances that had been piling up since my Emmaus weekend, pointing unmistakably to God's call for me to join Kairos. Susan was very supportive with only one constraint: that I only work one team per year in order to spend time with the children. I made a commitment to her and the kids to average one team per year.

But this was not all. The most improbable statistical odds were yet to happen. Our first Kairos #8 team meeting was the day before Super Bowl Sunday in late January 1996. On the morning of Super Bowl Sunday, I was driving the family to church at about 9:30 A.M. We live only about five minutes from church. Five-year-old Hope was in the back of the minivan and eight-year-old Oscar was in the middle seat of the van, singing and talking. Susan was in the front passenger seat. Within a minute or two, Oscar picked up some Sunday School handout or bulletin that he somehow plucked out of the trash that is characteristic of cars with families that have young children. We often joke that our minivan is a mobile trash dumpster. Oscar began reading the following Scripture from the parable of the sheep and the goats:

> For I was hungry and you gave me something to eat, I was thirsty and you gave me something to drink, I was a stranger and you invited me in, I needed clothes and you clothed me, I was sick and you looked after me, I was in prison and you came to visit me.
>
> Matthew 25:35-36

Susan and I had been visiting in the front seat, but as soon as we recognized this familiar Scripture, we ceased talking and listened. When Oscar finished the last sentence, I was approaching a stop sign at a six-lane road and I was in no condition to attempt crossing it, chills going up and down my spine. Susan and I looked at each other and she said, "Steve, God just gave you another signal." It was God speaking through Oscar, telling me in effect, "Steve, I've called you into prison ministry; you've been to one team meeting yesterday, don't even think about backing out." What are the odds that Oscar would just happen to pick up a piece of paper in a trashed-out car and read the two verses of Scripture that contain the heart of Kairos Prison Ministry ("I was in prison and you came to visit me"). I did some research and found that the Bible has 31,124 verses. Thus, the odds of picking out two verses randomly out of 31,124 verses is equal to one out of 15,562 verses.

What are the odds of all these circumstances happening in such a short time? Using the principle of probability through multiplication of the various denominators of each chance, the odds can be calculated as follows: 1/18 x 1/6 x 1/6 x 1/2 x 1/46 x 1/15,562 or one in 927,744,192 or one chance out of a little under a billion. This can be expressed as approximately 0.928×10^9. Do you think God engineered all these circumstances?

I know beyond a shadow of a doubt that this is where I am supposed to be, serving Christ in prison in one of His most distressing disguises. I have no idea why God called me into this ministry. Perhaps God knew that I needed to get over my prejudice toward this segment of society. I know God has a sense of humor. I believe God desires to stretch us. Thus, if we have particularly strong prejudices, then perhaps God desires to soften our hearts by calling us into ministries that we would otherwise strongly resist on our own inclination. People in my Sunday School class at the time were shocked when I announced that I was seeking support for Kairos since I hardly ever said anything in class. Christ told us that His power is made perfect in weakness. God perhaps calls some of us into ministries that we are naturally weak in so that He may be glorified.

It is one of the profoundest discoveries in life when you discern God's call as Oswald Chambers said. It is a special blessing because some people never find out the reason why they're here. When there is no uncertainty, no ambiguity, no confusion, there is a peace, joy, strength, and energy that comes from the Holy Spirit. I thank God for choosing me and being relentless in the circumstances He engineered in my life. I know for a fact that if it wasn't for Him I wouldn't have entered prison ministry in a million years, it flat-out wouldn't have happened. But because circumstances lined up so perfectly for me, I was ready to explore the path that God had laid before me. This call led me to explore walking in God's will.

I continue to be amazed that I am in prison ministry. Another amazing thing is how God has softened my attitude toward death-row inmates during these past few years. For many years I had been a vigorous proponent of capital punishment. If there was one group of people that I despised in society, it was the people locked up on death row. Now, after doing my own research and examining the evidence and praying about it, I came to the conclusion that I was ignorant. Once again God changed my thinking.

For those seeking the Truth, it is important to pay close attention to your circumstances. God often speaks to us through other people, the written word (a holy book and related books, articles, etc.), and circumstances. I find that when things line up, like a target in the cross hairs of a rifle, God's will is evident when circumstances are congruent with His word.

6

> If you are searching for God and do not know where to begin, learn to pray and take the trouble to pray every day. You can pray anytime, anywhere. . .You can pray at work - work doesn't have to stop prayer and prayer doesn't have to stop work. . .Tell Him everything, talk to Him. He is our father, He is father to us all whatever religion we are. We are all created by God, we are his children. We have to put our trust in Him and love Him, believe in Him, work for Him. And if we pray, we will get all the answers we need.
>
> Mother Teresa

SEEKING THE TRUTH

There are many faiths in the world. Most people adhere to the faith that they were brought up in. I know if I had been born into a Jewish family, the odds are that I would practice the Jewish faith. If I had been born in India, the odds are that I would practice the Hindu faith. You receive instruction and indoctrination as a young child which is reinforced over the years by parents, relatives, friends, teachers, and religious leaders. Thus, we are usually born into a certain faith and more or less come to accept the tenets of that particular faith over time.

I would like to challenge every person to seek the Truth directly from God. It is good to observe others in learning one's faith and receive training from knowledgeable people, but ultimately it is our responsibility to seek the Truth on our own. It is incumbent upon us to eventually go it alone in seeking the Truth. We must do our own rigorous research and assiduous analysis. We must learn to think well. This includes not only studying one's own existing faith but the other major faiths as well to discern God's will for humanity. God is Truth. God is perfect love. We must seek the faith that comes closest to achieving God's perfection. Perfect love drives out fear. A person who is already secure in his or her own faith should have no fear exploring other major faiths. God gives us free will and you are free to choose whatever faith you discover to be the Truth. But how can you know what God's will for humanity is unless you do your own research and analysis? How can you intellectually defend your position, with integrity, unless you have researched, studied, and analyzed other faiths? Only you can establish with confidence what the Truth is by seeking the Truth for yourself.

Pursuing the Truth by asking God for guidance takes courage. Courage is the fortitude to stay the course, to persevere no matter what the obstacles. It might mean going against the training of your parents, relatives, and ethnic group that has a track record of thousands of years of beliefs, rituals, and traditions. But what is ultimately more important: relying on the truth from humans or on what God is telling you directly? I have a close friend who is a member of another faith. He told me that he was not convertible because that would be disrespectful to his deceased parents. But what is worse: being disrespectful to your parents or being disrespectful to God because you opted not to seek the Truth from Him? Who is the best source for the Truth: your parents or God?

Getting to know God is a life-long process. It is a marathon, an endurance event. You can have the best coaches, the best equipment, the best nutrition, the best training books, the best medical care, the best training partners, the best environment, but nobody can run the marathon for you. When Frank C. Shorter, gold and silver medalist in the marathon in the 1972 Munich and 1976 Montreal Olympic Games, was asked by reporters if special food was a key to his success, he responded to the effect, "Vitamins, bee pollen, yogurt, tofu. . . .maybe, I don't know. But I do know one thing: You don't run 26.2 miles at less than 5 minutes per mile on good looks and a secret recipe." Not even Bill Gates with his untold wealth can buy you a marathon finish. Nobody can put in the miles in preparation for you. It's your body that has to go through the trials and tribulations in training in order to have a chance at finishing the marathon. When you show up at the start of the marathon, it is you and you alone against 26.2 miles (42.2 kilometers). So it is with getting to know God. You can have the best rabbis, the best imams, the best teachers, preachers, and monks, the best religious study materials and holy books, etc. but only you can get to know God personally for yourself. What is more important: to know God personally or rely on what you've been spoon-fed all your life? It takes guts to seek the Truth. But how else can you defend your faith unless you have intellectual integrity. How can you defend your position if you haven't truly scrutinized other principal faiths? How do you know what God's will is for humanity unless you've done your own research, study, and analysis? You can't. Therefore every person should seek the Truth on their own. As the late George Sheehan, M.D. stated, we were born to be participants, not spectators in the drama of life. We must not rely solely on what is spoon-fed us; we must seek the Truth for ourselves and nobody can do that for us. We must eventually come to grips with who God is and what His will is for humanity.

> We were not created to be spectators. Not made to be onlookers. Not born to be bystanders. You and I cannot view life as a theatergoer would, pleased or displeased by what unfolds. You, as well as I, are producer, playwright, and actor making, creating and living the drama on stage. Life must be lived. Acted out. The play we are in is our own.
>
> There are reasons, of course, to observe others. To learn how something is done. And to see the human body or soul or intellect in its perfection. We watch others so that their skill becomes our skill, their wisdom becomes our wisdom, their faith becomes our faith. But eventually we must go it alone. Find our own skill, our own wisdom, *our own faith* [my emphasis]. Otherwise we will die without having learned who we are or what we can accomplish. And we will die without having an inkling of the meaning of it all.[18]

I am convinced that if people sought the Truth for themselves that eventually most people on the planet would align with one religion because God's will is perfect and pleasing. There will never be unanimity because there is no absolute proof which religion is the Truth. If there was absolute proof, there would be no need for faith which is a gift God desires to give us. God wants us to come to Him with the faith of little children so that we can get to know Him. After much study and research, I believe that God has offered a preponderance of evidence that bolsters one religion. But that is my own conclusion. You are encouraged to embark on your own quest for the Truth to find out for yourself what you think is God's plan for humanity.

It is also useful to note that many scientific truths were held for hundreds, if not thousands of years, before being shattered by continuing research and analysis that proved them false. Just because fallible human beings have practiced a certain faith for X number of years doesn't mean that particular faith is God's will for humanity. What counts is not what human beings think and will; what matters is what God's will is. Only God can help you discover the Truth. Go to Him in prayer and earnestly ask Him to help you discover, develop, and deploy the Truth.

There are three "original" sins according to M. Scott Peck, the noted psychiatrist and author: pride, fear, and laziness. Most of us believe our own faith is the best because of our human pride. We naturally adhere to what our parents and ancestors believed. Thus, pride is an obstacle to seeking the Truth. We think there is no need to explore other faiths because ours is right. Fear is another obstacle in seeking the Truth. We are afraid of what we might find, especially if it leads us to another faith. We are afraid of the cognitive dissonance and the repercussions of going against our parents and ancestors. Finally, laziness obstructs us from seeking the Truth. It takes energy and effort to research, study, and analyze other faiths and to pray to God, to really listen to God, for discerning His will. It is much easier to simply take what you've been taught without critically thinking for yourself.

There is a man whom I greatly admire who overcame the big three sins in seeking the Truth for himself. His name is Louis Lapides and his story is an amazing one as documented in Lee Strobel's excellent book *The Case for Christ*. Lapides grew up in a Jewish family, attending a conservative Jewish synagogue in Newark, New Jersey. His family never discussed the Messiah and it was never an issue in the Hebrew school he attended. Jesus was only referenced in derogatory terms. Lapides, when he was first presented the New Testament, had pre-conceived notions that it was a handbook on anti-Semitism. He thought the American Nazi Party would have found it useful as a guidebook. Lee Strobel was saddened to hear this, thinking how many other Jewish children have grown up thinking Christians are their enemies.

Lapides' spiritual quest was engendered by difficulties in his youth. The divorce of his parents when he was 17 led to a rebellious attitude. He didn't feel a personal relationship with God through Judaism. He was drafted and served time in Vietnam, where he experienced or witnessed suffering, death, drugs, and some anti-Semitism. Because of his isolation, he began delving into Eastern religions and philosophies and began visiting Buddhist temples in Japan. Lapides came home from Vietnam, with a penchant for marijuana and a desire to become a Buddhist priest. He attempted to live a spartan lifestyle to offset the wrongs of his earlier life but he realized he could never overcome his past misdeeds. He got depressed and began experimenting with LSD.

Seeking a new start in his life, he moved to California.

> I went to Buddhist meetings, but that was empty. Chinese Buddhism was atheistic, Japanese Buddhism worshiped statues of Buddha, Zen Buddhism was too elusive. I went to Scientology meetings, but they were too manipulative and controlling. Hinduism believed in all these crazy orgies that the gods would have and in gods who were blue elephants. None of it made sense; none of it was satisfying.[19]

In 1969, a tumultuous time in America, Lapides found himself on Sunset Strip in Los Angeles, observing an evangelist who had chained himself to an eight-foot cross in protest of local tavern owners who had evicted him from his storefront ministry. Some Christians on the sidewalk challenged Lapides' thinking on the Old and New Testaments. When Jesus' name was mentioned, Lapides replied with his standard response: "I'm Jewish, I can't believe in Jesus." Then a pastor challenged him by asking Lapides if he was knowledgeable of the messianic prophecies. This caught Lapides off guard and the pastor began reeling off some of the prophecies from the Old Testament. Lapides was startled because he knew that Jewish Scriptures were being quoted and he was ignorant of any references to Jesus being in the Old Testament. Lapides initially agreed to read the Old Testament but not the New Testament. The pastor concurred, saying:

> Just read the Old Testament and ask the God of Abraham, Isaac, and Jacob - the God of Israel - to show you if Jesus is the Messiah. Because he *is* your Messiah. He came to the Jewish people initially, and then he was also the Savior of the world.[20]

Lapides was intrigued enough to begin poring over the Old Testament, searching for references to the Messiah. When Lapides read Isaiah 53, he was stopped dead in his tracks by the explicit prophecy of a Messiah 700 years prior to Jesus walking the earth.

> Who has believed our message and to whom has the arm of the Lord been revealed? He grew up before him like a tender shoot, and like a root out of dry ground. He had no beauty or majesty to attract us to him, nothing in his appearance that we should desire him. He was despised and rejected by men, a man of sorrows, and familiar with suffering. Like one from whom men hide their faces he was despised, and we esteemed him not. Surely he took up our infirmities and carried our sorrows, yet we considered him stricken by God, smitten by him, and afflicted. But he was pierced for our transgressions, he was crushed for our iniquities; the punishment that brought us peace was upon him, and by his wounds we are healed. We all, like sheep, have gone astray, each of us has turned to his own way; and the Lord has laid on him the iniquity of us all. He was oppressed and afflicted, yet he did not open his mouth; he was led like a lamb to the slaughter and as a sheep before her shearers is silent, so he did not open his mouth. By oppression and judgment he was taken away. And

> who can speak of his descendants? For he was cut off from the land of the living; for the transgression of my people he was stricken. He was assigned a grave with the wicked, and with the rich in his death, though he had done no violence, nor was any deceit in his mouth. Yet it was the Lord's will to crush him and cause him to suffer, and though the Lord makes his life a guilt offering, he will see his offspring and prolong his days, and the will of the Lord will prosper in his hand. After the suffering of his soul, he will see the light of life and be satisfied; by his knowledge my righteous servant will justify many, and he will bear their iniquities. Therefore, I give him a portion among the great, and he will divide the spoils with the strong, because he poured out his life unto death, and was numbered with the transgressors. For he bore the sin of many, and made intercession for the transgressors.
>
> Isaiah 53:1-12

Lapides recognized the description in Isaiah as that of the Jesus he had seen as a child passing Catholic churches: the suffering Jesus who had been "pierced for our transgressions" as he "bore the sin of many." Lapides recognized the consistency of Jesus being the sacrificial lamb of God with the Jewish practice of animal sacrifices in the Old Testament for the atonement of sins.

> So breathtaking was this discovery that Lapides could only come to one conclusion: it was a fraud! He believed that Christians had rewritten the Old Testament and twisted Isaiah's words to make it sound as if the prophet had been foreshadowing Jesus.
>
> Lapides set out to expose the deception. "I asked my stepmother to send me a Jewish Bible so I could check it out myself," he told me. "She did, and guess what? I found that it said the same thing! Now I really had to deal with it."[21]

As Lapides continued to uncover prophecy after prophecy regarding the Messiah, his skepticism melted to the point that he was able to take a dramatic leap - reading the New Testament.

> Matthew's initial words leaped off the page: "A record of the genealogy of Jesus Christ the son of David, the son of Abraham . . ."
>
> Lapides' eyes widened as he recalled the moment he first read that sentence. "I thought, Wow! Son of Abraham, son of David - it was all fitting together! I went to the birth narratives and thought, Look at this! Matthew is quoting from Isaiah 7:14: 'The virgin will be with child and will give birth to a son.' And then I saw him quoting from the prophet Jeremiah. I sat there thinking. You know, this is about Jewish people. Where do the Gentiles come in? What's going on here?
>
> "I couldn't put it down. I read through the rest of the gospels, and I realized this wasn't a handbook for the American Nazi Party; it was an interaction between Jesus and the Jewish community. I got to the book of Acts and - this was incredible! - they were trying to figure out how the Jews could bring the story of Jesus to the Gentiles. Talk about role reversal!"[22]

After continued prayer and seeking God's will, Lapides accepted Christ into his heart. Lapides used the word "whole" to describe the peace that he felt, a wholeness that he had never felt before. Integrity is another description of wholeness. Yet, Lapides knew he was risking ostracism from his parents. They were joyful that his desire for drugs had ended and his emotional health seemed much improved but they were dismayed to find out that Jesus was behind the transformation. Lapides went on to earn a bachelor's degree in theology from Dallas Baptist University as well as a master of divinity and a master of theology degree in Old Testament and Semitics from Talbot Theological Seminary. Lapides met his wife, Deborah, also Jewish and a disciple of Christ. In an amazing circumstance engineered by God, she took him to her church, the same one that was pastored by the minister who had challenged him to read the Old Testament on Sunset Strip. Lapides went on to start Beth Ariel Fellowship, a home for Jews and Gentiles seeking wholeness in Jesus.

Lee Strobel posed a penetrating question to Lapides: "If the prophecies were so obvious to you and pointed unquestionably toward Jesus, why don't more Jews accept him as their Messiah?"

> It was a question Lapides has asked himself a lot during the three decades since he was challenged by a Christian to investigate the Jewish Scriptures. "In my case, I took the time to read them," he replied. "Oddly enough, even though the Jewish people are known for having high intellects, in this area there's a lot of ignorance.
>
> "Plus you have countermissionary organizations that hold seminars in synagogues to try to disprove the messianic prophecies. Jewish people hear them and use them as an excuse for not exploring the prophecies personally. They'll say, 'The rabbi told me there's nothing to this.'
>
> "I'll ask them, 'Do you think the rabbi just brought up an objection that Christianity has never heard before? I mean, scholars have been working on this for hundreds of years! There's great literature out there and powerful Christian answers to those challenges.' If they're interested, I help them go further."
>
> I wondered about the ostracism a Jewish person faces if he or she becomes a Christian. "That's definitely a factor," he said. "Some people won't let the messianic prophecies grab them, because they're afraid of the repercussions - potential rejection by their family and the Jewish community. That's not easy to face. Believe me, I know."[23]

Lapides is an example of a man who overcame pride, fear, and laziness in seeking the Truth. Here is a man who has humility, courage, and diligence. Lapides mentions how many Jews simply take instructions from seminars and rabbis without doing their own thinking and research. Intellectual integrity demands commitment, guts, and effort. Lapides took time and effort to actually read the Old and New Testaments himself.

Lee Strobel presented similar stories as that of Louis Lapides in his book *The Case for Christ.*

> I reflected on how many times I had encountered similar stories [as Louis Lapides], especially among successful and thoughtful Jewish people who had specifically set out to refute Jesus' messianic claims.
>
> I though about Stan Telchin, the East Coast businessman who had embarked on a quest to expose the "cult" of Christianity after his daughter went away to college and received *Y'shua* (Jesus) as her Messiah. He was astonished to find that this investigation led him - and his wife and second daughter - to the same Messiah. He later became a Christian minister, and his book that recounts his story, *Betrayed!,* has been translated into more than twenty languages.
>
> There was Jack Sternberg, a prominent cancer physician in Little Rock, Arkansas, who was so alarmed at what he found in the Old Testament that he challenged three rabbis to disprove that Jesus was the Messiah. They couldn't, and he too has claimed to have found wholeness in Christ.
>
> And there was Peter Greenspan, an obstetrician-gynecologist who practices in the Kansas City area and is a clinical assistant professor at the University of Missouri-Kansas City School of Medicine. Like Lapides, he had been challenged to look for Jesus in Judaism. What he found troubled him, so he went to the Torah and Talmud, seeking to discredit Jesus' messianic credentials. Instead he concluded that Jesus did miraculously fulfill the prophecies.

> For him, the more he read books by those trying to undermine the evidence for Jesus as the Messiah, the more he saw the flaws in their arguments. Ironically, concluded Greenspan, "I think I actually came to faith in *Y'shua* by reading what detractors wrote."
>
> He found, as have Lapides and others, that Jesus' words in the gospel of Luke have proved true: "Everything must be fulfilled that is written about me in the Law of Moses, the Prophets and the Psalms" (Luke 24:44). It was fulfilled, and only in Jesus - the sole individual in history who has matched the prophetic fingerprint of God's anointed one.[24]

Lapides notes that people who don't take time to do their own research are ignorant. The offspring of pride and laziness are arrogance and ignorance. It is far easier to simply take at face value what others tell you; it requires very little thinking. Thinking is hard work and can result in cognitive dissonance when new information creates friction with previously held thoughts. And human beings will go to great lengths to avoid the pain of cognitive dissonance. Lapides is a man who thinks well. Not thinking well is one of the major curses of humanity because it leads to ignorance which breeds bigotry and prejudice, precluding us from reaching the human potential.

M. Scott Peck, in his book *The Road Less Traveled and Beyond*, discusses thinking.

> Thinking is difficult. Thinking is complex. And thinking is - more than anything else - a process, with a course or direction, a lapse of time, and a series of steps or stages that lead to some result. To think well is a laborious, often painstaking process until one becomes accustomed to being "thoughtful." Since it is a process, the course or direction may not always be clear-cut. Not all the steps or stages are linear; nor are they always in the same sequence. Some are circular and overlap with others. Not everyone seeks to achieve the same result. Given all this, if we are

> to think well, we must be on guard against simplistic thinking in our approach to analyzing crucial issues and solving the problems of life.[25]

People are generally comfortable in their existing framework and don't want to rock the boat. People lack the guts to reach beyond their comfort zone, no matter where that leads them. They are too lazy to expend time and energy to think well.

> It is no surprise that many people resist the arduous efforts involved in continually monitoring and revising their thinking . . . Yet if all the energy required to think seems troublesome, the lack of thinking causes far more trouble and conflict for ourselves as individuals and for the society in which we live.[26]

In the history of the world there has always been war, strife, and civil disobedience. What if every person put down their weapons and began thinking well? What if people would study holy books of other faiths and denominations and/or objective, reputable books discussing the major religions of the world? Even if people, after doing their own research, study, and analysis - their own thinking - their own praying and listening to God, adhered to their own faith they would have a much better understanding of other peoples' faith. This would promote peace. Thinking well is how I overcame my strong prejudice against prisoners - I spent time with them in their environment and most importantly, I applied the Kairos motto: "listen, listen, love, love." I expended energy listening to men in prison. Not only should we think well, but we should listen to one another, to try to understand another person's faith and come to our own conclusion what God's will for humanity is.

The other sin Lapides overcame was fear - fear of rejection from his family and Jewish community. It takes guts to think well because, if you are truly open-minded and analytical, you don't know the end result, the potential ramifications. Thinking well is integrity, letting the chips fall where they may. To think or not to think is the real question.

God gave us a brain to think with. He wants us to think well. Our sins of pride, laziness, and fear hinder our brain from thinking well. Peck continues:

> Just as our capacity for learning depends on thinking, our capacity for thinking well depends on learning . . . When we are young, our dependency on those who raise us shapes our thinking and what we learn. And given our lengthy dependence, we are at risk of developing thinking patterns that have become ingrained, even seemingly irreversible. If we have adults in our young lives who help us to learn to think well, we benefit in a multitude of ways. If we have adults in our young lives whose own thinking is suspect, disordered, or otherwise limited, our thinking will be impaired by what we learn and don't learn from them. But it would be nonsense to presume that we are doomed. As adults, we no longer have to depend on others to tell us what to think or do.[27]

As adults it is imperative that we throw off the constraints imposed by our backgrounds that hinder thinking well. We must exercise our freedom to think well to fulfill our human potential.

God is Truth. He created us to be loved and to love. He desires us to know Him. He blessed us with brains to think well. God wants us to seek His will for humanity and for our individual lives.

APPENDIX

Another interesting view from a Jew for Jesus is presented below. Zola Levitt, at the time of the publication of the following article, hosted a weekly television program, *Zola Levitt Presents*, on the FAM and TBN networks. He wrote a guest column in the May 30, 1998 *Dallas Morning News* entitled "Jesus: He remains the Jew's Jew."

> In response to Rabbi Jordan S. Ofseyer's column last week, "A Jewish view on Jews for Jesus," let's imagine for a moment that Jesus really was the Jewish Messiah. In that case, I would expect to have the Old Testament full of prophecies about Him, which it is.

I would expect Him to have given His message in the only Jewish country in the world, which He did. I would expect Him to choose Jewish disciples and Jewish apostles, which He did.

I would expect that the New Testament, the Bible inspired by Him, would be written by Jewish authors and published by them, which it was. I would expect that all of His original followers would have been Jews, which they were, and that every generation would contain Jewish Believers (or "Jews for Jesus"), which they have.

I would also expect that the unbelieving Jews would turn away from Scripture, which would tend to constantly remind them of the Messiah they missed. I would expect a new kind of Judaism to become invented by a new kind of priesthood, the rabbis. And I would expect that Judaism, without its Messiah, would become fragmented, argumentative and diverse, which it has. I would expect Jewish people to become disenchanted with synagogue worship and a majority to just give it up, which is happening.

The rabbi wants Jewish Believers to call themselves Christians, but they never did this. The original Jews who believed in Messiah didn't stop being Jewish but rather felt that they had found the fulfillment of the Jewish hope. The biggest problem they had was deciding whether they should let non-Jews participate in this totally Jewish faith.

When Rabbi Ofseyer says that Jews who believe in their Messiah are no longer Jewish, I wonder how that happens. Does a Jew stop being a Jew if he becomes an atheist? a materialist? a follower of a cult? None of those would make a Jew stop being a Jew. Oddly, the rabbis argue that those Jews who believe the Torah with all their heart and believe that

Yeshua (Jesus) fulfills all that Moses and the prophets foretold are the only ones who cease to be Jews.

As for me, I was totally convinced of the Messiah by the Jewish Scripture. Isaiah 53, written by a Jewish prophet to a Jewish audience in the Old Testament - along with 300 other prophecies - convinced me. I was thoroughly educated in the synagogues with Bar Mitzvah and Confirmation, but now at last I understand what it means to be truly Jewish. I have a new understanding of, and love for, Israel. And despite my many failings, my life as a Messianic Jew feels complete and fulfilling. Truly this is really living.

In the New Testament, I read that Jesus told the devout Jew Nicodemus, "You must be born again" (John 3:3). I saw that Paul, a rabbi of Israel, advised that the good news of the Messiah is to go "to the Jew first" (Romans 1:16). He appealed to us, "Brethren, my heart's desire and prayer to God for Israel is that they might be saved" (Romans 10:1). And he proclaimed, "For I also am an Israelite. . .God hath not cast away His people" (Romans 11:1-2). Paul was sent among Gentiles, but his heart remained with his own people.

All Jews who believe in the Messiah weep for their own people who, like the rabbi, mean all that they say with the best of intentions but are without faith in the Messiah, who said, "I am not sent but unto the lost sheep of the house of Israel" (Matthew 15:24).

What really happened is this. Jesus came to the Jews because He was their Messiah. After some believed in Him and found how wonderful their lives had become, they wished to share this good news with everyone who would *listen* [my emphasis], including the Gentiles. The Gentiles believed in great numbers, and the Jews continued to come per capita. Today we have a thriving Gentile church containing Jewish Believers who want nothing more than to do what their first-century brethren did - share their faith - and they especially have warm hearts toward the Jewish people, their own.

Far from being deceptive, Jews for Jesus are merely trying to give their landsmen the greatest of all gifts.

7

> For centuries the phrase "as predicted by the prophets" was one of the most powerful influences on people coming to faith. Justin the Martyr credited his conversion to the impression made on him by the Old Testament's predictive accuracy. The brilliant French mathematician Blaise Pascal also cited fulfilled prophecies as one of the most important factors in his faith.
>
> Philip Yancey

WHAT ARE THE ODDS?

As a high school baseball player I was fortunate to have had a coach who was a former major league catcher. He taught us much about the intricacies of baseball. We communicated during our times at bat and on the bases through signals. The coaches and players memorized signals that would enable us to know what to do in any given situation. We had signals for bunting, taking a pitch, and hit-and-run situations with men on base. The first-base coach performed different arm and hand movements in addition to vocal guidance in communicating to the batter who had just hit the ball whether to run across first base into the right-field foul territory, or to round the base and hold, preparing to either return to first base or go for second base should a throwing error or some mental error occur, or to go flat-out to second, observing where the ball was and listening for the third base coach's exhortations. We also tried to steal signals from the catcher, primarily from second base, but sometimes from the other bases if the catcher was sloppy. The second-base runner, before the pitch was delivered, would flash a signal to the batter, notifying him of the type of pitch that would be delivered. The extra knowledge could mean the difference between a base hit and an out, given the necessity of making split-second decisions at the plate.

I like to use baseball as an analogy to view God and His assistant coaches. As a Christian, I view God as the owner and general manager and Jesus Christ as the Head (of the Church) Coach. God's will is known to His Son, who, as our Head Coach, is our liaison with the front office. I view the major and minor prophets of Israel as the assistant coaches. As a non-Christian, you could view God as the owner, general manager, and head coach. God sent signals to His assistant coaches who in turn relayed the signals to the players in Israel. Sometimes the players were not pleased with the signals being relayed to them and they rebelled against the assistant coaches, and by inference, God. What are these signals communicated by God? They are prophecies or predictions.

The Bible is replete with prophetic signals handed down by God to His chosen assistant coaches. According to the *Encyclopedia of Biblical Prophecy* by J. Barton Payne, Pd.D. (1922-1979) there are 737 separate matters predicted in the Bible that have been fulfilled. There are 1,817 predictions when including those repeated in different books of the Bible. Of these 1,817 referenced predictions, 1,239 are in the Old Testament and 578 are in the New Testament. This is a remarkable revelation when you consider this kind of track record, unparalleled in history. Think about it: 737 prophecies in the Bible have been fulfilled. It seems that somebody who has this kind of track record would warrant being paid attention to. What if a stockbroker accurately predicted 737 major moves in the stock market? Would you say this stockbroker was credible? God has generated 737 predictions that have been fulfilled. Anybody who doubts the Bible is the inspired Word of God should think carefully about this evidence.

There have been many books written about the fulfillment of biblical prophecies, both academically and fictionally such as the *Left Behind* series by Tim LaHaye and Jerry B. Junkins. Continuing archaeological discoveries buttress the accuracy of biblical accounts. However, few books have documented the mathematical probability of prophecies being fulfilled. I uncovered one such book entitled *Science Speaks* by Peter W. Stoner, M.S. and Robert C. Newman, S.T.M., Ph.D. Lest anyone question the credibility of this book, check out the foreword of this book by H. Harold Hartzler, Ph.D. of the American Scientific Affiliation:

> The manuscript for *Science Speaks* has been carefully reviewed by a committee of the American Scientific Affiliation members and by the Executive Council of the same group and has been found, in general, to be dependable and accurate in regard to the scientific material presented. The mathematical analysis included is based upon principles of probability which are thoroughly sound and Professor Stoner has applied these principles in a proper and convincing way.[28]

Professors Stoner and Newman relied on input from several hundred college students over ten years to estimate the probability of eleven Old Testament prophecies being fulfilled and eight prophecies being fulfilled by Jesus Christ. Stoner tempered the probability estimates by his own judgment in favor of conservatism. Obviously these probability estimates are subjective. Each reader can estimate their own probabilities if they disagree with the estimates used by Stoner and Newman. The main point to emphasize is that the fulfillment of just these few prophecies is so infinitesimally small as to be immeasurable. It is even more staggering when considering that 737 prophecies have been fulfilled in the Bible.

The rest of this chapter will deal with some specific prophecies that have been fulfilled by Jesus Christ. Jesus said:

> You diligently study the Scriptures because you think that by them you possess eternal life. These are the Scriptures that testify about me. [John 5:39].

> This is what I told you while I was still with you: Everything must be fulfilled that is written about me in the Law of Moses, the Prophets, and the Psalms.

Luke 24:44

Christ is saying that the Old Testament testifies to His life through prophecies. It is the fulfillment of these prophecies generated by God through the prophets that provides crucial evidence whether Christ is the Messiah.

Josh McDowell refers to these prophecies as providing God's address for His Son. This address, emanating from the fulfillment of numerous prophecies in one man, would allow humanity to realize beyond a shadow of a doubt that this was God's perfect and pleasing will. McDowell, in his book *A Ready Defense*, states:

> The task of matching up God's address with one man is further complicated by the fact that all the prophecies of the Messiah were made at least 400 years before He was to appear. Some might disagree and say that these prophecies were written after the time of Christ and fabricated to coincide with His life. This might sound feasible until you realize that the Septuagint, the Greek translation of the Hebrew Old Testament, was translated around 150-200 B.C. This Greek translation shows that there was at least a two-hundred-year gap between the prophecies being recorded and their fulfillment in Christ.
>
> Certainly God was writing an address in history that only the Messiah could fulfill. . . .What were some of those details? And what events had to precede and coincide with the appearance of God's Son?
>
> To begin, we need to go way back to Genesis 3:15. Here we have the first messianic prophecy. In all of Scripture, only one man was "born of the seed of a woman" - all others are born of the seed of a man. Here is the one who will come into the world and undo the works of Satan ("bruise His head").
>
> In Genesis 9 and 10 God narrowed the address down further. Noah had three sons, Shem, Japheth, and Ham. Today all of the nations of the world can be traced back to these three men. But in this passage, God effectively eliminated two-thirds of them from the line of Messiahship. The Messiah will come through the lineage of Shem.
>
> Continuing on to the year 2000 B.C., we find God calling a man named Abraham out of Ur of the Chaldees. With Abraham, God became still more

specific, stating that the Messiah will be one of his descendants (Genesis 12; 17; 22). All the families of the earth will be blessed through Abraham. Abraham had two sons, Isaac and Ishmael, but many of his descendants were eliminated when God selected his second son, Isaac (Genesis 17, 21).

Isaac had two sons, Jacob and Esau, and God chose the line of Jacob (Genesis 28; 35:10-12; Numbers 24:17). Jacob had twelve sons, out of whom developed the twelve tribes of Israel. God singled out the tribe of Judah for Messiahship and eliminated 11/12ths of the Israelite tribes. And of all the family lines within Judah's tribe, the line of Jesse was the divine choice (Isaiah 11:1-5). One can see the probability of Jesus being the Messiah building.

Jesse had eight children and in 2 Samuel 7:12-16 and Jeremiah 23:5 God eliminated 7/8ths of Jesse's family line: We read that God's man will not only be of the seed of a woman, the lineage of Shem, the race of the Jews, the line of Isaac, the line of Jacob, the tribe of Judah, but that He will also be of the house of David.

A prophecy dating 1012 B.C. (Psalm 22:6-18, cf. Zechariah 12:10 and Galatians 3:13) also predicts that this man's hands and feet will be pierced (i.e., He will be crucified). This description was written eight hundred years before crucifixion began to be practiced by the Romans.

Isaiah 7:14 adds that this man will be born of a virgin - a natural birth of unnatural conception, a criterion beyond human planning and control. Several prophecies recorded in Isaiah and the psalms describe the social climate and response that God's man will encounter: His own people, the Jews, will reject Him and the Gentiles will believe in Him

> (Isaiah 8:14; 28:16; 49:6; 50:6; 52:53; 60:3; Psalms 22:7,8; 118:22). There will be a forerunner for Him (Isaiah 40:3; Malachi 3:1), a voice in the wilderness, one preparing the way before the Lord, a John the Baptist.
>
> Notice, too, the seven ramifications of a prophecy (Zechariah 11:11-13; cf. Psalm 41, Jeremiah 32:6-15, and Matthew 27:3-10) that narrows the drama down even further. Here God indicates the Messiah will be (1) betrayed, (2) by a friend, (3) for 30 pieces, (4) of silver, that will be (5) cast onto the floor, (6) of the Temple, and (7) used to buy a potter's field.
>
> In Micah 5:2 God eliminated all the cities of the world and selected Bethlehem, with a population of less than a thousand, as the Messiah's birthplace.
>
> Then through a series of prophecies He even defined the time sequence that would set His man apart. For example, Malachi 3:1 and four other Old Testament verses (Psalm 118:26; Daniel 9:26; Zechariah 11:13; Haggai 2:7-9) require the Messiah to come while the Temple of Jerusalem is still standing. This is of great significance when we realize that the Temple was destroyed in A.D. 70 and has not since been rebuilt.
>
> The precise lineage; the place, time, and manner of birth; people's reactions; the betrayal; the manner of death. These are just a fraction of the hundreds of details that made up the address to identify God's Son, the Messiah, the Savior of the world.[29]

J. Barton Payne, in his book *Encyclopedia of Biblical Prophecy*, delineated 127 prophecies that were fulfilled in the life of Christ. This is simply a staggering number. However, if one never reads the Old and New Testaments, ignorance will prevail as it does in so much of the world. What are the odds that one man would fulfill all of these prophecies? No one has done the math for all 127 prophecies, but mathematician Peter Stoner analyzed the odds of one man fulfilling just eight of these 127 prophecies in his book *Science Speaks*. Stoner shows that if the prophecies were not offered by God, no man would have fulfilled any number of them.

He will be born in Bethlehem

> But you, Bethlehem Ephrathah, though you are small among the clans of Judah, out of you will come for me one who will be ruler over Israel, whose origins are from of old, from ancient times.

Micah 5:2

According to J. Barton Payne, a suggested dating for Micah is 739-710 B.C., or over 700 years before Christ was born.

> This prophecy predicts that the Christ is to be born in Bethlehem. Since this is the first prophecy to be considered there are no previously set restrictions, so our question is: One man in how many, the world over, has been born in Bethlehem?
>
> The best estimate which we can make of this comes from the attempt to find out the average population of Bethlehem, from Micah down to the present time, and divide it by the average population of the earth during the same period. One member of the class was an assistant in the library so he was assigned to get this information. He reported at the next meeting that the best determination of the ratio that he could determine was one in 280,000. Since the probable population of the earth has averaged less than two billion, the population of Bethlehem has averaged less than 7,150. Our answer may be expressed in the

form that one man in 7,150/2,000,000,000 or one man in 2.8×10^5 was born in Bethlehem.[30]

He will be a forerunner to Christ

> "See, I will send my messenger, who will prepare the way before me. Then suddenly the Lord you are seeking will come to his temple; the messenger of the covenant, whom you desire, will come," says the Lord Almighty.

Malachi 3:1

Payne dates Malachi's ministry to approximately 430 B.C.

> Our question here is: Of the men who have been born in Bethlehem, one man in how many has had a forerunner to prepare his way? John the Baptist, of course, was the forerunner of Christ. But since there appears to be no material difference between the people born in Bethlehem and those born any other place in the world, the question can just as well be general: One man in how many, the world over, has had a forerunner to prepare his way?
>
> The students said that the prophecy apparently referred to a special messenger of God, whose one duty was to prepare the way for the work of Christ, so there is a further restriction added. The students finally agreed on one in 1,000 as being extremely conservative. Most of the members thought the estimate should be much larger. We will use the estimate as 1 in 10^3.[31]

Jesus will enter Jerusalem in triumph on the colt of a donkey

> Rejoice greatly, O Daughter of Zion! Shout, Daughter of Jerusalem! See, your King comes to you, righteous and having salvation, gentle and riding on a donkey, on a colt, the foal of a donkey.

Zechariah 9:9

Payne places Zechariah's ministry as a prophet from 520 to 479 B.C.

Stoner framed the question for this prophecy as one man in how many, who was born in Bethlehem and had a forerunner, entered Jerusalem as a king riding on a colt, the foal of a donkey. This question is so restrictive that Stoner considered an equivalent question: One man in how many, who has entered Jerusalem as a ruler, entered riding on a colt, the foal of a donkey?

> The students said that this was a very hard thing to place an estimate on. They knew of no one but Christ who had so entered. The students thought that at least in more modern times any one entering Jerusalem as a king would use a more dignified means of transportation. They agreed to place an estimate of 1 in 10^4. We will use 1 in 10^2.[32]

He will be betrayed by a friend and His hands will be pierced

> If someone asks him, 'What are these wounds in your hands?' he will answer, 'The wounds I was given at the house of my friends.'

Zechariah 13:6

Christ was betrayed by Judas, one of His disciples. This caused Jesus to be crucified, involving piercing of the hands.

> There seems to be no relation between the fulfillment of this prophecy and those which we have previously considered. We may then ask the question: One man in how many, the world over, has been betrayed by a friend, and that betrayal has resulted in his being wounded in his hands?
>
> The students said that it was very rare to be betrayed by a friend, and still rarer for the betrayal to involve wounding in the hands. One in 1,000 was finally agreed upon, though most of the

students would have preferred a larger number. So we will use the 1 in 10^3.[33]

Jesus will be betrayed for 30 pieces of silver

I told them, "If you think it best, give me my pay; but if not, keep it." So they paid me thirty pieces of silver.

Zechariah 11:12

The question here is very simple: Of the people who have been betrayed, one in how many has been betrayed for exactly thirty pieces of silver?

The students thought this would be extremely rare and set their estimate as one in 10,000, or 1 in 10^4. We will use 1 in 10^3.[34]

The 30 pieces of silver will be thrown into the house of the Lord

And the Lord said to me, "Throw it to the potter" - the handsome price at which they priced me! So I took the thirty pieces of silver and threw them into the house of the Lord to the potter.

Zechariah 11:13

This is extremely specific. All thirty pieces of silver are not to be returned. They are to be cast down in the house of the Lord, and they are to go to the potter. You will recall that Judas in remorse tried to return the thirty pieces of silver, but the chief priest would not accept them. So Judas threw them down on the floor of the temple and went and hanged himself. The chief priest then took the money and bought a field of the potter to bury strangers in. Our question is: One man in how many, after receiving a bribe for the betrayal of a friend, had returned the money, had it refused, and thrown it on the floor in the house of the Lord, and then had it used to purchase a field from the potter?

The students said they doubted if there had ever been another incident involving all of these items, but they agreed on an estimate of one in 100,000. They were sure that this was very conservative. So we use the estimate of 1 in 10^5.[35]

He was silent at his defense

He was oppressed and afflicted, yet he did not open his mouth; he was led like a lamb to the slaughter, and as a sheep before her shearers is silent, so he did not open his mouth.

Isaiah 53:7

Isaiah prophesied from approximately 740 to 700 B.C. Here Jesus was compared to a lamb being brought to the slaughter because He did not open His mouth in his defense.

One man in how many, after fulfilling the above prophecies, when he is oppressed and afflicted and is on trial for his life, though innocent, will make no defense for himself?

Again my students said they did not know that this had ever happened in any case other than Christ's. At least it is extremely rare, so they placed their estimate as one in 10,000 or 1 in 10^4. We will use 1 in 10^3.

He was crucified

Dogs have surrounded me; a band of evil men has encircled me, they have pierced my hands and feet.

Psalm 22:16

This is a psalm of King David whose reign was approximately 1000 B.C., long before crucifixion was invented.

The Jews are still looking for the coming of Christ; in fact, He might have come any time after these prophecies were written up to the present time, or even on into the future. So our question is: One man

> in how many, from the time of David on, has been crucified?
>
> After studying the methods of execution down through the ages and their frequency, the students agreed to estimate this probability at one in 10,000 or 1 in 10^4, which we will use.[36]

Stoner goes on to describe the staggering statistical odds of one man fulfilling eight prophecies.

> If these estimates are considered fair, one man in how many men, the world over, will fulfill all eight prophecies? This question can be answered by applying our principles of probability. In other words, by multiplying all of our estimates together, or 1 in $2.8 \times 10^5 \times 10^3 \times 10^2 \times 10^3 \times 10^3 \times 10^5 \times 10^3 \times 10^4$. This gives 1 in 2.8×10^{28}, where 28 means that we have 28 ciphers following the 2.8. Let us simplify and reduce this number by calling it 1 in 10^{28}. Written out this number is 1 in 10,000,000,000,000,000,000,000,000,000.
>
> This is thc answer to the question: One man in how many men has fulfilled these eight prophecies? But we are really concerned with the answer to the question: What is the chance that any man might have lived from the day of these prophecies down to the present time and have fulfilled all of the eight prophecies? We can answer this question by dividing our 10^{28} by the total number of people who have lived since the time of these prophecies. The best information available indicates the number to be about 88 billion or 8.8×10^{10}. To simplify the computation let us call the number 10^{11}. By dividing these two numbers we find the chance that any man might have lived down to the present time and fulfilled all eight prophecies is 1 in 10^{17}.
>
> Let us try to visualize this chance. If you mark one of ten tickets, and place all of the tickets in a hat, and

> thoroughly stir them, and then ask a blindfolded man to draw one, his chance of getting the right ticket is one in ten. Suppose that we take 10^{17} silver dollars and lay them on the face of Texas. They will cover all of the state two feet deep. Now mark one of these silver dollars and stir the whole mass thoroughly, all over the state. Blindfold a man and tell him that he can travel as far as he wishes, but he must pick up one silver dollar and say that this is the right one. What chance would he have of getting the right one? Just the same chance the prophets would have had of writing these eight prophecies and having them all come true in any one man, from their day to the present time, providing they wrote using their own wisdom.
>
> Now these prophecies were either given by inspiration of God or the prophets just wrote them as they thought they should be. In such a case the prophets had just one chance in 10^{17} of having them come true in any man, but they all came true in Christ.
>
> This means that the fulfillment of these eight prophecies alone proves that God inspired the writing of those prophecies to a definiteness which lacks only one chance of 10^{17} of being absolute.[37]

This is particularly impressive considering that these eight prophecies involve four prophets spanning between 740 B.C. and 430 B.C. and a Davidic psalm written approximately 1000 B.C.

Stoner goes on to address possible concerns that the estimates of the probability of the fulfillment of these prophecies are too liberal or large, with a suggestion that the numbers should be reduced. Stoner challenges people to furnish their own probabilities, and if they are smaller, he suggests adding a few more of the 127 prophecies fulfilled in Christ. The result: the same number will be reestablished or perhaps exceeded. Stoner concludes: "Any man who rejects Christ as the Son of God is rejecting a fact proved perhaps more absolutely than any other fact in the world."[38]

Indeed, it was Stoner's remarkable analytical results of the fulfillment of messianic prophecies that helped convince Louis Lapides that Jesus was the promised Savior of the world. When Lee Strobel posed the question to Lapides in *The Case for Christ* if it was possible "that Jesus merely fulfilled the prophecies by accident," Lapides responded:

> Not a chance. The odds are so astronomical that they rule that out. Someone did the math and figured out that the probability of just eight prophecies being fulfilled is one chance in one hundred million billion. That number is millions of times greater than the total number of people who've ever walked the planet![39]

Strobel had studied this same statistical analysis by mathematician Peter W. Stoner when he was on his own quest for the Truth.

> Stoner also concluded that the probability of fulfilling forty-eight prophecies was one chance in a trillion, trillion, trillion, trillion, trillion, trillion, trillion, trillion, trillion, trillion, trillion, trillion, trillion!
>
> Our minds can't comprehend a number that big. This is a staggering statistic that's equal to the number of minuscule atoms in a trillion, trillion, trillion, trillion, billion universes the size of our universe!
>
> "The odds alone say it would be impossible for anyone to fulfill the Old Testament prophecies," Lapides concluded. "Yet Jesus - and only Jesus throughout all of history - managed to do it."[40]

The list of messianic prophecies related to the first advent of Christ is overwhelming when statistical probabilities are applied. In addition to the prophecies analyzed by Stoner, some of my favorite prophecies are listed below:

- The virgin Mary will conceive a child through the Holy Spirit
- He will come from the Semitic branch of humanity
- Within this branch, His descent will be from the family of Abraham

- His family will be non-Levitical
- He will come from the royal tribe of Judah
- He will be a descendant of Ruth
- He will be a descendant of King David
- He will be born in Bethlehem
- Jesus will be a branch from Nazareth
- He will grow up in lowly circumstances
- He will be anointed 483 years following the decree from Artaxerxes to Nehemiah to restore and rebuild Jerusalem
- He will be a prophet like Moses
- Christ's ministry will include the healing of diseases
- He will suffer from thirst and pierced limbs as men gamble for His clothes
- Men will scorn and mock Him at His crucifixion
- He will be killed 3½ years after the commencement of His ministry
- Christ's body will suffer no broken bones
- But His body will be pierced on the cross
- In honor of His sinlessness he will be buried in the tomb of a rich man

Shavuot is a holiday that Jewish people celebrate based on their acceptance of the Torah from God and conversion to Judaism. It is customary during Shavuot to read the Book of Ruth. Ruth leaves her own land and people to join the people of her mother-in-law (Naomi), the Israelites, after both become widows. Ruth's commitment in converting to Judaism so impressed the Jews that the Torah says the Messiah will be her descendant. Jesus is a descendant of Ruth, who was the mother of Obed, who was the father of Jesse, who was the father of King David.

It is interesting to note that there were 14 generations from Abraham to David, 14 generations from David to the Babylonian exile, and 14 generations from the exile to Jesus Christ. Christ's lineage through his earthly father, Joseph, as predicted in Isaiah 11:1, would be a shoot emanating from the stump of Jesse (the father of David), "from his roots a Branch will bear fruit." Matthew's Gospel carefully delineates 42 generations from Abraham to Christ. So

Christ was predicted to come from the Abrahamic-Davidic line and that he would be born in Bethlehem, the same birthplace of David. We've already seen that the odds of a man being born in Bethlehem, from Micah's prediction over 700 years before Christ was born, that would be the Christ, is about 0.0000036%. How about the odds of Isaiah's prediction over 700 years before Christ's birth that Christ would come out of the Davidic line? How about the combined odds of Christ coming out of the Davidic line and being born in David's hometown? It is safe to say that the probability is remote for just these two prophecies coming true.

One of the most impressive prophecies in all of the Old Testament is the prediction by Daniel that the Messiah would enter Jerusalem in 483 years, nearly half a millennium, after the decree to restore and rebuild Jerusalem. While Daniel was speaking and praying, the angel Gabriel, who had appeared to Daniel in an earlier vision:

> . . . .came to me in swift flight about the time of the evening sacrifice. He instructed me and said to me:
>
> "Daniel, I have now come to give you insight and understanding. As soon as you began to pray, an answer was given, which I have to tell you, for you are highly esteemed. Therefore, consider the message and understand the vision:
>
> Seventy 'sevens' are decreed for your people and your holy city to finish transgression, to put an end to sin, to atone for wickedness, to bring an everlasting righteousness, to seal up vision and prophecy, and to anoint the most holy.
>
> Know and understand this: From the issuing of the decree to restore and rebuild Jerusalem until the Anointed One, the ruler, comes, there will be seven 'sevens', and sixty-two 'sevens.' It will be rebuilt with streets and a trench, but in times of trouble. After the sixty-two 'sevens', the Anointed One will be cut off and will have nothing. The people of the ruler who will come will destroy the city and the sanctuary.

> The end will come like a flood: War will continue until the end, and desolations have been decreed. He will confirm a covenant with many for one 'seven.' In the middle of the 'seven' he will put an end to sacrifice and offering. And on a wing of the temple, he will set up an abomination that causes desolation, until the end that is decreed is poured out on him."

Daniel 9:21-27

Interpretation of the 70 Weeks

The "sevens" are considered "weeks" in the text. However, there is evidence that the "sevens" really translate into periods of seven years. Thus, the 7 and 62-week periods referenced in the text are understood as 69 seven-year periods. In Daniel 9:27, there is a reference to a final "seven." An expert in this interpretation is Harold W. Hoehner, chairman of the Department of New Testament Literature and Exegesis at Dallas Theological Seminary. He holds a Ph.D. degree from Cambridge University. Hoehner notes in his book *Chronological Aspects of the Life of Christ* that in Hebrew a "unit of seven" may be interpreted different ways depending on the particular context. In Daniel 9:24-27, the Hebrew term means units of seven years or a total of 490 years for all 70 units of seven. Hoehner supports his conclusion interspersed with several Hebrew words or phrases. Since I don't understand Hebrew, I will merely insert brackets [] to note the use of Hebrew where Hoehner uses actual Hebrew language. Hoehner's interpretation of the "sevens" is supported by several logical reasons.

> In this passage [Daniel 9:24-27] the term [] refers to units of seven years and thus Daniel is speaking of seventy of these units of seven years or a total of 490 years. The reasons for this conclusion are as follows:
>
> First, in the context Daniel had been thinking in terms of years as well as multiples of (ten times seven) of years (Daniel 9:1-2).

Second, Daniel had been considering Jeremiah 25:11 and 29:10 regarding the seventy-year captivity. The captivity was a result of violating the sabbatical year, which was to have been observed after every six years (2 Chron. 36:21; cf. Lev. 26:34-35, 43). Each year of captivity represented one seven-year cycle in which the seventh or Sabbath year had not been observed. Thus it is clear that the context refers to years, not days. The seventy-year captivity was due to the Jews having violated seventy sabbatical years over a 490-year period and Daniel now saw seventy units of sevens decreed for another 490 years into Israel's future. This can be diagramed in the following way:

UNITS OF SEVENTY		
70 x 7 Sabbatical Years Violated	70-Year Captivity	70 x 7 Decreed Years Remaining
Lev. 26:34-35, 43	Jer. 25:11, 29:10	Daniel 9:24-27
490 years in past	Daniel's Day	490 years in future

Third, the only other usage of [] by Daniel is in 10:2, 3 where the phrase [] is literally "three units of seven days" or twenty-one days. This has reference to Daniel's mourning for three weeks since the word [] is included. The very fact that Daniel adds [] indicates that he did not want his readers to think of the unit of seven the same way it was used in chapter nine. Everyone would have realized that Daniel would not have fasted twenty-one years, but the fact that he inserted [] "days" in 10:2, 3 when it was not necessary would seem to indicate that he *would* have used [] in 9:24-27 if there he meant 490 "days." Therefore, in Daniel 9:24-27 Daniel was referring to years and not days.

Fourth, it is impossible to fit the events described in 9:24-27, regardless of the *terminus a quo* [Latin,

> meaning "starting point"], into 490 days or weeks. Only that number of years is viable.
>
> Fifth, in 9:27 the covenant that will be confirmed for one "unit of seven" [] will be broken in the middle of that unit of seven. If one accepts the [] as a unit of seven years, this would mean that the covenant will be broken at the three and one-half year point and the last three and one-half years will be a time of trouble and desolation. This fits well with the trouble described by the temporal note "time, times, and a half a time" in Daniel 7:25 and 12:7 as well as in Revelation 12:14.
>
> Sixth, although the term [] does not refer to years elsewhere in the Bible it has this meaning in the Mishnah [Mishnah: Baba Metzia ix. 10; Sanhedrin v. 1].
>
> In conclusion the term [] in Daniel 9 most reasonably refers to a unit of seven years. To make it anything else does not make good sense. However, for the sake of clarity this unit of seven years will be called "week(s)" for the remainder of this chapter, for it is simpler to refer to seventy "weeks" than to seventy "units of seven years." Therefore, Daniel's reference to seventy weeks means a period of 490 years.[41]

The Beginning of the 70 Weeks

Daniel 9:25 notes the starting point of the seventy weeks is the issuance of a command to restore and rebuild Jerusalem with streets (plaza) and a trench (moat) during difficult times. Hoehner continues his description:

> Three things are to be noted in the description of the rebuilding of Jerusalem. First the words [] ("to restore and to rebuild") suggest that the city was raised to its former state. It is not a partial rebuilding but a complete restoration.

> Second, the words [] ("plaza and moat") give weight to the position for a complete restoration of the city. . . .Commentators are divided on how to apply the two words [] to Daniel 9:25, but it is best to take the first word *plaza* as referring to the interior of the city and the second word *trench* as referring to a moat going around the outside of the city. Part of Jerusalem's natural defenses consisted of a great cutting in the rock along the northern wall, which is still visible, for the purpose of building a defense wall. . . .
>
> Third, it should be noted that the rebuilding of Jerusalem would be done in times of distress or oppression.
>
> In conclusion, then, Daniel describes the rebuilding of Jerusalem as being a complete restoration during troublous times.[42]

The Issuance of the Decree to Begin Rebuilding

Hoehner discusses four possibilities when the issuance of the decree to commence rebuilding Jerusalem was given. The most likely scenario, Hoehner concludes, is the decree from Artaxerxes to Nehemiah.

> The final decree is that of Artaxerxes to Nehemiah in 444 B.C. to rebuild the city of Jerusalem (Neh. 2:108). Several factors commend this decree as the one prophesied by Daniel (9:25) for the commencement of the seventy weeks. First, there is a direct reference to the restoration of the city (2:3,5) and of the city gates and walls (2:3,8). Second, Artaxerxes wrote a letter to Asaph to give materials to be used specifically for the walls (2:8). Third, the Book of Nehemiah and Ezra 4:7-23 indicates that certainly the restoration of the walls was done in the most distressing circumstances, as predicted by Daniel (Dan. 9:25). Fourth, no later decrees were given by the Persian kings pertaining to the rebuilding of Jerusalem. . . .

> In conclusion, this is the only decree that adequately fits the strictures given in Daniel 9:25. Hence this decree of Artaxerxes is considered the *terminus a quo* of the seventy weeks. . . .the decree of Artaxerxes (2:1) occurred in Nisan (March/April) of 444 B.C. Therefore, Nisan 444 B.C. marks the *terminus a quo* of the seventy weeks of Daniel 9:24-27.[43]

J. D. Wilson concurs with Hoehner's assessment.

> This decree then is the "commandment to restore and rebuild Jerusalem." There is no other decree authorizing the restoration of the city. This decree authorizes the restoration and the book of Nehemiah tells how the work was carried on. The exigencies of their various theories have led men to take some other decree for the *terminus a quo* of their calculations, but it is not apparent how any could have done so without misgivings. This decree of Nehemiah 2 is the commandment to restore and rebuild Jerusalem; no other decree gives any permission to restore the city. All other decrees refer to the building of the Temple and the Temple only.[44]

The Completion of the 69 Weeks

The next step is to determine what constitutes a year. Hoehner makes a convincing case that a 360-day year is relevant.

- the ancient calendars of India, Persia, Babylonia, Assyria, Egypt, Central and South America, and China were based on 12 30-day months.
- the prophetic literature in the Bible uses a 360-day year. In Revelation 11:2 and 13:5, 42 months is referenced; in Revelation 11:3 and 12:6, 1,260 days is referenced. Thus, each month equals 30 days.
- according to Genesis 7:11, the flood began on the 17th day of the second month. According to Genesis 8:4 the flood ended on the 17th day of the seventh month, exactly five months later. Genesis 7:24 and 8:3 state that the duration of the flood

> was 150 days. Thus, five months equals 150 days or 30 days per month.[45]

Hoehner concluded that the decree to rebuild Jerusalem occurred sometime in Nisan 444 B.C. He assumed the date of the issuance of this decree occurred on Nisan 1, 444 B.C. or March 5. Although this can't be proven, it fits with the prediction of 483 years between the issuance of the decree to rebuild Jerusalem and the coming of the Messiah in conjunction with recent scholarship that puts Christ's death on April 3, A.D. 33.

Using a 360-day year, Hoehner computes the terminal day of the 69 weeks (69 x 7 = 483 years) predicted in Daniel 9:25:

> Multiplying the sixty-nine weeks by seven years for each week by 360 days gives a total of 173,880 days. The difference between 444 B.C. and A.D. 33, then, is 476 solar years [since only one year expired between 1 B.C. and A.D. 1, the total is 476, not 477]. By multiplying 476 by 365.24219879 [days per solar year] or by 365 days, 5 hours, 48 minutes, 45.975 seconds, one comes to 173,855.28662404 days or 173,855 days, 6 hours, 52 minutes, 44 seconds. This leaves only 25 days to be accounted for between 444 B.C. and A.D. 33. By adding 25 days to March 5 (of 444 B.C.), one comes to March 30 (of A.D. 33) which was Nisan 10 in A.D. 33. This is the triumphal entry of Jesus into Jerusalem.[46]

Hoehner presents convincing evidence that the only logical day for Christ's crucifixion was Friday, April 3, A.D. 33 [Christ was "cut off" as predicted in Daniel 9:26] which corresponds to Christ's triumphal entry on the colt of a donkey into Jerusalem on Monday, March 30, A.D. 33 as predicted in Zechariah 9:9. Thus, what Christians celebrate as Palm Sunday is really Palm Monday.

There is considerable debate on the date of Christ's crucifixion, generally ranging from A.D. 21 to 36. Hoehner's conclusion is as follows:

> To attempt to come to a concrete date, one must examine all the evidence at hand. First, it was seen that the officials at Christ's trial were Caiaphas and Pilate who were in office simultaneously from A.D. 26 to 36. This eliminates the A.D. 21 date. Next, in examining the day of crucifixion it was concluded that it occurred on Friday, Nisan 14. With the help of astronomy the only possible years on which Friday, Nisan 14 occurred were A.D. 27, 30, 33, and 36. One can eliminate A.D. 27 and 36 when one looks at the ministry of Christ, leaving only A.D. 30 and 33 as feasible dates. However, upon further examining the evidence of astronomy and the life of Christ the most viable date for the death of Christ was A.D. 33. This date is confirmed when one looks into history for it not only fills several passages of the Gospels with meaning but it also prevents the charge that the Gospels are inaccurate in some parts of the passion narrative. Here, then, is the case for the A.D. 33 date for the crucifixion of our Lord, more specifically Friday, April 3, A.D. 33.[47]

There are no doubt scholars and academicians who will argue that Christ was born in December 5 B.C. or January 4 B.C. ad nauseam. People will differ in their opinions of when the decree was issued to rebuild Jerusalem and when Christ rode into Jerusalem on that penultimate week that radically transformed history. But given God's impeccable and flawless track record of fulfilling hundreds of prophecies, can anyone really doubt the accuracy of this prophecy? Our inability to precisely and consensually track the period of this prophecy does not invalidate the accuracy of God's prophecy.

In conclusion, two events had to materialize between the end of the 69 weeks and the beginning of the 70th week:

- the "cutting off" of the Messiah.
- the destruction of the city and sanctuary (Temple)

Jerusalem and the Temple were destroyed in A.D. 70 by Titus the Roman. Therefore, based on Daniel's prediction, the Anointed One had to come and be killed between March 30, A.D. 30 and A.D. 70. Thus, this prophecy was fulfilled.

What are the odds of a prophet who lived during the Babylonian exile in 605-539 B.C. predicting the triumphal entry of the Messiah into Jerusalem 483 years after the issuance of a decree to restore and rebuild Jerusalem? I don't know. One thing is for sure, though, the odds are infinitesimal. The probability would be akin to me, having never flown a plane before or taken any instructional training, sneaking into the tightly-guarded Joint Reserve Base - Naval Air Station in Fort Worth, Texas, stealing an F-16 fighter jet, flying to San Francisco, descending over the Bay, performing a 360-degree barrel role under the Golden Gate Bridge with a martini on my lap without the olive falling out, and landing on an aircraft carrier at night.

The amazing number and depth of prophecies that were fulfilled in Christ is simply staggering. It defies comprehension. Certainly the statistical probabilities of so many prophecies coming true in Christ is one of the most compelling pillars of evidence supporting Christ's claim of who He was and is: the Messiah.

In *The Case for Christ*, Lee Strobel asked Louis Lapides, the Christian convert from Judaism, if the passages that Christians identify as messianic prophecies are really intended to point to the coming of the Messiah, or do Christians simply cite them out of context and misinterpret them.

> Lapides sighed. "You know, I go through the books that people write to try to tear down what we believe. That's not fun to do, but I spend the time to look at each objection individually and then to research the context and the wording in the original language," he said. "And every time, the prophecies have stood up and shown themselves to be true."[48]

Despite the impressive array of predictions and fulfillment thereof, the prophets of Israel often met with failure in communicating God's messages to the populace. Israel's history, like all of humanity, is characterized by cycles of greatness and failure. God ultimately had to forecast the coming of a Messiah to let people know in no uncertain terms that He had a perfect plan for salvation and the forgiveness of sins.

8

> It is a harder task to deny than to accept a direct relation between prediction and fulfillment in the case of such passages as Psalm 22.
>
> W. J. Farley

A MESSIANIC PSALM

There are 13 messianic psalms, of which Psalm 22 is the most impressive in my opinion. According to the late J. Barton Payne, Ph.D. from Princeton Theological Seminary and former professor of Old Testament at Covenant Theological Seminary, in his book *Encyclopedia of Biblical Prophecy*, Psalm 22 is one of three psalms in which all verses (31) are messianic. The psalms are closely connected to King David, whose reign was around 1000 B.C., with 73 of its 150 chapters ascribed to him, including Psalm 22. Five of the anonymously labeled psalms are also ascribable to David by reference of other Scriptures. It is probably true that a number of other psalms are attributable to him. Since the Messiah was prophesied to come from David's lineage, it is crucial to pay careful attention to what David wrote. Dr. Payne gives an overview of the predictive importance of the Psalter in his book.

> When Jesus told His disciples, "This is what I told you while I was still with you: Everything must be fulfilled that is written about me in the Law of Moses, the Prophets and the Psalms" (Luke 24:44), He confirmed not simply the predictive character of the Psalter - including its Messianic statements, which specifically foretold His coming - but also its importance as representing, along with the Law and the Prophets, one of the three major divisions of the OT [Old Testament] canon. For according to the most ancient description of the organized Hebrew Bible, that of Josephus in NT [New Testament] times, the third division of Israel's canon consisted of but four

> books, containing hymns to God and precepts for the conduct of human life. In this poetic subdivision of the OT Scriptures, which came later to be identified as the "Writings," the Psalter thus holds first place, being followed by Proverbs, Ecclesiastes, and the Song of Solomon. Psalms is by far the largest of the four: its Hebrew text requires almost as many pages as does Jeremiah's (which is the longest in the Bible); and its total of 2,526 verses is the greatest for any volume of Scripture. Furthermore, when one recalls that the Song of Solomon contains no predictive matter whatsoever and that the prophetic verses of the two wisdom books of Proverbs and Ecclesiastes do not exceed 3% of their whole, with none of even this minimal amount being directly Messianic, it is no wonder that our Lord limited His designation for the third division of the canon to the Book of Psalms. Here, by way of contrast, appear some 59 separate predictions; and their verses, while amounting to only 10% of the Psalter, still total 242. Of these, moreover, 101 are directly anticipatory of Jesus Christ, they occur in 13 different Messianic psalms, and they constitute the greatest single block of predictive matter concerning the Savior to be found anywhere in the OT.[49]

Some might argue that Psalm 22 merely referred to David's plight and that it was just a coincidence that many of David's statements applied to Christ. However, as stated earlier in this book, there are no coincidences in life, only circumstances engineered or orchestrated by God. Many of the references in Psalm 22 went beyond David's sufferings. The late John F. Walvoord, Ph.D. and former Chancellor of Dallas Theological Seminary, addressed this issue in his book *The Prophecy Knowledge Handbook*.

> This psalm [Psalm 22] is considered one of the messianic psalms because some of the expressions in the psalm go far beyond any sufferings which David himself experienced. There was no known incident

> in the life of David that exactly corresponded to what the psalm stated. What may have been true of David as a type of one suffering was literally fulfilled by the sufferings of Christ.[50]

His pierced hands and feet (verse 16) and lots cast over his garments (verse 18) were not true of David. Indeed, the piercing of hands and feet was an obvious reference to the Crucifixion, approximately 800 years before the Romans invented it.

If one accepts the premise that the Bible is God-breathed or Spirit-led, then it is evident that these prophecies are accurately and divinely written. The Holy Spirit of inspiration had in view the fulfillment of these psalms in Christ. As Louis Berkhof cautions, "Scripture contains a great deal that does not find its explanation in history, nor in the secondary authors, but only in God as the *Auctor primarius* [primary author]."[51] J. R. Sampey elaborates on this theme in an article in the *International Standard Bible Encyclopedia* (ISBE).

> Rationalistic critics insist that to apply part of a psalm to David and part to Christ introduces confusion. They contend that the language refers to the psalmist and to him alone, and that the application of certain verses to our Lord Jesus is only by way of accommodation. This theory ignores the presence and activity of the Holy Spirit altogether; and when men talk of psychological impossibilities, they may be talking nonsense; for who of us can understand fully the psychological experience of men while receiving revelations from God? The real author of inspired prophecies is the Holy Spirit. His meaning is that which the reverent interpreter most delights to find. . . .We ought not to be surprised that we should be unable to explain fully the method of the Holy Spirit's activity in guiding the thought of the prophets and psalmists in their predictions of the sufferings of Christ and the glories that should follow them.[52]

Another author, Milton S. Terry, describes this theme as applied to Psalm 2, another psalm characterized by Payne as containing all messianic verses.

> The second psalm [which Payne describes as Christ speaking in the First Person] was composed in spiritual ecstasy. David became a seer and prophet. The Spirit of Jehovah spoke within him, and his word was upon his tongue (II Sam 23:20 ["The Spirit of the Lord spoke through me; his word was on my tongue."]). . . .He is lifted into visionary ecstasy, transcending all earthly royalty and power. He sees Jehovah enthroning his Anointed upon Zion, the mountain of his holiness. . . .Thus, the second psalm is seen to be no mere historical ode, composed upon the royal inauguration of David or Solomon, or any other earthly prince. A greater than David or Solomon arose in the psalmist's vision. . . .the Son of Jehovah whom the kings of the earth are counseled to kiss. . . .It is only as the interpreter attains a vivid apprehension of the power of such ecstasy that he can properly perceive or explain the import of any Messianic prophecy.[53]

Payne classifies Psalm 22 as one in which Christ speaks in the First Person. "Psalm 22 is the one chapter in the Psalter in which the Messiah speaks forth the entire composition."[54] Sampey declares, "Every sentence can be applied to Jesus without straining its meaning. If David took up his harp to sing of his own sorrows, the Spirit of God guided him to describe those of a greater."[55]

The initial verse of Psalm 22, "My God, my God, why have you forsaken me? Why are you so far from saving me, so far from the words of my groaning?" was quoted by Christ as recorded in Matthew 27:46 and Mark 15:34.

Verses 6 and 7 state: "But I am a worm and not a man, scorned by men and despised by the people. All who see me mock me; they hurl insults, shaking their heads." This was amplified by Isaiah 300 years later in Chapter 53 around 700 B.C. (see Chapter 6 of this book for the text of Chapter 53). The NT Scriptures dealing with the mocking of Christ include Matthew 27:28-31 and 39, Mark 15:17-20 and 29, and Luke 23:36. Samples from each NT book, respectively, are presented below.

- They stripped him and put a scarlet robe on him, and then twisted together a crown of thorns and set it on his head. They put a staff in his right hand and knelt in front of him and mocked him. "Hail, king of the Jews!" they said. They spit on him, and took the staff and struck him on the head again and again. After they had mocked him, they took off the robe and put his own clothes on him. Then they led him away to crucify him. . . .Those who passed by hurled insults at him, shaking their heads. . . .
- They put the purple robe on him, then twisted together a crown of thorns and set it on him. And they began to call out to him, "Hail, king of the Jews!" Again and again they struck him on the head with a staff and spit on him. Falling on their knees, they paid homage to him. And when they had mocked him, they took off the purple robe and put his own clothes on him. Then they led him out to crucify him. . . .Those who passed by hurled insults at him, shaking their heads. . . .
- The soldiers also came up and mocked him. . . .

Verse 8 states: "He trusts in the Lord; let the Lord rescue him. Let him deliver him, since he delights in him." The NT Scripture dealing with this passage is Matthew 27:43. "He trusts in God. Let God rescue him now if he wants him, for he said, 'I am the Son of God.'"

Verse 14 states: "I am poured out like water, and all my bones are out of joint. My heart has turned to wax; it has melted away within me." John 19:33-34 alludes to Jesus being poured out like water. "But when they came to Jesus and found that he was already dead, they did not break his legs. Instead, one of the soldiers pierced Jesus' side with a spear, bringing a sudden flow of blood and water." John continues in verses 36-37: "These things happened so that the scripture would be fulfilled: 'Not one of his bones will be broken,'

[Exodus 12:46 and Numbers 9:12, regarding the command not to break the sacrificial Passover lamb's bones] and, as another scripture says, 'They will look on the one they have pierced.'" [Zechariah 12:10 which states: "And I will pour out on the house of David and the inhabitants of Jerusalem a spirit of grace and supplication. They will look on the one they have pierced, and they will mourn for him as one mourns for an only child, and grieve bitterly for him as one grieves for a first-born son."].

Alexander Metherell, M.D., Ph.D. was interviewed by Lee Strobel in *The Case for Christ*. He described the prophecy of "all my bones are out of joint" in verse 14 by noting the result of hanging on the cross.

> First of all, his arms would have immediately been stretched, probably about six inches in length, and both shoulders would have become dislocated - you can determine this with simple mathematical equations. This fulfilled the Old Testament prophecy in Psalm 22, which foretold the Crucifixion hundreds of years before it took place [and was even invented] and says, "My bones are out of joint."[56]

Regarding verse 14's reference to the heart turning to wax and melting away, Dr. Metherell described the impact of the Crucifixion on Christ's heart.

> Once a person is hanging in the vertical position, crucifixion is essentially an agonizingly slow death by asphyxiation. . . .As the person slows down his breathing, he goes into what is called respiratory acidosis - the carbon dioxide in the blood is dissolved as carbonic acid, causing the acidity of the blood to increase. This eventually leads to an irregular heartbeat. In fact, with his heart beating erratically, Jesus would have known that he was at the moment of death, which is when he was able to say, "Lord, into you hands I commit my spirit." And then he died of cardiac arrest.[57]

Verse 15 states in part: ". . . .and, my tongue sticks to the roof of my mouth. . . ." This is a reference to thirst. John 19:28 quotes Jesus on the cross saying, "I am thirsty."

Verse 16 states: "Dogs have surrounded me; a band of evil men has encircled me, they have pierced my hands and my feet." This is an obvious reference to the Crucifixion. The "dogs" were evil men.

Verse 18 states: "They divide my garments among them and cast lots for my clothing." John 19:23-24 states: "When the soldiers crucified Jesus, they took his clothes, dividing them into four shares, one for each of them, with the undergarment remaining. This garment was seamless, woven into one piece from top to bottom. 'Let's not tear it,' they said to one another. 'Let's decide by lot who will get it.'"

W. J. Farley concludes: "It is a harder task to deny than to accept a direct relation between prediction and fulfillment in the case of such passages as Psalm 22. . . ."

9

> Everything in Christ astonishes me. His spirit overawes me, and his will confounds me. Between him and whoever else in the world, there is no possible term of comparison. He is truly a being by himself. . . .I search in vain in history to find the similar to Jesus Christ, or anything which can approach the gospel. Neither history, nor humanity, nor the ages, nor nature, offer me anything with which I am able to compare it or to explain it. Here everything is extraordinary.
>
> Napoleon

THE DRAFTING OF A SUPERSTAR

No one in history has even remotely performed the number and quality of miracles that Jesus Christ did, a strong indicator of Christ's claim to be God's Son, and hence, the Truth. The miracles are further evidence of His Messiahship. Jesus' incomparable miracles, works, wonders, and signs are evidence of God sanctioning Jesus' ministry.

This chapter will use baseball, America's traditional sport and now an Olympic sport, to illustrate many of these miracles in an analogous fashion. As Christ said in John 14:11:

> Believe me when I say that I am in the Father and the Father is in me; or at least believe on the evidence of the miracles themselves.

After relaying an impressive and unrivaled number of meticulous signals through a host of prophets over several hundred years, God, as promised, drafted His Son to enter the world's major leagues to compete with the best teams and players 2,000 years ago. Many fans were unaware of this momentous event out of pride, fear, and laziness which bred arrogance and ignorance. Jesus kept a low profile for approximately the first 30 years of his life as He toiled in spring training, preparing Himself for the major league games He was destined to play. God appointed Jesus as a player-coach and He formed a team that eventually became known as the Apostles, a rag-tag team of players that He scouted during the last days of spring training before being called up to the majors.

His first game was one that He was not expecting to play since He was merely a fan in attendance at a wedding reception at the ballpark in Cana in Galilee. Jesus' mother was in the stands as were some of the disciples (who later formed the Apostles team). The opposition threw a curve ball culminating in a called third strike at the plate as the wine was completely depleted. Jesus' mother was most distressed since the game looked hopeless and she pleaded with Jesus to enter the game. Jesus rather emphatically told Mary not to sweat the loss of the game because there was nothing He could do since His time in spring training was not finished yet. Then Jesus looked at the dugout and received a signal from God that He could enter the game, and thus make His debut as a major league ballplayer. Jesus, of course, was very excited to have this opportunity to play the game that He was destined to play after three decades of arduous training. So Jesus quickly slugged a home run by transforming six stone jars filled with 20 to 30 gallons of water into wine, heroically saving the game in the bottom of the ninth.

As impressive as His debut was, Jesus was traveling to an away game in Samaria when He came across a player who had not yet heard of His exploits in game one. She was a Samaritan woman drawing some water from a well to replenish the water cooler in their dugout for their game later that day. Jesus asked her if He could have a drink. The Samaritan woman was shocked that a male would even be addressing her, much less a Jewish male since Jews and Samaritans drank from separate fountains. Then Jesus began tossing her a few pitches from his vast repertoire of pitches, tossing sliders, change-ups, curve balls, and even a knuckleball or two. Jesus talked to her about living water, eternal life, and inquired about her husband. She hit the ball weakly back to Jesus on the mound when she responded that she didn't have a husband. Then Jesus reared back and hurled a fastball that left her reeling at the plate, when He responded: "You are right when you say you have no husband. The fact is, you have had five husbands, and the man you now have is not your husband. What you have just said is quite true." At this overpowering display of control, the woman declared that He must be a prophet with pitching prowess. Then she said she was aware that a superstar was forecasted to enter the major leagues at some point. Jesus basically responded by saying "You're looking at the superstar, sister." Well, the lady was so pumped up that she immediately went back to her town to tell the folks that she had encountered the superstar that was to check into the major leagues. Many ballplayers in Samaria were duly impressed and began tracking the performance of Jesus from that time forward.

After two days of playing ball in Samaria, Jesus headed back to the ballpark in Cana in Galilee where He had made his successful debut. A royal official whose son lay near death in Capernaum heard Jesus was in town for that night's ball game and he pleaded with Jesus to heal his son. Jesus basically replied that He didn't have time to visit his son because He was due at the ballpark so He said "You may go. Your son will live." Bingo, another home run for Jesus. What was particularly impressive was that the father later found out that the time his son's fever dissipated was the seventh hour (1 PM), the exact time that Christ slugged the home run.

Jesus embarked on another road trip, this time to the heart of the big leagues in Israel's capital, Jerusalem. Jesus' first ball game was at the ballpark near the Sheep Gate. However, many fans were laying around outside the ballpark who were disabled (blind, lame, paralyzed). Many of these fans simply wanted to see the game and some had yearned to play the game since they were little kids. Jesus looked at one fellow and found out that he had been incapacitated for 38 years. Jesus said something to the effect, "Hey, you want to play ball in tomorrow's game?" The prospect replied, "Man, I would give anything just to get up and walk." So Jesus basically said, "Go ahead, make my day." At that the man was cured; he picked up his mat and walked. Unfortunately for Jesus, the Jewish players got upset because this home run occurred on the Sabbath, a day in which no games or even batting practice was allowed. The Jewish players rebuked the former invalid for violating the Sabbath by picking up his mat. So what that this man had waited patiently for 38 years to do so and it just happened to occur on a Sabbath. Oh well, some folks just can't take a joke. Jesus basically told the man, "Don't sweat it; I have a no-cut contract with God that allows me to take hitting practice on the Sabbath."

John the Baptist, after being ejected from the league and banished to a prison for criticizing the umpires, sent word through his disciples, asking Jesus if he was the superstar who was to come or if someone else was being groomed for the big leagues. Jesus told the boys: "Go and tell Big John what you hear and see: The blind are visiting art museums, the lame are purchasing running shoes, the lepers are entering beauty contests, the deaf are attending symphony concerts, the hungry are managing grocery stores, the disenfranchised are buying franchises, the people with little clothing are managing department stores, the homeless are building houses for Habitat for Humanity, the destitute are becoming rich in the kingdom of heaven and buying mutual funds, the dead are trading their cemetery plots for mansions, the sick are participating in triathlons, the orphans are being adopted, the widows are being given life-time annuities, the prisoners are being set free by the truth, death row inmates are being pardoned, and the mentally disabled are being treated with medication, understanding, and compassion."

Jesus' next game was to be played across the Sea of Galilee at a place near the Sea of Tiberias. Attendance at the ball games was swelling because of Jesus' hitting sprees and pitching prowess. About 5,000 men were in the concession stand areas waiting to buy food and drinks when it became evident that the vendors hadn't made it to the ballpark yet. One boy working in the stadium had gathered up five loaves of bread and two small fish from the game before. Jesus asked one of His teammates, Philip, where they could buy food to feed the fans. Philip was perplexed, saying numbly that it would take more than eight months' wages to buy the food necessary to feed the fans. The Apostles were fearful of the fans becoming unruly with a full-scale riot breaking out like an international soccer game. So Jesus instructed the Apostles to tell the crowd to sit down. Jesus gave thanks for the loaves and fish and converted these paltry amounts into enough food to feed the multitudes. Fans were amazed; exclaiming that they had already witnessed a great game before the real game had even begun. At another stadium the same thing happened with 4,000 men and an untold number of women and children but this time with seven loaves and a few small fish. The vendors knew then that it was no use going on strike because their monopoly on supplying the stadiums had ended.

After the ball game some of Jesus' team set off across the lake for Capernaum where they had a road game the next day. Jesus missed the boat but joined them after they had rowed three and a half miles. His method of travel? A rather unorthodox mode of travel known as walking on water. The team members were getting used to Jesus' skills but this one topped the earlier performances and they were frightened when they first saw Him traversing the water. Jesus calmed them down and immediately the boat reached the shore where they were heading. Nothing like beating boat lag.

One day Jesus and the Apostles were traveling by boat to an away game. Jesus was tired from playing several days in a row and was asleep in the boat when a furious storm came up, washing waves over the boat and nearly swamping it. The disciples were mighty shook up and woke Jesus who immediately calmed the storm. The Apostles knew then that they could count on not having any games rained out.

Jesus was offering a coaching clinic one day to some eager prospects when all of a sudden some all-stars from the preeminent Pharisees team showed up with a woman who they said was caught in thc act of adultery. Based on the baseball rules written under Commissioner Moses, such an act warranted beaning without a helmet. The all-stars asked Jesus what he thought they should do. Jesus continued his coaching clinic by writing some instructions in the sand with his finger. The all-stars pressed their case, knowing that they had fooled Jesus with their devilish knuckleball and with a quick two strikes and no balls. Jesus calmly straightened up and swung at the next pitch, rocketing a rifle shot over the right-field fence. Jesus, an accomplished switch-hitter, often preferred hitting to right field because He was a righteous man. Jesus told the all-stars point blank: "If any one of you is without sin, let him be the first to throw a fastball at her head." Again, Jesus resumed his coaching clinic, writing some more instructions on the ground, and acting annoyed at this latest interruption. The all-stars gradually shuffled off, amazed at the ability of Jesus to protect the plate with two strikes and no balls. Jesus straightened up again and asked the accused, "Woman, where are they? Has no one thrown a fastball at your head?" "No one, sir." she said. "Then neither do I throw a fastball at you," Jesus declared. "Go now and leave your life of sin." The crowd erupted into enthusiastic applause at this unscheduled home-run derby.

The Apostles team had the day off since it was a Sabbath when Jesus came across a man who had been born blind. The disciples, steeped in the culture of the day, knew that this man was either a big screw-up or his parents were, otherwise God would not have inflicted this blindness on him from the word go. Jesus set the boys straight on their faulty thinking, saying that neither the man nor his parents had sinned, causing this disability. Jesus then turned to the disciples and said, "Boys, how would you like to play a pick-up game today?" For Jesus so loved baseball that he was willing to give his life to play the game. So Jesus calmly strode to the mound, spit on the ground and made some mud with the saliva, formulating the famed spitball that had fooled so many batters. Jesus hurled the pitch which sent the blind man reeling into the Pool of Siloam. When the blind man emerged from the pool his eyes were opened and he could see his field of dreams for the first time in his life. The man was ecstatic and began sharing the miraculous news with his neighbors.

The all-stars on the Pharisees team soon found out about it and their first instinct was that Jesus must not be on God's team because he continued to play ball on the Sabbath. The Pharisees confronted the man's parents about it. They confirmed that he was their son and had been born blind, but they refrained from addressing how the miraculous cure materialized because they feared getting kicked out of the league (the Pharisees were jealous of Jesus' flawless baseball record and threatened any of His players and fans). The blind man tried to set them straight with how only someone doing God's will could open a blind person's eyes, but the Pharisees' spiritual blindness was a more profound handicap than had been the blind man's lack of physical eyesight.

Jesus and the disciples faced the same opponent at Bethsaida when some folks brought him a blind man. Once again Jesus relied on his trusty spitball, directly spitting on the man's eyes this time. The man could see but his vision was still blurry. Jesus reared back and threw another pitch, this time completely restoring the man's vision.

Jesus continued amazing the crowds with his pitching, base running, catching, and hitting. He "single"-handedly snatched victory from the jaws of the diseased, the demon-possessed, the disabled, and even the dead. Nothing Satan or the all-stars threw at him could defeat his skills. One of his most impressive victories occurred during an unscheduled game en route to their toughest opponent yet, overcoming the death of a ruler's young daughter. While the team was traveling down a dusty road to this most important match-up, a woman who had been subject to bleeding for 12 years broke through security and simply touched Jesus' uniform, thinking that if she could just get Jesus' autograph she would be healed. Jesus whirled around, knowing someone had touched his uniform. He saw the woman; trembling with fear at having been so brazen, but Jesus told her to step up to the plate and He tossed her an easy pitch. She smacked a home run and was healed.

After this exhibition, Jesus continued on with the Apostles to the scheduled game where death had already claimed victory. The Apostles were overwhelmed at the odds of winning a game that was seemingly already over, muttering among themselves how they could not possibly pull this one out. What's the sense in playing a game when the outcome has already been determined, thought the Apostles. Although their best player had worked wonders in every game, nobody could defeat death. Death was final. This game was over before they even got to the stadium. The Apostles, who had enjoyed winning every game they had started with Jesus, were dejected that they would finally lose their first game.

As Jesus approached the stadium, He saw flute players and a noisy crowd. He told the crowd to go away. Then He told the crowd that the girl was not dead but merely asleep. At this absurd assertion, the people laughed, knowing that Jesus had finally met His match. The people thought Jesus had finally lost His mental acuity. Then

Jesus slowly approached the mound, fingering the ball, looking for a signal from God on what pitch to throw. Deep in concentration, Jesus slowly began his delivery, reaching out with every ounce of courage to the young girl, gently grabbing her hand, and assisting her to her feet. Death took a called third strike that day and the crowd went nuts when the girl exited the stadium, signing autographs alongside Jesus. The Apostles were stunned as the concept of death being defeated sunk in. The impossible had become possible. No longer was it just the blind who saw, the deaf who heard, the mute who talked, the lame who walked, and the diseased who were cured. Now it was the dead who lived. Yikes! The Apostles were pumped up because now they knew that nobody could defeat them.

Because demand for tickets was increasing at every game the Apostles played, Jesus sent out the 12 Apostles on their own to play with His own power to drive out demons and cure diseases. Demand continued mushrooming and Jesus appointed 72 others to go out in pairs of players to take on all opponents. Major league baseball was quickly becoming a huge success much to the consternation of the all-star teams in Jerusalem who had reigned supreme for hundreds of years. Their dynasties were threatened by this upstart bunch of yahoos from the backwoods and hick towns of Judea. The glory boys began plotting to take Jesus out since they knew without Jesus, the Apostles would be just some other ho-hum bush-league team that wouldn't stand a chance against the more talented and experienced players in Jerusalem.

Once again Jesus and the Apostles hit the road when they came across a widow's only son being carried out in a coffin near the town gate of Nain, where they had a scheduled game the next day. Jesus wanted to rest but couldn't resist the chance to get in a little extra practice. So Jesus stepped up to the plate and crashed a towering homer well beyond the town gate as the young man rose from the coffin and rejoined his mom. Naturally the crowd was stunned at this unexpected display of baseball skill, never before witnessing anything like it. Of course, the next day's game was immediately sold out.

One of the most spectacular games the Apostles played was when they defeated a demon that had possessed a man for quite some time. No one had been able to defeat this demon. Jesus threw three quick strikes and tossed the demon into a herd of 2,000 pigs roaming outside the stadium, who rushed into a nearby lake and drowned. Of course, the man who was released from the grip of this demon was relieved, but the vendors who had counted on many hot dogs from the pigs were greatly displeased.

Another memorable game was played in the vicinity of the Decapolis when Jesus and the Apostles played against a man who was deaf and mute. Once again Jesus relied on the spitball to retire this man's ailments, first putting his fingers in the man's ears and then spitting and touching the man's tongue. Immediately the man's ears were opened and his tongue loosened and he began speaking plainly. The crowd loved it.

And now Christ and the Apostles were preparing for their greatest game to date. An up-and-coming player named Lazarus, the brother of two devoted fans, Mary and Martha, had fallen ill and was put on the disabled list. When Jesus first heard that Lazarus had been put on the disabled list he decided to put in two more days of practice on their home field before traveling to Judea. The Apostles were upset because the ballpark where they would play was one of the most hostile in the league; these fans had not just thrown tomatoes at them last time they were in town, but stones. The Apostles thought that Lazarus was sick, but not that sick. Jesus acknowledged that Lazarus had been removed from the disabled list and put on permanent waivers from playing the game. The Apostles had seen Jesus overcome death in a few earlier games but they still thought it was a fluke. So they naturally were very wary about playing such a tough game in such a hostile environment. When Jesus arrived at the stadium, Martha, one of his biggest fans, came out to greet him. She told Him that if He had arrived on time Lazarus would have been on the winning team instead of going down to defeat. Jesus was deeply moved by the grief expressed by the sisters and Lazarus' friends, even shedding some tears.

Jesus composed Himself and looked to God for signals on how to proceed with this historic situation. The tension mounted in the stadium as Jesus studied the situation, immersing Himself in deep prayer. Jesus flashed a signal to Martha to remove the stone from the grave so the game could resume. Martha resisted saying that the game had been over for four days and that a foul odor would emanate from behind the stadium walls. Jesus again flashed the signal for Mary to remove the stone and this time she did. The crowd was on its feet, but the silence was deafening. All eyes were fastened on Jesus as he stood on the mound, a solitary figure up against death, the most feared opponent of human beings. Most folks in the crowd had not seen the earlier games in which Jesus had beat death, and many of them were skeptical of the press reports they had read, thinking there was some hoax or logical explanation behind these so-called victories. God and Jesus went through another exchange of prayers and signals, then Jesus slowly began His delivery, the one the Apostles had seen so many times before. But this time Christ delivered His hardest pitch yet, smoking the inside of the plate leaving Death quivering in its wake, taking a called third strike, and muttering to the umpire, "I didn't even see that last pitch. Did you see it?" The umpire retorted, "I didn't see the pitch either, but it sounded like a strike." At that moment, Lazarus calmly walked out of the dugout, wrapped in his grave clothes. Jesus told the trainer to retire Lazarus' grave clothes in the Hall of Fame and put Lazarus' uniform on. Lazarus trotted out to the field amidst a thunderous and prolonged standing ovation as Christ tipped His hat to His Father and walked off the mound.

Meanwhile, the perennial teams in Jerusalem were getting more and more upset at the outstanding record compiled by the Apostles. Not only were the Apostles winning, but they were playing flawless ball, shutting out demons, disease, and death, and crushing their opponents. The power teams in Jerusalem knew that their only hope at restoring parity to the league was to terminate Jesus with extreme prejudice. So they plotted to take Him out during the World Series in Jerusalem the very next week.

The last game Jesus played before being hauled before the authorities in Jerusalem was when He was arrested for playing the game too well. One of the Apostles was so upset that he lost his temper and hacked off an opposing player's ear. Jesus rebuked the Apostle. Jesus said, "We play fair and square. No sliding in with your spikes high, no illegal pitches, no bean balls." Then Jesus turned to the opposing player and said, "Sorry about that, mate," and healed him by touching his ear.

Oh how the Apostles wanted to keep playing; they had experienced their field of dreams, witnessing amazing comeback victories, blazing pitches, dazzling pick-off moves, towering home runs, exciting base running. They had compiled a perfect won-loss record. And now their greatest player was being hauled off to court for monopolizing their league with victory after victory. The Apostles were glum as they trudged into Jerusalem, hoping that this was merely a breather in their quest to play the big boys - the Pharisees and Sadducees and Sanhedrin. But alas, their dream of playing in the World Series was shattered when the religious authorities turned Jesus over to be crucified by the Romans. The Apostles were crushed, perplexed, depressed. They had experienced miracle after miracle, victory after victory for the preceding three years, and now it had all come down to their superstar being killed on a cross. The anger of the authorities was so intense, the Apostles laid low that weekend, keeping a very low profile so as to preserve their own lives. The Apostles knew that their winning streak was over with their superstar in the grave. From the giddiness of being on top of the world to the gut-wrenching blow of such a devastating strike, the Apostles had experienced the widest range of emotions in a few hours time. And now they hung their heads in sadness and shame, wondering how they could even go on. Yes, indeed, the Apostles had taken a called third strike with the bases loaded. The game was over and the Apostles' grieving had pierced a new depth while the religious authorities were celebrating the defeat of the undefeated. No more Christ. God had been defeated ignominiously. The crowd exited the stadium as the score read Satan - 1, God - 0. There would be no more games since the Apostles' superstar had been terminated. The real World Series was over.

On Sunday morning, however, the biggest Superstar of all shouted, "Play ball! This game is not over; it's just beginning." God motioned for Jesus to get up from the grave, just as Jesus had told Lazarus to come out of the grave. Some lady fans were the first to see Jesus in His resurrection uniform and they were afraid and overjoyed at the same time. They ran to tell the Apostles, who were skeptical, yet hopeful. Nearly 500 people, some individually, some in pairs and some in larger groups, saw Jesus in His resurrection uniform during the next 40 days. Then God drafted Jesus back into heaven. The Apostles were pumped up, knowing that Jesus would soon send them the Holy Spirit to continue their ballplaying. And for the next two millennia, the nucleus of the Apostles team, a mere mustard seed, spawned the Christian league, now the largest in the world.

The Apostles Perform Miracles

Not only did Jesus perform miracles, he empowered his apostles to do likewise. This testifies to Christ's authority since he was the source of their power. As God performed miracles through Moses, so too did Jesus perform miracles through the apostles. Therefore, God's power is tantamount to Jesus' power. Christ could not have performed miracles or empowered his apostles to perform miracles had not God sanctioned Jesus to do it. God never performed miracles through Muhammad nor any of Muhammad's followers. How could Moses perform miracles if he was an imposter? How could Christ and his apostles perform miracles if they were imposters?

The array of miracles performed by the apostles is impressive. Peter and John healed a man crippled from birth by invoking the name of Jesus Christ. According to Acts 5:12, "The apostles performed many miraculous signs and wonders among the people." According to Acts 8:6-7, "When the crowds heard Philip and saw the miraculous signs he did, they all paid close attention to what he said. With shrieks, evil spirits came out of many, and many paralytics and cripples were healed." Acts 8:13 states, "Simon himself believed and was baptized. And he followed Philip everywhere, astonished by the great signs and miracles he saw."

Peter presided over the resurrection of a dead woman as documented in Acts 9:36-40:

> In Joppa there was a disciple named Tabitha (which, when translated, is Dorcas), who was always doing good and helping the poor. About that time she became sick and died, and her body was washed and placed in an upstairs room. Lydda was near Joppa;

> so when the disciples heard that Peter was in Lydda, they sent two men to him and urged him, "Please come at once!"
>
> Peter went with them, and when he arrived he was taken upstairs to the room. All the widows stood around him, crying and showing him the robes and other clothing that Dorcas had made while she was still with them.
>
> Peter sent them all out of the room; then he got down on his knees and prayed. Turning toward the dead woman, he said, "Tabitha, get up." She opened her eyes, and seeing Peter she sat up.

Paul had a miraculous conversion on the road to Damascus and was empowered to perform miracles. Acts 14:8-10 states:

> In Lystra there sat a man crippled in his feet, who was lame from birth and had never walked. He listened to Paul as he was speaking. Paul looked directly at him, saw that he had faith to be healed and called out, "Stand up on your feet!" At that, the man jumped up and began to walk.

Paul presided over the resurrection of a dead man in Acts 20:9-12. Acts 19:11-12 states:

> God did extraordinary miracles through Paul, so that even handkerchiefs and aprons that had touched him were taken to the sick, and their illnesses were cured and the evil spirits left them.

The God who performed miracles through Jesus and the apostles is incontrovertible evidence of Jesus' Messiahship because Christ claimed he was the Messiah. If Christ was an imposter, God would not have performed miracles through him and his apostles.

10

Of course, I quite agree that the Christian religion is, in the long run, a thing of unspeakable comfort. But it does not begin in comfort; it begins in the dismay I have been describing, and it is no use at all trying to go on to that comfort without first going through that dismay. In religion, as in war and everything else, comfort is the one thing you cannot get by looking for it. If you look for truth, you may find comfort in the end; if you look for comfort you will not get either comfort or truth - only soft soap and wishful thinking to begin with and, in the end, despair. Most of us have got over the pre-war wishful thinking about international politics. It is time we did the same about religion. . . .

If you are a Christian you do not have to believe that all the other religions are simply wrong all through. If you are an atheist you do have to believe that the main point in all the religions of the whole world is simply one huge mistake. If you are a Christian, you are free to think that all these religions, even the queerest ones, contain at least some hint of the truth. When I was an atheist I had to try to persuade myself that most of the human race have always been wrong about the question that mattered to them most; when I became a Christian I was able to take a more liberal view. But, of course, being a Christian does mean thinking that where Christianity differs from other religions, Christianity is right and they are wrong. As in arithmetic - there is only one right answer to a sum, and all other answers are wrong: but some of the wrong answers are much nearer being right than others.

C. S. Lewis

ADDITIONAL EVIDENCE

I believe Christianity is God's will for humanity. I believe when you examine the evidence and witness first-hand the transformation of some of the least of the least in a three-day period deep inside a maximum-security prison that the probability of Christianity being the Truth is greater than any other religion or faith. I have arrived at this conclusion after years of study, research, analysis, prayer, and observations of the circumstances in my life that have been engineered by God. This book is a documentation of my quest for the Truth. This chapter summarizes some of the rationale presented in earlier chapters that led me to this conclusion as well as introduce additional evidence that has convinced me that Christianity has the greatest probability of being the Truth.

Where there is hatred, strife, and separation there is Satan. Where there is love, peace, and unity there is God. In the beginning there was paradise on earth in the Garden of Eden. God created man and woman and there was love, peace, joy, and communion with God in a virtually perfect environment. There was perfect unity.

The only constraint God put on Adam and Eve was to not partake of the fruit from the tree of the knowledge of good and evil. God warned them that they would die if they disobeyed Him. Adam and Eve disobeyed God and they lost the chance to live forever.

> And the Lord God said, "The man has now become like one of us, knowing good and evil. He must not be allowed to reach out his hand and take also from the tree of life and eat, and live forever."

Genesis 3:22

This first prophecy regarding the fall of man, if the fruit of the knowledge of good and evil was consumed, was fulfilled by the spiritual death of Adam and Eve and eventually their physical death. In consummating the prophecy of death, God added other prophecies including the curse on the serpent, greatly increased pain in childbearing, husbands ruling over their wives, and the curse on the ground which resulted in thorns and thistles hindering food production and increased hardship and toil for humanity.

Choices and Consequences

So early in the Bible we see that there is a price to be paid for disobedience. The first talk we deliver to the prisoners during a Kairos Prison Ministry weekend is entitled "Choices." Choices have consequences as any good parent instructs his or her child. God's will was for mankind to live in paradise on earth forever, in perfect communion with Him or a plurality of God as indicated by the references to "us" and "our" in Genesis. These references support the concept of the trinity (God, Christ, and the Holy Spirit).

- Then God said, "Let *us* make man in *our* image, in *our* likeness, and let them rule over the fish of the sea and the birds of the air, over the livestock, over all the earth, and over all the creatures that move along the ground." [Genesis 1:26].
- And the Lord God said, "The man has now become like one of *us*, knowing good and evil." [Genesis 3:22a].

But heaven on earth was shattered when sin raised its ugly head. When mankind capitulated to the temptation offered by the crafty serpent, an act of supreme disobedience, there was a staggering price to be paid by all of humanity.

The Old Testament of the Bible is replete with examples of disobedience and consequences. Cain murdered Abel and was cursed with unfertile soil that would yield no crops and relegated to be a restless wanderer on the earth (a classic description of a homeless person).

God got so upset with humanity's wholesale disobedience that he destroyed the world with a flood, sparing only the righteous Noah and his family and the animals.

One of the greatest examples of the consequence of choice comes from Abram and Sarai's plan to begin a family through Sarai's maidservant, Hagar.

> And Abram said, "You have given me no children, so a servant in my household will be my heir." Then the word of the Lord came to him: "This man will not be your heir, but a son coming from your own body will by your heir."

Genesis 15:3-4

The option of having a child through Hagar, borne out of frustration at growing old without children and their impatience with God's timing, was antithetical to the unity of one man and one woman becoming one flesh (Genesis 2:24).

> Now Sarai, Abram's wife, had borne him no children. But she had an Egyptian maidservant named Hagar; so she said to Abram, "The Lord has kept me from having children. Go, sleep with my maidservant; perhaps I can build a family through her."
>
> Abram agreed to what Sarai said. So after Abram had been living in Canaan ten years, Sarai his wife took her Egyptian maidservant Hagar and gave her to her husband to be his wife. He slept with Hagar, and she conceived.
>
> When she knew she was pregnant, she began to despise her mistress. Then Sarai said to Abram, "You are responsible for the wrong I am suffering. I put my servant in your arms, and now that she knows she is pregnant, she despises me. May the Lord judge between you and me."
>
> "Your servant is in your hands," Abram said. "Do with her whatever you think best." Then Sarai mistreated Hagar; so she fled from her.

Genesis 16:1-16

Here we see dissension between Abram and Sarai and between Sarai and Hagar. Sarai blames Abram even though it was her suggestion that he sleep with Hagar. When Hagar knows she is pregnant, she begins to despise Sarai. And no doubt Sarai is jealous and resentful of Hagar. Sarai's animosity drives Hagar away. Clearly the lack of patience in waiting for God's timing in creating a family caused much heartache for Abram and Sarai. Their choice, however, has had even more profound, persistent, and pernicious consequences for humanity.

An angel of the Lord told Hagar:

> "You are now with child and you will have a son. You shall name him Ishmael, for the Lord has heard of your misery. He will be a wild donkey of a man; his hand will be against everyone and everyone's hand against him, and he will live in hostility toward all his brothers."

Genesis 16:11-12

The Jewish ethnicity and faith emanated from Abram (who became Abraham) and Sarai (who became Sarah) through their son Isaac. The Arabs, who largely adhere to the Islamic faith today, emanated from Abraham and Hagar's son Ishmael. Ishmael was the offspring of an Egyptian woman and a Jewish man whereas Isaac was the offspring of a Jewish man and woman. According to Hebrew tradition, the offspring of a Jewish female is Jewish but the same does not hold for the offspring of a Jewish male who is paired with a non-Jewish woman. Thus, this fissure in the Abrahamic lineage between the two I's (Isaac and Ishmael) was the epicenter of a titanic social earthquake that has caused much havoc, heartache, and hostility for the past 4,000 years with profound ramifications for much of the world. Indeed, there has probably been no other ethnic rivalry in history that remotely approaches the intensity and duration of the enmity between the Jews and Arabs or Muslims. These two groups are cousins. Regrettably they have proven to be killing cousins instead of kissing cousins for much of history. And yet, God predicted this hostility in the foregoing Scripture ["He will be a wild donkey of a man; his hand will be against everyone and everyone's hand against him, and he will live in hostility toward all his brothers."].

Although God heeded Abraham's request that Ishmael be blessed, He made it clear, "But my covenant I will establish with Isaac, whom Sarah will bear to you by this time next year." [Genesis 17:21].

> I will bless her [Sarah] and will surely give you a son by her. I will bless her so that she will be the mother of nations; kings of peoples will come from her."

> Abraham fell facedown; he laughed and said to himself, "Will a son be born to a man a hundred years old? Will Sarah bear a child at the age of ninety?" And Abraham said to God, "If only Ishmael might live under your blessing!"
>
> Then God said, "Yes, but your wife Sarah will bear you a son, and you will call him Isaac. *I will establish my covenant with him as an everlasting covenant for his descendants after him.* And as for Ishmael, I have heard you: I will surely bless him; I will make him fruitful and will greatly increase his numbers. He will be the father of twelve rulers, and I will make him into a great nation. *But my covenant I will establish with Isaac*, whom Sarah will bear to you by this time next year." When he had finished speaking with Abraham, God went up from him.

Genesis 17:16-22

God's will then was for the Jewish faith to be the chosen path at this critical juncture since God identified Isaac as the offspring of Abraham and Sarah to be the recipient of God's covenant. God's will is unity; Satan's will is division. Satan rejoiced when Judaism and the forerunner of Islam emerged from the choice of Abraham and Sarah, a decision that continues to have enormous reverberations 4,000 years later. It is my hypothesis that the enmity between the forerunners of the Arabs and the Jews created a propitious environment for the Arabs to enthusiastically embrace Muhammad in 570-632 A.D., whom, Muslims believe, was the prophet in which Islam reached its definitive shape. Because of the hostility between these two ethnic groups for thousands of years, it would have been highly improbable that the Jews would accept the Arabs into their faith even if the Arabs were so inclined to seek reconciliation and inclusion. This is also my hypothesis why many African-Americans have embraced Islam: because of the horrible racism that still exists in America (although improved from when our nation was founded) and the historical remnants of the degrading conditions of slavery imposed by white Christians, some African-Americans don't want to be associated with the white Christian church. And who can blame them.

Along this same line of reasoning, Arabs had no interest in embracing Christianity which was born out of Judaism; indeed, Christians view their religion as being the prophetic fulfillment of Judaism. Thus, we have God's will of one faith (Judaism) eventually splintering into two other major world religions: Islam and Christianity. Thus, out of one faith comes three major world religions and, according to Scriptures, these three faiths will become tantamount to one faith again upon Christ's second coming.

> Your attitude should be the same as that of Christ Jesus:
>
> Who, being in very nature God, did not consider equality with God something to be grasped, but made himself nothing, taking the very nature of a servant, being made in human likeness. And being found in appearance as a man, he humbled himself and became obedient to death - even death on a cross! Therefore, God exalted him to the highest place and gave him the name that is above every name, that at the name of Jesus every knee should bow, in heaven and on earth and under the earth, and every tongue confess that Jesus Christ is Lord, to the glory of God the Father.

Philippians 2:5-11

As the angel told Ishmael's mother (Hagar), Ishmael's "hand will be against everyone and everyone's hand against him, and he will live in hostility toward all his brothers." [Genesis 16:12]. There certainly has been hostility between Arabs and Jews for thousands of years. Perhaps out of antipathy toward the Jews and early Christians, the field was ripe for the germination and flourishing of the Islamic faith among the descendants of Ishmael. However, the Islamic faith does not seem to stand on a firm foundation since God clearly and incisively told Abraham that His covenant would be with Isaac, not Ishmael, and it would be an everlasting covenant for his descendants after him. God agreed to bless Ishmael and his descendants but God clearly chose not to establish His covenant with Ishmael's branch.

Therefore, the inscrutability of Muslims adhering to a faith that was not established by God's covenant is an impenetrable mystery for Jews and Christians.

God is perfection. He sanctifies marriage - the union of one man and one woman. Abraham and Sarah had been married for many years when out of frustration to conceive a child, Sarah suggested Abraham have relations with Hagar. How could God logically establish His covenant with a descendant from a second wife? Establishing the covenant with Ishmael would be antithetical to God's perfection and sanctification of marriage. Logically God could only establish His covenant with Isaac who was the offspring of Abraham's and Sarah's marriage. Recall the dialogue between Abram and God in Genesis 15:3-4.

> And Abram said, "You have given me no children; so a servant in my household will be my heir." Then the word of the Lord came to him: "This man will not be your heir, but a son coming from your own body will by your heir."

The Scripture is most explicit regarding God's covenant with Isaac, and not with Ishmael.

The apostle Paul amplifies this split in his letter to the Galatians:

> Tell me, you who want to be under the law, are you not aware of what the law says? For it is written that Abraham had two sons, one by the slave woman and the other by the free woman. His son by the slave woman was born in the ordinary way; but his son by the free woman was born as the result of a promise.
>
> These things may be taken figuratively, for the women represent two covenants. One covenant is from Mount Sinai and bears children who are to be slaves: This is Hagar. Now Hagar stands for Mount Sinai in Arabia and corresponds to the present city of Jerusalem, because she is in slavery with her children. But the Jerusalem that is above is free, and she is our mother. For it is written:

> "Be glad, O barren woman, who bears no children; break forth and cry aloud, you have not labor pains; because more are the children of the desolate woman than of her who has no husband." [Isaiah 54:1]
>
> Now you, brothers, like Isaac, are children of promise. At that time the son born in the ordinary way persecuted the son born by the power of the Spirit. It is the same now. But what does the Scripture say? "Get rid of the slave woman and her son, for the slave woman's son will never share in the inheritance with the free woman's son." [Genesis 21:10]. Therefore, brothers, we are not children of the slave woman, but of the free woman.

Galatians 4:21-31

This construct of going from one faith to three faiths and back to one faith achieves God's will of unity and is analogous to the Trinity in Christian theology. From one God comes three Persons - God, Jesus, and the Holy Spirit - and from these three Persons comes one God. According to the Bible, when Jesus Christ comes again, many people around the world will be drawn to Him because of His brilliant majesty. Philip Yancey discusses the second coming of Christ and how Jews and Christians are waiting for a Messiah.

> I have a Jewish friend who sometimes leads tour groups in Israel. He quickly learned that the real money in such tour groups comes from evangelical Christians on pilgrimage to "the Holy Land." It went against his grain to study the details of Jesus' life, for his parents had always forbidden mention of Jesus' name. As he did so, though, and as he got to know Christian tourists who knew more about Jewish history than he did, he was struck by an astonishing convergence.
>
> He learned that the conservative Christian groups believed world history was moving toward a culmination in which Israel would play a crucial

> role. They kept talking about the "second coming" of Jesus, quoting the prophecies he had learned in Hebrew school. As he listened to them, he realized that he and they were waiting for the same thing: a Messiah, a Prince of Peace, to restore justice and peace to a badly fractured planet. The Christians anticipated Messiah's second coming; as a Jew, he was still looking for the first coming. "Wouldn't it be amazing," he once told me, "if we found out we were all waiting for the same person."
>
> To the question, *Why doesn't God act*? Jews and Christians have the same answer, with one crucial difference. Jews believe that God will act, by sending the Messiah. Christians believe that God has acted, by sending the Messiah, and will act once more, by sending him again, this time in power and glory, not in weakness and humility.[58]

It is also very possible that Jesus' paradoxical statement that the first shall be last, and the last, first may apply to the Jews in toto (not counting Jewish Christians). The Jews were the people chosen by God to be His vehicle to reach the world. Did they succeed? Christianity is the world's largest faith with Christians comprising one-third of the world's population. There are about as many Jews today as there were 2,000 years ago. You do the math. The Jews were the first people chosen; they may also be the last group to accept Jesus Christ as their Messiah.

There are numerous examples of disobedience and consequences in the Old Testament. Some are summarized below.

Choices	Consequences
Adam and Eve partake of the fruit of the tree of the knowledge of good and evil	Greatly increased pain in childbearing and increased hardship associated with work

Choices	Consequences
Cain kills Abel	Cain is banished from his homeland to be a wanderer the rest of his days
Sexual depravity in Sodom and Gomorrah	Sodom and Gomorrah destroyed
No one in Lot's family to look back at the destruction of Sodom and Gomorrah	Lot's wife looked back and she became a pillar of salt
Israelites worshiped a golden calf	The Lord struck the people with a plague
Moses to speak to a rock to bring forth water; Moses strikes rock twice with staff causing water to gush out	Moses denied entry into the Promised Land
People are told to go into Promised Land but refuse	Forced to wander for 40 years in the wilderness
After Joshua died, Israelites disobeyed God intermittently between judges by worshiping other gods	Israel defeated intermittently by enemies

Choices	Consequences
Saul disobeys God by not keeping his commands	God rejects Saul as King and replaces him with David
David commits adultery with Bathsheba and conspires to have Bathsheba's husband murdered	The son born out of wedlock died on the 7th day
Satan rose up against Israel and incited David to take a census of Israel	Three options from God: three years of famine, three months of being conquered by Israel's enemies, or a plague - a plague was chosen with 70,000 casualties

Much of Israel's history in the Old Testament was characterized by a litany of righteous kings interspersed among evil kings with God's wrath eventually punishing the Israelites in various modes, such as being partially or totally conquered by enemies such as the Assyrians and Babylonians. So God has exhibited a track record of consequences following disobedience or poor choices.

It is my contention that given God's track record it can be logically deduced that if God's will is for humanity to be reconciled to Him through His Son (and this conclusion must be reached independently by every individual to ensure intellectual integrity) then people who are aware of this but refuse to believe it will have to pay a price. The initial group to reject God's plan were most of the Jews.

> This again is a great contradiction: though he was a Jew, his followers were not Jews.
>
> Voltaire

Jesus predicted that a price would have to be paid for their refusal to see, hear, understand, and accept God's will. Jesus states:

> Woe to you, because you build tombs for the prophets, and it was your forefathers who killed them. So you testify that you approve of what your forefathers did; they killed the prophets, and you build their tombs. Because of this, God in his wisdom said, "I will send them prophets and apostles, some of whom they will kill and others they will persecute." Therefore this generation will be held responsible for the blood of all the prophets that has been shed since the beginning of the world, from the blood of Abel to the blood of Zechariah, who was killed between the altar and the sanctuary. Yes, I tell you, this generation will be held responsible for it all.

Luke 11:47-51

As Jesus was making his triumphal entry into Jerusalem on what Christians traditionally celebrate as Palm Sunday, he was deeply saddened.

> As he approached Jerusalem, and saw the city, he wept over it and said, "If you, even you, had only known on this day what would bring you peace - but now it is hidden from your eyes. The days will come upon you when your enemies will build an embankment against you and encircle you and hem you in on every side. They will dash you to the ground, you and the children within your walls. They will not leave one stone on another, because you did not recognize the time of God's coming to you."

Luke 19:41-44

Jesus laments Jerusalem's resistance in another passage:

> O Jerusalem, Jerusalem, you who kill the prophets and stone those sent to you, how often I have longed to gather your children together, as a hen gathers her chicks under her wings, but you were not willing. Look, your house is left to you desolate.

Matthew 23:37-38

Of course, Daniel had predicted this over half a millennium earlier when he prophesied about the coming of the Messiah and the subsequent destruction of Jerusalem and the temple. Indeed of all the prophecies fulfilled by Christ this is one of the most impressive.

Some of the consequences of the Jews' disobedience was the destruction of Jerusalem in A.D. 70, the Crusades, and the Holocaust. Indeed, Christ predicted the destruction of Jerusalem:

> As he was leaving the temple, one of his disciples said to him, "Look, Teacher! What massive stones! What magnificent buildings!"
>
> "Do you see all these great buildings?" replied Jesus. "Not one stone here will be left on another; every one will be thrown down."

Mark 13:1-2

I'm not saying it was God's will for the Crusades and Holocaust to happen because God is the source of all goodness; He does not cause suffering because that would be antithetical to His nature. It was God's will for the Jews to accept His Son as the Messiah and, as with all choices, there are consequences and trade-offs. Jesus predicted suffering for the Jews in the New Testament. The horror of the Holocaust resulted in an incomprehensible and unparalleled tragedy: approximately six million Jews perished at the hands of the Nazis. It is estimated that, as a result of the Holocaust, the Jewish population today is roughly equivalent to what it was 2,000 years ago with the same proportion living in Palestine.[59] What often is forgotten or not mentioned is that there were 37,600,000 civilian and military deaths in World War II with Russia suffering 20,000,000 deaths, more than World War I's 17,000,000 deaths. The economic cost has been calculated at $1.6 trillion[60]. Many Christians paid a huge price.

Hardening the Heart

All of us share the blame in Christ's death because we are all sinners and Christ died for the forgiveness of sins. Can most of the Jews of 2,000 years ago be blamed for their refusal to accept Jesus Christ as their Messiah? In my view, the Jews can't be blamed because God hardened their hearts, just like he did Pharaoh when Pharaoh repeatedly refused to allow the Jews to leave Egypt. Why did God harden their hearts? I don't know. But there is evidence that the apostle Paul believed God hardened the Jews' hearts and he gives some rationale for this belief.

> What then shall we say? Is God unjust? Not at all! For he says to Moses, "I will have mercy on whom I have mercy, and I will have compassion on whom I have compassion." [Exodus 33:19].
>
> It does not, therefore, depend on man's desire or effort, but on God's mercy. For the Scripture says to Pharaoh: "I raised you up for this very purpose, that I might display my power in you and that my name might be proclaimed in all the earth." [Exodus 9:16]. Therefore, God has mercy on whom he wants to have mercy, and he hardens whom he wants to harden.

Romans 9:14-18

> What then? What Israel sought so earnestly it did not obtain, but the elect did. The others were hardened, as it is written: "God gave them a spirit of stupor, eyes so that they could not see and ears that they could not hear, to this very day."

Romans 11:7-8

> But to this day the Lord has not given you a mind that understands or eyes that see or ears that hear.
>
> Deuteronomy 29:4

> The Lord has brought over you a deep sleep: He has sealed your eyes (the prophets); he has covered your heads (the seers).
>
> Isaiah 29:10

> And David says: "May their table become a snare and a trap, a stumbling block and a retribution for them. May their eyes be darkened so they cannot see, and their backs be bent forever." [Psalm 69:22-23].
>
> Romans 11:9-10

And there is a well-known passage from Isaiah that speaks of God's hardening His chosen people's hearts.

> He [God] said, "Go and tell this people: "Be ever hearing, but never understanding; be ever seeing, but never perceiving. Make the heart of the people calloused; make their ears dull and close their eyes. Otherwise they might see with their eyes, hear with their ears, understand with their hearts, and turn and be healed."
>
> Isaiah 6:9-10

Isaiah's passage is so important that it appears in Acts 28:26-27 and in all four Gospels [Matthew 13:14, Mark 4:12, Luke 8:10, and John 12:40]. If repetition is an indication of the importance of a message, then it can be inferred that God's message through Isaiah is compelling.

Paul described the hardening of the Pharisees:

> They are darkened in their understanding and separated from the life of God because of the ignorance that is in them due to the hardening of their hearts.
>
> Ephesians 4:18

An interesting perspective on the hardening of hearts is found in the *Disciple Study Manual* for Genesis, Exodus, Luke, and Acts.

> What do we know about human power? That it is not easily surrendered, not voluntarily given up. Do people abandon their economic leverage? Not usually. Do governments yield their control without a struggle? Not normally. Revolutions take place to overthrow entrenched tyrants.
>
> Many readers of Exodus have difficulty with Pharaoh's "hard heart." Most perplexing is the phrase "I will harden his heart, so that he will not let the people go" (Exodus 4:21). References to the hardening of Pharaoh's heart appear eighteen times in Exodus 4-14. The thought is expressed three different ways: 1) God hardened Pharaoh's heart; 2) Pharaoh hardened his own heart; and 3) Pharaoh's heart was hardened. They have the same meaning. The word *hardened* sometimes means to be strong or stubborn. It can mean to be heavy, dull, or unresponsive. It means unyielding, severe, obstinate. Such is the mind of those who enslave.
>
> The Hebrew speaks of the heart not as the center of emotions but as the seat of the will. So we are speaking of decisions, the gritting of teeth, the making up of one's mind, the clenching of fists.
>
> God hardens no one's heart who has not first hardened it himself or herself. Yet does not the Word of God, intended to soften, become, to the one who resists, a cause of hardening? Is not rejecting God a cause of growing insensitivity and increasingly calloused conscience?[61]

God used the hardening of Pharaoh's heart to glorify God since Pharaoh's magicians could not replicate many of the calamities inflicted by God or reverse them. The Hebrews would know incontrovertibly that God delivered them from the Egyptians. Thus, the Hebrews could not take credit for their deliverance. Likewise, God hardened the hearts of the Jews to glorify God through God's appeal to the Gentiles. God reached the Gentiles despite the Jews' obstinacy. As God's chosen people, the Jews were God's instrument to bless the nations.

> Abraham will surely become a great and powerful nation, and all nations on earth will be blessed through him.

Therefore, only God could have overcome the obstacle of most of the Jews to bless the Gentiles and the vast majority of Jews couldn't take credit for it.

The *Disciple Study Manual* touches on parallels between Moses and Jesus in delivering salvation.

> Jewish people read the Hebrew Scriptures (Old Testament) in light of the Exodus. We might say that the entire Old Testament was written down in the afterglow of Exodus. That miraculous opening of the sea was the moment of salvation for the Hebrews. Salvation history looks back on that moment when God acted to save the covenant people. Just as Christians read the New Testament in light of the resurrection of Jesus, when his death threatened to end all, so Jewish people reflect their entire faith experience out of the day they were given new life in freedom. The Bible is built on two dramatic moments of divine intervention, the Exodus of Moses and the resurrection of Jesus. Any reader who fails to understand this stance of faith will miss the reality of Scripture.[62]

Parallels: Moses and Jesus	
God performed miracles through Moses. Miracles included imposition of plagues and other calamities and in most cases (except death of firstborn son) their reversal. Pharaoh rejected the miracles.	God performed miracles through Jesus. The Pharisees, Sadducees, teachers of the law, chief priests, and other leaders of Jewish society rejected the miracles.
God hardened Pharaoh's heart (and other leaders of society).	God hardened the hearts of the leaders of the Hebrews.
God favorably disposed common people to have soft hearts toward the Hebrews. (Ex. 11:2-3, 3:21-22, and 12:36).	Jesus evoked common sinners to be drawn to him. He had a soft heart toward common sinners, whereas Jesus harshly rebuked the Pharisees and other Jewish leaders ("brood of vipers, hypocrites, blind guides, blind fools, blind men"). "Blessed are the poor in spirit, for theirs is the kingdom of God." [Matt. 5:3]. Cursed are the haughty and arrogant in spirit, for theirs is the kingdom of man.
God delivered the Hebrews from bondage to Pharaoh.	God delivered the people who believed in Jesus from bondage to sin.

Parallels: Moses and Jesus	
God glorified Himself by defeating the false gods/ idols of the Egyptians which weren't able to perform the same miracles as Moses did (the few that they did replicate were allowed by God). (Ex. 14:4 and 17-18). God glorified himself through the hardening of Pharaoh's heart.	God glorified Himself through defeating the false idols (to wit, slavish devotion to rules and regulations) of the Hebrews through the power of the resurrection miracle (saved by faith through grace, not by works or slavish devotion to rules and regulations). God glorified Himself by not allowing the Jewish leaders to get credit for being the vehicle through which salvation came.
God could have stopped with one plague or calamity, and had he not hardened Pharaoh's heart, Pharaoh possibly would have let the Hebrews go. The Hebrews probably would not have been in awe of God as much as they were after several miracles (i.e., plagues and their removal).	God could have not hardened the Pharisees' hearts further and maybe they would have been receptive to Christ. The Jews were the chosen people to bring blessings to the nations. The Pharisees and other leaders of society rejected Jesus because he threatened their power structure and prestige. However, God circumvented their obstinacy and Christianity became the world's largest faith. The Pharisees and their comrades derailed a whole segment of Jews for the past 2,000 years but God's will could not be thwarted.
God did not want Israelites to think they were responsible for their freedom	God did not want people to think they were responsible for their salvation. People are saved through God's grace, not by their works.

Parallels: Moses and Jesus	
God chose Pharaoh to display his power. (Ex. 9:16). But God would not be derailed by his obstinacy. He delivered freedom for the Hebrews through Moses.	God chose the Hebrews to display his power by bringing blessings to the nations. But God would not be derailed by their obstinacy and stiff necks. He delivered salvation to the Jews and Gentiles through Jesus.
Pharaoh had power. Lord Action said, "Power tends to corrupt and absolute power corrupts absolutely." Pharaoh did not want to give up his power. His economy was built on slave labor. His wealth was derived from slavery.	The Pharisees and other Hebrew leaders did not want to yield their power and prestige in society.

Of course not all the Jews' hearts were hardened since the first Christians were Jews. However, many of the Jews who accepted Jesus as the Messiah were from the lower echelon of society. They were humble; they didn't have much to lose. God exalted them through their faith in Christ. The Jews from the upper echelon of society, however, had much more to lose; the exalted were humbled. In Romans 9-11, Paul addresses the failure of many Jews, his own people, to accept Christ as their Messiah. Paul did not believe that the Jews were no longer God's chosen people. Instead, he believed that God hardened the Jews' hearts for two reasons: 1) Israel's unfaithfulness and 2) God's desire to make the Jews jealous of the Gentiles and thereby attract more of them to Christ.

> Again I ask: Did they stumble so as to fall beyond recovery? Not at all! Rather, because of their transgression, salvation has come to the Gentiles to

> make Israel envious. But if their transgression means riches for the world, and their loss means riches for the Gentiles, how much greater riches will their fullness bring!
>
> I am talking to you Gentiles. Inasmuch as I am the apostle to the Gentiles, I make much of my ministry in the hope that I may somehow arouse my own people to envy and save some of them.

Romans 11:11-14

It was hard for most Jews to accept Jesus Christ as their Messiah because His teachings were so radical and so foreign to their traditions, rules, and laws that had governed them for 2,000 years. Jesus' contemporaries were also expecting a powerful earthly ruler like King David who would defeat the Romans. Instead of being a strong political Messiah, Jesus was rather weak since he wound up hanging on a cross. As Philip Yancey put it, "The Jews objected so strongly to Jesus because, despite his audacious claims, he did not match their conception of what God is like; they rejected him for not measuring up."[63]

Today, most Jews still refuse to accept Christ as their Messiah. Thus, modern Jews have 4,000 years of traditions, rules, and laws behind them. How hard it must be to convert to Christianity after this much investment. However, the question that must be asked is: "What is the best option for me on an ex ante (going forward) basis?" People who blindly adhere to a course or path without investigating options because they and their ancestors have invested so much for millennia commit intellectual bankruptcy. Just because there are thousands of years of investment behind a faith doesn't make it in accordance with God's will. This is analogous to an economics principle called the sunk-cost fallacy. People who gauge a prior investment in a project as being relevant to their decision whether to accept or reject continuing the project commit the sunk-cost error. An example is presented below:

> Sunk costs are like spilt milk: they are past and irreversible outflows. Because sunk costs are bygones, they cannot be affected by the decision to

> accept or reject the project, and so they should be ignored.
>
> This fact is often forgotten. For example, in 1971 Lockheed sought a federal guarantee for a bank loan to continue development of the TriStar airplane. Lockheed and its supporters argued it would be foolish to abandon a project on which nearly $1 billion had already been spent. Some of Lockheed's critics countered that it would be equally foolish to continue with a project that offered no prospect of a satisfactory return on that $1 billion. Both groups were guilty of the so-called sunk-cost fallacy; the $1 billion was irrecoverable and, therefore, irrelevant.[64]

The question of eternal salvation depends on a decision as soon as you have satisfied yourself what the Truth is. The past, while important, is a sunk cost. The future is what counts; discovering your eternal destiny is the most important investment you will ever make.

A Firebrand named Paul

One of the most compelling facts that has bolstered my faith in Christianity is the miraculous transformation of a man named Saul. No knowledgeable person would consider Saul of Tarsus to have been a follower of Christ. Indeed, the evidence documents the precise opposite. Saul was a champion antagonist of Christians; he despised Christians and persecuted them, tracking them down in surrounding communities to bring them back to Jerusalem for prosecution. Josh McDowell, in a synthesis of his earlier books as compiled by Bill Wilson in his book *A Ready Defense*, states:

> When we come to the apostle Paul, we find what some would say is the greatest evidence for the truth of the Christian faith. Here is a man cut completely from the cloth of Jewish culture. Fashioned by it and steeped in it, he was probably one of the most intense protagonists of the day for rabbinic Judaism.[65]

Paul essentially describes himself as a Pharisee's Pharisee. The Pharisees were a Jewish sect holding the religious power in Palestine during Christ's ministry. These "separated ones" believed that their detailed descriptions of how to obey the law were equal in authority to the Mosaic law and that their meticulous adherence to these rules, rituals, and traditions made them the only righteous Jews alive.

> I want you to know, brothers, that the gospel is not something that man made up. I did not receive it from any man, nor was I taught it; rather, I received it by revelation from Jesus Christ.
>
> For you have heard of my previous way of life in Judaism, how intensely I persecuted the church of God and tried to destroy it. I was advancing in Judaism beyond many Jews of my own age and was extremely jealous for the traditions of my fathers. But when God, who set me apart from birth and called me by his grace, was pleased to reveal his Son in me so that I may preach him among the Gentiles, I did not consult any man, nor did I go up to Jerusalem to see those who were apostles before I was, but I went immediately into Arabia and later returned to Damascus.

Galatians 1:11-17

> If anyone else thinks he has reasons to put confidence in the flesh, I have more: circumcised on the eighth day, of the people of Israel, of the tribe of Benjamin, a Hebrew of Hebrews; in regard to the law, a Pharisee; as for zeal, persecuting the church; as for legalistic righteousness, faultless.
>
> But whatever was to my profit I now consider loss for the sake of Christ. What is more, I consider everything a loss compared to the surpassing greatness of knowing Christ Jesus my Lord, for whose sake I have lost all things. I consider them rubbish, that I may gain Christ and be found in

> him, not having a righteousness of my own that comes from the law, but that which is through faith in Christ - the righteousness that comes from God and is by faith. I want to know Christ and the power of his resurrection and the fellowship of sharing in his sufferings, becoming like him in his death, and so, somehow, to attain to the resurrection from the dead.

Philippians 3:4-11

In Lee Strobel's book, *The Case for Christ*, Professor J. P. Moreland was questioned about Paul's conversion.

> "As a Pharisee, he hated anything that disrupted the traditions of the Jewish people. To him, this new countermovement called Christianity would have been the height of disloyalty. In fact, he worked out his frustration by executing Christians when he had a chance," Moreland replied.
>
> "Suddenly he doesn't just ease off Christians but joins their movement! How did this happen? Well, everyone agrees Paul wrote Galatians, and he tells us himself in that letter what caused him to take a 180-degree turn and become the chief proponent of the Christian faith. By his own pen he says he saw the risen Christ and heard Christ appoint him to be one of his followers."
>
> I was awaiting for Moreland to make his point, so I could challenge him with an objection by Christianity critic Michael Martin. He said that if you count Paul's conversion as being evidence for the truth of the Resurrection, you should count Muhammad's conversion to Islam as being evidence for the truth that Jesus was not resurrected, since Muslims deny the Resurrection!
>
> "Basically, he says the evidential values of Paul's conversion and Muhammad's conversion cancel each

other out," I told Moreland. "Frankly, that seems like a good point. Won't you admit that he's right?"

Moreland didn't bite. "Let's take a look at Muhammad's conversion," he said with confidence in his voice. "No one knows anything about it. Muhammad claims he went into a cave and had a religious experience in which Allah revealed the Koran to him. There's no other eyewitness to verify this. Muhammad offered no publicly miraculous signs to certify anything.

"And someone easily could have had ulterior motives in following Muhammad, because in the early years Islam was spread largely by warfare. Followers of Muhammad gained political influence and power over the villages that were conquered and 'converted' to Islam by the sword.

"Contrast that with the claims of the early followers of Jesus [who did not use warfare to spread their faith], including Paul. They claimed to have seen public events that other people saw as well. These were things that happened outside their minds, not just in their minds.

"Furthermore, when Paul wrote 2 Corinthians - which nobody disputes he did - he reminded the people in Corinth that he performed miracles when he was with them earlier. He'd certainly be foolish to make this statement if they knew he hadn't."

"And your point?" I asked.

"Remember," he said, "it's not the simple fact that Paul changed his views. You have to explain how he had this particular change of belief that completely went against his upbringing; how he saw the risen Christ in a public event that was witnessed by others, even though they didn't understand it; and how he

> performed miracles to back up his claim to being an apostle."[66]

Saul was on the road to Damascus with other men to bring back Christians as prisoners to Jerusalem to be killed. On the way, Jesus appeared to Saul, and asked, "Saul, Saul, why do you persecute me?" Saul was struck blind by the light that flashed from heaven. After three days of blindness, Saul was healed by Jesus' empowering of Annanias, one of the Christians in Damascus that Saul had been hunting. Saul saw Jesus, was converted, and changed his name to Paul. For Paul it was a life-shattering epiphany when he saw the risen Christ, inspiring him to become the foremost champion of Christianity in the early years. Paul's transformation from persecutor to proponent of Christians emanating from his lightning-bolt experience on the road to Damascus, witnessed by other men, is one of the most powerful pieces of evidence for the truth of the resurrection.

Josh McDowell in *A Ready Defense* describes Paul's conversion:

> And how about Paul, the religious persecutor of the Christians? This Jewish fanatic so hated the followers of Christ that he obtained special permission to go to other cities and incarcerate Christ's disciples. He ravaged the church.
>
> But something happened to this persecutor. He turned from an antagonist to a protagonist of Jesus. He was transformed from a murderer to a Christian missionary. He changed from a bitter interrogator of Christians to one of the greatest propagators of the Christian faith.
>
> The irony is that Paul began to confound the Jewish authorities "by proving Jesus is the Christ," the Son of God (Acts 9:22). He was eventually killed for his devotion to Christ. What happened? This historical explanation is Paul's statement that Jesus "appeared to me also" (1 Corinthians 15:8, Acts 9:3-22).[67]

Paul knew beyond a shadow of a doubt that Christ was real because he had seen Him. This confidence in the truth of the resurrection gave Paul rock-solid courage to persevere no matter what the cost. Paul describes the sufferings he endured for the sake of promoting Christ:

> What anyone else dares to boast about - I am speaking as a fool - I also dare to boast about. Are they Hebrews? So am I. Are they Israelites? So am I. Are they Abraham's descendants? So am I. Are they servants of Christ? (I am out of my mind to talk like this.) I am more. I have worked much harder, been in prison more frequently, been flogged more severely, and been exposed to death again and again. Five times I received from the Jews the forty lashes minus one. Three times I was beaten with rods, once I was stoned, three times I was shipwrecked, I spent a night and a day in the open sea, I have been constantly on the move. I have been in danger from rivers, in danger from bandits, in danger from my own countrymen, in danger from Gentiles; in danger in the city, in danger in the country, in danger at sea; and in danger from false brothers. I have labored and toiled and have often gone without sleep; I have known hunger and thirst and have often gone without food; I have been cold and naked.

2 Corinthians 11:21-27

Paul was imprisoned at least three times; he suffered a serious physical ailment; and died a martyr with tradition holding that he was beheaded in Rome. Now why would a man who was in the elite echelon of Hebrew society with many comforts voluntarily forgo all that status to endure 25 years of agony to spread the word of Jesus, and eventually lose his very life? The only logical explanation is that Paul knew with absolute certainty that Christ was real because he had appeared to him, eyeball to eyeball, so to speak.

On Saturday during a Kairos weekend, a clergy meditation entitled "Who is Jesus Christ?" is shared with the prisoners. This meditation is found in the *Pre-Kairos and the Kairos Weekend Manual* [Kairos Manual] and states in part:

> He [Paul] was extremely intelligent, and if there had been anything false about Jesus' life, death, and resurrection, Paul, more than anyone, would have known. There can be no doubt, Jesus' death and resurrection is true![68]

Eyewitnesses to the Resurrection

The resurrection of Jesus Christ is the fulcrum of Christianity. Christianity would not exist without the Resurrection. Had not Jesus been raised from the dead, he would have been no more than a great teacher, perhaps consigned to a brief description in some textbook. St. Paul put it this way:

> For if the dead are not raised, then Christ has not been raised either. And if Christ has not been raised, your faith is futile; you are still in your sins. Then those also who have fallen asleep in Christ are lost. If only for this life we have hope in Christ, we are to be pitied more than all men.

1 Corinthians 15:16-19

Jon Meacham, in a *Newsweek* article entitled "From Jesus to Christ", writes:

> From the beginning, critics of Christianity have dismissed the Resurrection as a theological invention. As a matter of history, however, scholars agree that the two oldest pieces of New Testament tradition speak to Jesus' rising from the dead. First, the tomb in which Jesus' corpse was placed after his execution was empty; if it were not, then Christianity's opponents could have produced his bones. (Matthew also says the temple priests tried to bribe Roman guards at the tomb, saying, "Tell people, `His disciples came by night and stole him away while we were asleep'"[Matthew 28:13] - implying the body was in fact gone.)[69]

However, the Roman guards who allowed the Roman seal on the tomb to be broken faced the death penalty. And how could all the Roman guards (anywhere from 4 to 16 men) be asleep when it would take a number of disciples to move the boulder at the entrance to the tomb? And how could the Roman guards tell it was the disciples who were removing the body if they were asleep?

Matthew records in his Gospel:

> The next day, the one after Preparation Day, the chief priests and the Pharisees went to Pilate. "Sir," they said, "we remember that while he was still alive that deceiver said, 'After three days I will rise again.' So give the order for the tomb to be made secure until the third day. Otherwise, his disciples may come and steal the body and tell the people that he has been raised from the dead. This last deception will be worse than the first."
>
> Take a guard," Pilate answered. "Go, make the tomb as secure as you know how." So they went and made the tomb secure by putting a seal on the stone and posting the guard.
>
> Matthew 27:62-66

The purpose of the seal was to discourage anyone from disturbing the contents of the grave. According to Josh McDowell in his book *A Ready Defense*:

> After the guard inspected the tomb and rolled the stone in place, a cord was stretched across the rock. This was fastened at either end with sealing clay. Finally, the clay packs were stamped with the official signet of the Roman governor. . .The consequences of breaking the seal were severe. The FBI and CIA of the Roman Empire were called into action to find the man or men responsible. When they were apprehended, it meant automatic execution by crucifixion upside down. Your guts ran into your throat. So people feared the breaking of the seal.[70]

Those who dismiss the resurrection of Jesus often view the disciples as either naive bumpkins with a penchant for supernatural phenomena or cunning conspirators who concocted a seamless story so fantastic as a way to ignite their new religion.

As for the first view of the disciples being naive bumpkins, quite the opposite is portrayed in the Gospels. If anything, the disciples were among the most skeptical of the events of Easter morning, completely dismissing the reports that the women brought back to them from the open tomb. Even after Jesus appeared to some of them in His resurrected body, some still doubted.

The second view, a clever, unimpeachable conspiracy or cover-up, also crumbles upon closer scrutiny. Charles Colson, a key participant in the conspiratorial Watergate fiasco, reports that cover-ups only succeed if all the conspirators are confident, competent, and consistent in their story. The disciples utterly failed as competent conspirators.

The trembling disciples were locked away, frightened of the same fate that befell Jesus. They were so terrified they delegated the women to go to the tomb to finish the embalming process. The disciples were in no condition to fabricate a resurrection or risk their lives by taking the corpse.

Philip Yancey, in his book *The Jesus I Never Knew*, writes:

> According to all four Gospels, women were the first witnesses of the resurrection, a fact that no conspirator in the first century would have invented. Jewish courts did not even accept the testimony of female witnesses. A deliberate cover-up would have put Peter or John or, better yet, Nicodemus in the spotlight, not built its case around reports from women. Since the Gospels were written several decades after the events, the authors had plenty of time to straighten out such an anomaly - unless, of course, they were not concocting a legend but recording the plain facts.
>
> A conspiracy also would have tidied up the first witnesses' stories. Were there two white-clad figures

> or just one? Why did Mary Magdalene mistake Jesus for a gardener? Was she alone or with Salome and another Mary? Accounts of the discovery of the empty tomb sound breathless and fragmentary. The women were "afraid yet filled with joy," says Matthew [28:8]; "trembling and bewildered," says Mark [16:8]. Jesus makes no dramatic, well-orchestrated entrance to quell all doubts; the early reports seem wispy, mysterious, confused. Surely conspirators could have done a neater job of depicting what they could later claim to be the hinge event of history.[71]

Anyone who has served as a juror knows the many conflicting testimonies of the same events. Even observers of a simple car wreck can have widely varying views of what they saw. Thus, despite the apparent illogicality of different details in the Gospels regarding the resurrection (on who initially observed the empty tomb; the number of angels at the tomb; the varying appearances of Jesus' resurrected body in terms of appearing as flesh and blood and at others, being able to walk through walls; the easy recognition of him by some and others' inability to recognize him until Jesus identified himself), the fact that there are disparate views actually is consistent with human behavior. One thing is certain, the Gospels are in agreement with the tomb being empty and the appearance of the resurrected Jesus to some of the people.

What accounts for the leery disciples' transformation from fear and doubt to courage and conviction "about the empty tomb and its significance in the history of salvation - that through his death and resurrection Jesus would redeem humankind?" as Jon Meacham asks in *Newsweek*. Meacham answers:

> Perhaps recollections of the words of Jesus himself. Though many scholars rightly raise compelling questions about the historical value of the portraits of Jesus in the Gospels, the apostles had to arrive at their definition of his messianic mission somehow, and it is possible that Jesus may have spoken of these things during his lifetime - words that came flooding back to his followers once the shock of his resurrection had

> sunk in. On historical grounds, then, Christianity appears less a fable than a faith derived in part from oral or written traditions dating from the time of Jesus' ministry and that of his disciples. "The Son of Man is delivered into the hands of men, and they shall kill him; and after that. . .he shall rise the third day," Jesus says in Mark [9:31], who adds that the disciples at the time "understood not that saying, and were afraid to ask him." [9:32].
>
> That the apostles would have created such words and ideas out of thin air seems unlikely, for their story and their message strained credulity even then. Paul admitted the difficulty: ". . .we preach Christ crucified, a stumbling-block to Jews and folly to Gentiles." [1 Corinthians 1:23]. A king who died a criminal's death? An individual's resurrection from the dead? A human atoning sacrifice? "This is not something that the PR [public relations] committee of the disciples would have put out," says Dr. R. Albert Mohler, Jr., president of the Southern Baptist Theological Seminary in Louisville, Ky. "The very fact of the salvation message's complexity and uniqueness, I think, speaks to the credibility of the Gospels and of the entire New Testament."[72]

Therefore, we can see that the Roman guards had a very strong vested interest in not allowing the seal to be broken and the body stolen. Their lives depended on it. We can see that the Jewish authorities had a very strong vested interest in not having the body removed. Their goal of snuffing out Jesus depended on it. We can see that the disciples were in no condition to even contemplate removing the body, being locked in a room, paralyzed with shock, fear, and grief. Then who did remove the stone and the body? The only logical answer is that God removed the stone either directly or through one of His angels. According to Matthew's Gospel, God had one of His angels remove the stone.

After the Sabbath, at dawn on the first day of the week, Mary Magdalene and the other Mary went to look at the tomb.

> There was a violent earthquake, for an angel of the Lord came down from heaven and, going to the tomb, rolled back the stone and sat on it. His appearance was like lightning, and his clothes were white as snow. The guards were so afraid of him that they shook and became like dead men.

Matthew 28:1-4

This explains why the guards were not a factor in preventing the stone being removed. A violent earthquake and a confrontation with a powerful, supernatural angel would scare the daylights out of most humans.

> The angel said to the women, "Do not be afraid, for I know that you are looking for Jesus, who was crucified. He is not here; he has risen, just as he said. Come and see the place where he lay. Then go quickly and tell the disciples: 'He has risen from the dead and is going ahead of you into Galilee. There you will see him.' Now I have told you."

Matthew 28:5-7

But God did not have to remove the stone for Jesus to be resurrected. Since God is all-powerful, He could have resurrected Jesus in any manner He saw fit. As my pastor friend, Rev. John Thornton, Ph.D., put it: "God did not remove the stone to let Jesus out; He removed the stone to let humanity in." Indeed, to let us in on the greatest gift we could receive - the forgiveness of sins, reconciliation with God, and the promise of eternal life.

Josh McDowell, in his book *A Ready Defense*, discusses the impressive impact of witnesses to the resurrected Christ.

> One of the earliest records of Christ's appearing after the resurrection is by Paul (1 Corinthians 15). The apostle appeals to his audience's knowledge of the fact that Christ has been seen by more than five

hundred people at one time. Paul reminds them that the majority of these people were still alive and could be questioned.

Dr. Ewin M. Yamauchi, associate professor of history at Miami University in Oxford, Ohio, emphasizes:

> What gives a special authority to the list [of witnesses] as historical evidence is the reference to most of the five hundred brethren being still alive. St. Paul says in effect, "If you do not believe me, you can ask them."

Let's take the more than five hundred witnesses who saw Jesus alive after His death and burial and place them in a courtroom. Do you realize that if each of these five hundred people were to testify only six minutes each, including cross-examination, you would have an amazing fifty hours of firsthand eyewitness testimony? Add to this the testimony of many other eyewitnesses and you could well have the largest and most lopsided trial in history.[73]

The Apostles

When Christ was arrested in the Garden of Gethsemane, his disciples fled in fear. During Christ's trial, Peter denied Him three times. After Christ was crucified, the disciples were crushed, fearing for their own lives. They locked themselves in an upper room, hiding themselves from the authorities. But something materialized in a few days to totally transform this group of cowardly disciples into a bold platoon of soldiers who faced hardship and death without trepidation.

Josh McDowell in *A Ready Defense* explains not only the apostles' transformation but many other early Christian believers as well.

> The changed lives of those early Christian believers is one of the most telling testimonies to the fact of the resurrection. We must ask ourselves: What motivated

> them to go everywhere proclaiming the message of the risen Christ?
>
> Had there been visible benefits accruing to them for their efforts - such as prestige, wealth or increased social status - we might logically account for their actions. As a reward, however, for their wholehearted and total allegiance to this "risen Christ," these early Christians were beaten, stoned to death, thrown to the lions, tortured, crucified and subjected to every conceivable method of stopping them from talking. Yet they were the most peaceful of men, who physically forced their beliefs on no one. Rather they laid down their very lives as the ultimate proof of their complete confidence in the truth of their message.[74]

In addition to the 11 apostles, James, the brother of Jesus, was also transformed in a miraculous way.

Indeed, Jesus' family had been skeptical of Jesus' claim to be the Messiah. They were embarrassed by His words and, like others in that era, probably thought he was mentally unbalanced. James and his brothers mocked Jesus. Following Christ's humiliating death on the cross, Jesus' family joined the apostles in the upper room. What happened to James to turn his attitude completely around? James, like the other people in that upper room, saw the risen Christ. James became an early leader in the church and eventually died by stoning for his allegiance to his brother.

The clergy meditation on "Who is Jesus Christ?" in the Kairos manual discusses with the prisoners the resurrection and the price paid by the apostles and James, the brother of Jesus, for their devotion to the Person of Jesus Christ.

> He was crucified, died, and came back to life. He was resurrected. Some people think that His resurrection was a fake, that someone took His body out of the tomb.
>
> But the Romans would not have done that. They were the people who killed Him and they were guarding

> the tomb. [the death penalty was imposed by the Roman military authorities for guards leaving their night watch].
>
> The Jews would not have done it because those in power wanted Him dead and they didn't want any mystery about it like the disappearance of the body, so they asked for the guard.
>
> That leaves the apostles who remained in hiding in terror and fright when Jesus died. They were too afraid to do anything. When they saw Jesus among them again they rejoiced and started spreading the good news. Jesus gave them new strength.[75]

According to tradition, eleven of the original apostles and the later apostle, Paul, were tortured and killed for their work. I am indebted to Kenneth Wyatt's book *The Apostles*[76] for the following descriptions of the martyred deaths of the apostles.

Peter

Twice imprisoned in Rome, most historians agree, Peter was also martyred there. He met his death by being crucified with arms extended but head downward. Tradition tells us that Peter and Paul were put to death on the same day in Rome, though in different parts of the city. Peter's death, however, came only after an imprisonment of nine months in the horrible and dreaded jails of the Mamertine. He existed there in absolute darkness, forced to stand at all times because he was chained to an upright post in the center of a cell which was never cleaned. He endured vicious torture by experts at their craft. It seems impossible that he could have survived those terrible months to face his death on that inverted cross. Peter not only lived through those long days - he, with an undaunted evangelistic fervor, converted to Christ his two jailers and forty-seven others in the prison.

Andrew

The hands of Andrew were the hands of a fisherman and accustomed to handling rope; but this rope would symbolize his death as a martyr, for it is accepted that Andrew died in Achaia tied with rope to a cross shaped like an X.

James (son of Zebedee)

Also known as James the Great, he was one of the three men who comprised the inner ring of the Apostles: Peter, James, and John. James was the first apostle to be killed. He died by the sword.

John

John was also a son of Zebedee and the only apostle to die a natural death. He was the last to die. However, he endured torture. Tertullian places John with Peter in Rome, where, tradition tells us, John was boiled in oil and later poisoned. He survived each attempt on his life by a miraculous deliverance. While in Ephesus, John was banished to the island of Patmos, which was a penal colony just off the coast of Turkey. It was here in prison that the text of Revelation was given to the Apostle and was written down by him while in that dark cave which served as his cell.

Philip

Philip was tied to a cross and stoned to death.

Bartholomew

Bartholomew was flayed (meaning, skinned alive), and then, to complete his martyrdom, beheaded.

Matthew

Matthew was reported to have met martyrdom by crucifixion on a Tau cross. It was also reported that while Matthew was hanging on that cross, he was beheaded with a battle-ax.

Thomas

Tradition states that Thomas' martyrdom occurred when a king's lance or spear was thrust through the Apostle because Queen Tertia had been converted.

James (son of Alphaeus)

Also known as James the Less (or younger), this Apostle, tradition holds, was initially tossed by the Pharisees from the pinnacle of the temple; yet he was unhurt. Observing this, they pelted him with stones, but he was still able to get to his knees and pray for his oppressors. It was at this point that a fuller (a fuller was the laundryman of the times) rushed out and killed James with a crushing blow to his head with a laundry-stick, or fuller's bat. His body was then sawn in half.

Simon the Zealot

Tradition holds that he was martyred in Persia by being sawn in half.

Jude

Also known as Thaddaeus, this Apostle, according to legend, met death by being shot full of arrows.

Paul

Paul's many hardships have been previously discussed. He was finally beheaded in Rome.

If Jesus' resurrection was just a fraudulent conspiracy by the apostles, surely some of them would have confessed to avoid death. Nobody deliberately and freely dies for a lie. There's no rational reason why Paul and James, two skeptics, would have been converted and willingly die for their faith. Can you imagine twelve people accepting whippings, beatings, torture, imprisonment, and wrongful death from crucifixions, arrows, spear and sword thrusts, stonings, beheadings, and being sawn in half when they could have gone free by acknowledging the scam if there was one?

The Logicality of being a Liar, Lunatic or Lord

Jesus claimed He was God. Muhammad never claimed to be God. No Hindu ever claimed to be God. Buddha never claimed to be God. Indeed, Buddhism, strictly speaking, is more of a philosophy than a religion. William James in *The Varieties of Religious Experience* describes Buddhism as follows:

> There are systems of thought which the world usually calls religious, and yet which do not positively assume a God. Buddhism is in this case. Popularly, of course, the Buddha himself stands in place of a God; but in strictness the Buddhistic system is atheistic.[77]

Jesus' claim to be God is either true or false. If it is false and Jesus knew it was false, He is a liar and a deceiver. If He knew it was true, the claim is so preposterous that many would construe Him as a lunatic, especially in first-century Palestine. So the question is: Is Jesus a liar and/or a lunatic?

There is no evidence in the New Testament that Jesus ever lied. However, did He lie about His very identity? Was He an imposter? Josh McDowell addresses this dilemma in *A Ready Defense*:

> But if He was a liar, then He was also a hypocrite because He told others to be honest, whatever the cost, while He himself taught and lived a colossal lie. More than that, He was a demon, because He told others to trust Him for their eternal life. If He couldn't back up His claims and knew it, then He was unspeakably evil. Last, He would also be a fool because it was His claims to being God that led to His crucifixion.[78]

Many people, including Jews and Muslims today, claim Jesus was a good moral teacher but discount His claim to be God. Philip Yancey, in his book *The Jesus I Never Knew*, states: "Modern Israeli schoolchildren learn that Jesus was a great teacher, perhaps the greatest Jewish teacher, who was subsequently 'co-opted' by the Gentiles."[79] But how could a liar be a good moral teacher? His example of lying about His identity would be incongruent with being a good moral teacher. C. S. Lewis, former professor at Cambridge University and once an atheist, addressed this issue in his book *Mere Christianity.*

> I am trying here to prevent anyone saying the really foolish thing that people often say about Him: "I'm ready to accept Jesus as a great moral teacher, but I don't accept His claim to be God." That is the one thing we must not say. A man who was merely a man and said the sort of things Jesus said would not be a good moral teacher. He would either be a lunatic - on a level with the man who says he is a poached egg - or else he would be the Devil of Hell. You

> must make your choice. Either this man was, and is, the Son of God: or else a madman or something worse. You can shut Him up for a fool, you can spit at Him and kill Him as a demon; or you can fall at His feet and call Him Lord and God. But let us not come with any patronizing nonsense about His being a great human teacher. He has not left that open to us. He did not intend to. We are faced, then, with a frightening alternative. This man we are talking about either was (and is) just what He said or else a lunatic, or something else.[80]

If Jesus was a liar, it sure doesn't mesh with what we know of His teachings, His life, and the results of His life. When Christ is promulgated to the prisoners during a Kairos weekend, lives have been transformed for the better, alcoholics and drug addicts have been cured of their desire, racists have been healed of their bigotry, atheists have come to accept Christ, Muslims have been converted to Christ, gang members spewing venomous hate have become conduits of God's love and grace, immoral persons have become moral, a mechanic for the Mafia has become an ardent disciple of Jesus. An unnamed man who described himself as a "Warrior in Christ" from the Michael Unit, states:

> We have all been touched by the Lord during the four days and I would like to point out some of the things I personally witnessed when we got back to the wings Sunday evening. I saw posters torn off cell walls, porno magazines torn up and thrown in the trash, cigarettes and matches, and tobacco destroyed or thrown away. I saw new brothers and older brothers hugging and crying; I saw prayer groups form everywhere while other brothers were scrambling around trying to come up with enough Bibles to cover the new brothers' needs. The power of the Holy Spirit was absolutely palpable!
>
> Anyone not believing in miracles, should have been present here at the Michael Unit this past weekend.

> I saw convicted murderers, robbers, thieves, etc. crying like babies while reading letters from little children asking them to "be nice to God because we love God." We each now have a personal relationship with Jesus Christ and a new sense of worth. If God loves us, and you all love us, then we must be worthy of being loved.

Historian Philip Schaff remarks:

> How, in the name of logic, common sense, and experience, could an imposter - that is a deceitful, selfish, depraved man - have invented, and consistently maintained from the beginning to the end, the purest and noblest character known in history with the most perfect air of truth and reality? How could He have conceived and successfully carried out a plan of unparalleled beneficence, moral magnitude, and sublimity, and sacrificed His own life for it, in the face of the strongest prejudices of His people and age?[81]

Someone who lived as Jesus did, taught has He taught, and sacrificed His life for what He advocated could not have been a liar. This leaves the options of lunacy or lordship. Jesus' own family thought he was out of his mind and some accused him of being demon-possessed. Josh McDowell addressed the lunacy option in *A Ready Defense*:

> If it is inconceivable for Jesus to be a liar, then couldn't He actually have thought Himself to be God, but been mistaken? After all, it's possible to be both sincere and wrong. But we must remember that for someone to think himself God, especially in a fiercely monotheistic culture, and then to tell others that their eternal destiny depended on believing in him, is no light flight of fantasy but the thoughts of a lunatic in the fullest sense. Was Jesus Christ such a person?

> Someone who believes he is God sounds like someone today believing himself Napoleon. He would be deluded and self-deceived, and probably he would be locked up so he wouldn't hurt himself or anyone else. Yet in Jesus we don't observe the abnormalities and imbalance that usually go along with being deranged. His poise and composure would certainly be amazing if He were insane. . . .
>
> In light of the other things we know about Jesus, it's hard to imagine that He was mentally disturbed. Here is a man who spoke some of the most profound sayings ever recorded. His instructions have liberated many individuals from mental bondage.[82]

The profundities of Christ's teachings are second to none.

Lee Strobel, in *The Case for Christ*, interviewed Gary R. Collins, Ph.D. on the psychological aspects of Christ. Collins holds a doctorate in clinical psychology from Purdue University, has published approximately 150 articles and 45 books, and has been studying, teaching, and writing about human behavior for 35 years. Collins states:

> Well, it's true that people with psychological difficulties will often claim to be somebody they're not. . . .However, psychologists don't just look at what a person says. They'll go much deeper than that. They'll look at a person's emotions, because disturbed individuals frequently show inappropriate depression, or they might be vehemently angry, or perhaps they're plagued with anxiety. But look at Jesus: he never demonstrated inappropriate emotions. For instance, he cried at the death of his friend Lazarus - that's natural for an emotionally healthy individual.[83]

Strobel asserted that perhaps Jesus' angry exhibition in grabbing a whip, overturning the tables in the temple, and forcing shameless moneymakers from the Jewish temple was a form of inappropriate behavior. Collins replies:

Yes, he did, but it was a healthy kind of anger at people taking advantage of the downtrodden by lining their pockets at the temple. He wasn't just irrationally ticked off because someone was annoying him; this was a righteous reaction against injustice and the blatant mistreatment of people.

Other deluded people will have misperceptions. They think people are watching them or are trying to get them when they're not. They're out of contact with reality. They misperceive the actions of other people and accuse them of doing things they have no intention of ever doing. Again, we don't see this in Jesus. He was obviously in contact with reality. He wasn't paranoid, although he rightfully understood there were some very real dangers around him.

Or people with psychological difficulties may have thinking disorders - they don't carry on a logical conversation, they'll jump to faulty conclusions, they're irrational. We don't see this in Jesus. He spoke clearly, powerfully, and eloquently. He was brilliant and had absolutely amazing insights into human nature.

Another sign of mental disturbances is unsuitable behavior, such as dressing oddly or being unable to relate socially to others. Jesus' behavior was quite in line with what would be expected, and he had deep and abiding relationships with a wide variety of people from different walks of life.

He was loving but didn't let his compassion immobilize him; he didn't have a bloated ego, even though he was often surrounded by adoring crowds; he maintained balance despite an often demanding lifestyle; he always knew what he was doing and where he was going; he cared deeply about people, including women and children, who weren't seen

> as being important back then; he was able to accept people while not merely winking at their sin; he responded to individuals based on where they were at and what they uniquely needed.
>
> All in all, I just don't see signs that Jesus was suffering from any known mental illness. He was much healthier than anyone else I know - including me![84]

At the end of his teaching one day, many of the Jews were divided.

> Many of them said, "He is demon-possessed and raving mad. Why listen to him?" But others said, "These are not the sayings of a man possessed by a demon. Can a demon open the eyes of the blind?"

John 10:20-21

And therein lies one of the great buttresses of Christ being Lord. He backed up His sayings with miracles. Muhammad never performed any miracles nor did Buddha or any Hindu. Moses performed miracles but he never claimed to be God. Moses knew it was God who performed the miracles. Jesus' statements weren't boastful or hollow rhetoric. The miracles were His way of helping people believe in Him. Jesus also used miracles to back up His claim of having authority from God. He asked observers one time whether it was easier to simply say "your sins are forgiven" or command a lame person who had been afflicted for decades to "get up and walk." Clearly a simple statement would be far easier to make but Christ immediately backed up His authority by healing the lame man.

> Thomas said to him, "Lord, we don't know where you are going, so how can we know the way?"
>
> Jesus answered, "I am the way and the truth and the life. No one comes to the Father except through me. If you really knew me, you would know my Father as well. From now on, you do know him and have seen him."

> Philip said, "Lord, show us the Father and that will be enough for us."
>
> Jesus answered: "Don't you know me, Philip, even after I have been among you such a long time? Anyone who has seen me has seen the Father. How can you say, 'Show us the Father'? Don't you believe that I am in the Father, and that the Father is in me? The words I say to you are not just my own. Rather, it is the Father, living in me, who is doing his work. Believe me when I say that I am in the Father and the Father is in me; or at least believe on the evidence of the miracles themselves.

John 14:5-11

> The miracles I do in my Father's name speak for me... Do not believe me unless I do what my Father does. But if I do it, even though you do not believe me, believe the miracles, that you may know and understand that the Father is in me, and I in the Father.

John 10:25, 37-38

Nobody else in history has even remotely pulled off the breadth and depth, the quantity (34) and quality of miracles that Jesus Christ pulled off and also claimed to be God. Nobody, zip, zero, null set. Not Muhammad, not Buddha, not any Hindu. Collins states:

> Jesus wasn't just making outrageous claims about himself. He was backing them up with miraculous acts of compassion, like healing the blind. . . .Jesus didn't just claim to be God - he backed it up with amazing feats of healing, with astounding demonstrations of power over nature, with transcendent and unprecedented teaching, with divine insights into people, and ultimately with his own resurrection from the dead, which absolutely nobody else has been able to duplicate. So when Jesus claimed to be God, it wasn't crazy. It was the truth.[85]

And what is especially amazing is that Christ predicted his death and resurrection. Think about the audacity of Jesus to predict his own death and being raised on the third day.

> Then the Jews demanded of him, "What miraculous sign can you show us to prove your authority to do all this?"
>
> Jesus answered them, "Destroy this temple, and I will raise it again in three days."
>
> The Jews replied, "It has taken forty-six years to build this temple, and you are going to raise it in three days?" But the temple he had spoken of was his body. After he was raised from the dead, his disciples recalled what he had said. Then they believed the Scripture and the words that Jesus had spoken.

John 2:18-22

So we can see clearly that Jesus was not a liar or lunatic. In other words, how could a good moral teacher and prophet be a liar or a lunatic? Therefore, by logical deduction, He must be who He claims to be: God. As C. S. Lewis states:

> The historical difficulty of giving for the life, sayings and influence of Jesus any explanation that is not harder than the Christian explanation, is very great. The discrepancy between the depth and sanity and (let me add) *shrewdness* of His moral teaching and the rampant megalomania which must lie behind His theological teaching unless He is indeed God, has never been satisfactorily got over. Hence the non-Christian hypotheses succeed one another with the restless fertility of bewilderment.[86]

In conclusion, Christ was not a liar or lunatic. He claimed to be God which must be the truth if He was not a liar or lunatic. Jesus made a bold statement in John 14:6: "I am the way and the *truth* and the life. No one comes to the Father except through me." Anyone on a quest for the Truth has to acknowledge the power of this unambiguous statement. Notice that Jesus did not say that you can go to the Father through Muhammad, Buddha, or a Hindu. He said that nobody can go to the Father except through Him.

Paradoxes and Truth

When I first began reading the New Testament I was puzzled by many of Jesus' paradoxical statements. How could the last be first? How could you lose your life and save it? I kept rereading the New Testament, taking Bible study courses, and reading other books to gain insight. Over time I began to understand Jesus' paradoxical statements.

The noted psychiatrist and author M. Scott Peck states:

> If you want to think with integrity, and are willing to bear the pain involved, you will inevitably encounter paradox. . . .If a concept is paradoxical, that in itself should suggest that it smacks of integrity and has the ring of truth. Conversely, if a concept is not in the least paradoxical, you may suspect that it has failed to integrate some aspect of the whole. . . .
>
> If no pieces of reality are missing from the picture, if all the dimensions are integrated, you will probably be confronted by a paradox. When you get to the root of things, virtually all truth is paradoxical. The truth is, for example, that I am and I am not an individual. Thus, to seek the truth involves an integration of things that seem to be separate and look like opposites when, in reality, they are intertwined and related in some ways. Reality itself is paradoxical, in that while many things in and about life seem simple on the surface, they are often complex - although not always complicated. There is a difference, just as clear as the difference between simplism and simplicity. There is, in fact, a great simplicity to wholeness.[87]

The New Testament is replete with Christ's paradoxes which is another reason that I believe Christ is the Truth.

- "But many who are first will be last, and the last first." Mark 10:31

- "If anyone wants to be first, he must be the very last, and the servant of all." Mark 9:35
- "For whoever wants to save his life will lose it, but whoever loses his life for me and for the gospel will save it." Mark 8:35
- "Instead, whoever wants to become great among you must be your servant, and whoever wants to be first must be slave of all." Mark 10:43-44
- "Whoever finds his life will lose it, and whoever loses his life for my sake will find it." Matthew 10:39
- "For whoever wants to save his life will lose it, but whoever loses his life for me will find it." Matthew 16:25
- "But many who are first will be last, and many who are last will be first." Matthew 19:30
- "So the last will be first, and the first will be last." Matthew 20:16
- "Instead, whoever wants to become great among you must be your servant, and whoever wants to be first must be your slave." Matthew 20:26-27
- "For whoever exalts himself will be humbled, and whoever humbles himself will be exalted." Matthew 23:12
- "For whoever wants to save his life will lose it, but whoever loses his life for me will save it." Luke 9:24
- "For he who is least among you all - he is the greatest." Luke 9:48
- "Indeed there are those who are last who will be first, and first who will be last." Luke 13:30
- "For everyone who exalts himself will be humbled, and he who humbles himself will be exalted." Luke 14:11 and Luke 18:14
- "Whoever tries to keep his life will lose it, and whoever loses his life will preserve it." Luke 17:33
- "For judgment I have come into this world, so that the blind will see and those who see will become blind." John 9:39
- "I am the resurrection and the life. He who believes in me will live, even though he dies; and whoever lives and believes in me will never die. Do you believe this?" John 11:25-26

- "I tell you the truth, unless a kernel of wheat falls to the ground and dies, it remains only a single seed. But if it dies, it produces many seeds. The man who loves his life will lose it, while the man who hates his life in this world will keep it for eternal life." John 12:24-25
- "It is more blessed to give than to receive." [or as St. Francis puts it in his famous prayer, "For it is in giving that we receive."] Acts 20:35
- "My grace is sufficient for you, for my power is made perfect in weakness." 2 Corinthians 12:9

The last paradox was in response to the apostle Paul's pleading three times for the Lord to heal him of a serious affliction. Paul understood Christ's denial of healing because people would be more amazed at what Paul could overcome and achieve with Christ's love if he was weak by world standards. Paul states:

> Therefore I will boast all the more gladly about my weaknesses, so that Christ's power may rest on me. That is why, for Christ's sake, I delight in weaknesses, in insults, in hardships, in persecutions, in difficulties. For when I am weak, then I am strong.
>
> 2 Corinthians 12:9-10

In regard to the last paradox, Christ shows himself most vividly in those who are weak - children, the infirm, the imprisoned, the downtrodden, the disenfranchised, the destitute. Some of the most inspirational people I have met are new creations in Christ in prison and those who are disabled. I have run a number of marathons (26.2 miles or about 42 kilometers) and century bike rides (100 miles or about 161 kilometers) in honor of people who have serious diseases, from children with leukemia and muscular dystrophy to adults with breast cancer and multiple sclerosis. One of these people was my brother Paul, who suffered from the debilitating effects of multiple sclerosis for 25 years. He lost the use of his legs, bowel, and urinary functions. He had great difficulty communicating and ate via a stomach tube. He was hospitalized frequently. He suffered a major heart attack in his mid-40s and had congestive heart failure. He was a prisoner in his body, completely dependent on others. Yet, he persevered with a positive attitude. His motive for living, in spite of the hardships and indignity of such an insidious disease, was to be a shining light of Christ to others. He inspired prisoners to pray for him and to keep up the good fight in a harsh environment. Jim Huddleston, a prisoner, wrote the following letter, describing the impact of Paul's life on him.

> Dear Paul,
>
> Hi, it's me Jim. I hope this letter finds you in the best of your health and in high spirits. I'm doing fine myself! I hope you had a very nice merry Christmas and a happy new year!
>
> Paul, you are a real blessing to us here at the Michael Unit because you have so much spirit and love for God that you show us down here. Even when we think our life is so bad and it could not possibly get worse, someone like you, who goes through more trials and tribulations and pain in one day than we go through in a month, shows us how to accept the things we can not change by faith in our Lord Jesus Christ.
>
> Paul, you have given all of us here at the Michael Unit, that know you through your brother Steve, the will to continue our spiritual journey even when we think it is not worth it anymore. Steve has given us at the Kairos meetings some very emotional accounts of your courageous testimony.
>
> Paul, all of our hearts go out to you and you are in many of our prayers! Paul, thank you for showing someone like me, in prison, that even here we can learn in our imperfect hearts what love is because of someone like you who comes closer to showing love as Jesus Christ does.

Paul, thank you for being you and try not to lose faith in us that are weaker than you, OK! May God bless you and yours now and always.

Your brother in Christ, with love always
Jim
January 3, 2001

There is a pattern in the Old Testament of God deliberately choosing the underdog or the second- or last-born son or even daughter as the case may be. Abraham and Sarah's first child, via Hagar, was Ishmael. Normally the blessing would flow to the first-born male in Jewish families but God chose the second-born son, Isaac, to make a covenant with. Isaac's first-born son was Esau but his second-born son, Jacob, through a crafty scheme devised by Rebekah, deceived Isaac and received his blessing. Then, in a classic example of what goes around comes around, Jacob was deceived by Laban as documented in Genesis 29:16-30. Jacob wanted to marry the youngest daughter, Rachel. Jacob offered to work for Laban for seven years so he could marry Rachel. After his seven years was completed, Laban tricked Jacob into sleeping with Leah, the oldest daughter. Jacob was angry but Laban noted that it was not their custom to allow the younger daughter to be married first. So Jacob agreed to work another seven years before being allowed to marry Rachel. Thus, Rachel, the younger sister, was the one who received the blessing of Jacob's lineage. Of Jacob's 12 sons, Joseph was born 11th, yet he was the one that rose to power in Egypt. David, the greatest king in Israel's history, was just a young boy when he went up against Goliath. Samuel was told by God to anoint a new king in place of Saul and seven of Jesse's sons paraded before Samuel. None of them were selected. Samuel asked Jesse if there were any more sons and he responded that the youngest one was out tending sheep. Once again God chose the last to be first. So it is not surprising that when God chose to go from heaven to human he selected the weakest option for entry into the world, a helpless infant. Once again, God's power was made perfect in weakness.

One of the most powerful paradoxes in the Gospels is Jesus' startling statement: "For whoever wants to save his life will lose it, but whoever loses his life for me will save it." Dr. Lloyd John

Ogilvie, Chaplain of the United States Senate, author of more than 40 books including the popular devotional *God's Best for My Life*, and former senior pastor of Hollywood Presbyterian Church, discusses this paradox in his book *Longing to be Free*:

> Now we come to the essence of the essence of freedom in the Spirit. The center of the center of the truth about what it means to be a liberated person. And at that center is a powerful paradox. . . .
>
> A strange mystery of life is that the more we concentrate on realizing ourselves, the less we are the unique persons God destined us to be. . . .And so we stand at the crossroads. It is crucial to see the very different destinations of both roads: self-assertion and self-surrender. The destination of self-assertion is achievement of our purposes, plans, professional goals, and personality structure. The other road is the way of self-surrender to the Lord's purposes and plans for use and its destination is the transformation of our personality into His image. The first road ends in self-centeredness, the second in true self-realization.
>
> The reason so many Christians are not free is that they are trying to travel both roads at the same time. Or what's worse, they are determined to get the Lord to help them become what they want to be. . . .They will not be free and they will rob the people around them of their freedom until they discover and live the powerful paradox of being Christ's free person. Here it is in two challenging dimensions: Either deny yourself or be denied your unique self; either lose your life or you will lose the possibility of all your life was meant to be. Jesus stated the paradox pointedly: "If anyone desires to come after Me, let him deny himself, and take up his cross daily, and follow Me. For whoever desires to save his life will lose it, but whoever loses his life for My sake will

> save it. For what advantage is it to a man if he gains the whole world, and is himself destroyed or lost?" [Luke 9:23-25].
>
> Familiarity with these words from the New Testament can blunt their liberating power. At first Jesus' challenge sounds negative. But on further reflection, we discover that He has given us the profound secret of lasting freedom. . . .But how can the denial of self lead to understanding of the self? At the core of the seemingly negative idea is a very positive possibility. Jesus is calling for the denial of a lesser self for the freeing of greater self. We give up self-interest, self-determination, self-aggrandizement, and self-defensiveness. The goal is not the protection of ourselves but the achievement of a much more creative picture of ourselves. . . .
>
> Jim Elliot, the martyred missionary, once said, "He is no fool who gives what he cannot keep to gain what he cannot lose." That's our confidence. A life surrendered to Christ becomes His post-resurrection home. Our security is not in our adequacy, but in His unlimited power surging through us, changing our personalities, and guiding us in daring expression of the loved, forgiven, transformed person He is enabling us to be. John Henry Newman said, "Fear not that your life will come to an end, but rather that it shall never have a beginning."[88]

A classic example of a man denying himself was Eric Liddell in the movie *Chariots of Fire*, a favorite movie of runners. Ogilvie describes this man's stirring example in *Longing to Be Free*:

> Often obedience today makes it possible for Him to bless us with what He has prepared for a future day. That was illustrated vividly in the life of Eric Liddell in the movie *Chariots of Fire*.

> At the Paris Olympics in 1924, the Christian athlete denied himself the right to participate in running on Sunday. He held firm beliefs about observing the Sabbath. He would not contradict his convictions and refused to run the race for which he had spent years of arduous preparation. Later in the week, because of the magnanimity of a friend and the intervention of the Lord in arranging the circumstances, Liddell was given the opportunity to enter another race. In that event he won the gold medal, placing first in the race. What he denied himself one day because of obedience to the Lord was given him on another day. And Liddell gave the Lord the glory for his victory. The same denial of self marked the athlete's life in his subsequent witness to Christ in a Japanese concentration camp during World War II.[89]

I have experienced the abundant life Christ talked about in Kairos Prison Ministry. You can't put a price tag on the joy and peace I have experienced in serving Christ in this ministry. I have lost my life in service to Christ, yet I have found a more profound life of joy and peace. My love of Kairos is best described by a scene from the movie *Patton*, for which George C. Scott as Patton won the Oscar for best actor. Patton arrives to inspect a battlefield following a particularly fierce fight with the Nazis. He stares across a devastated landscape with charred tanks, overturned vehicles, twisted equipment, mangled bodies strewn across the fields dotted by fires spewing acrid, billowing black smoke. Patton straightens up, swells his chest and with a firm voice states: "God help me, I do love it so." That's how I feel about Kairos. There are times during a Kairos weekend when I'll find myself over in a corner of the gym, gazing across the battlefield between Jesus and Satan, watching the work of my free-world team members and prisoner stewards in winning souls to Christ, and I'll say to myself: "God help me, I do love it so."

It is interesting that the freest people are those who have given up having to have things or having to have their own way (foregoing the right to be right).

> In short, lives based on having are less free than lives based either on doing or on being, and in the interest of action people subject to spiritual excitement throw away possessions as so many clogs.[90]

The Beatitudes in chapter 5 of Matthew's gospel and chapter 6 of Luke's gospel are a litany of paradoxical statements regarding people, people who Philip Yancey describes as "lucky are the unlucky." Here Christ says that those who are the underdogs are the most blessed. Certainly Christ's life and ministry were especially attuned to the underdogs of society. His own birth in humble circumstances epitomizes an underdog beginning. Although the world idolizes the wealthy and powerful, the strong and the beautiful, the athletic and successful, God exalts the humble. Blessed are the poor in spirit, the hungry, the mournful, the insulted, the powerless, the oppressed, the persecuted, the hated. Unlucky are the rich, the well fed, the esteemed, the powerful, the exalted. Those who are desperate may turn to God for help and, if so, they are truly blessed. The poor in spirit don't have all the trappings of this world to obscure their vision of God. C. S. Lewis describes this concept in *The Problem of Pain*:

> The dangers of apparent self-sufficiency explain why Our Lord regards the vices of the feckless and dissipated so much more leniently than the vices that lead to worldly success. Prostitutes are in no danger of finding their present life so satisfactory that they cannot turn to God: the proud, the avaricious, the self-righteous, are in that danger.[91]

During a Kairos weekend, we invite to the banquet prisoners who have done terrible deeds, who are reviled by society, the least of the least. They can't repay us and we tell them not to thank us. The joy we receive from watching Christ at work is our reward. Our example is based on Christ's exhortation:

> When you give a luncheon or dinner, do not invite your friends, your brothers or relatives, or your rich neighbors; if you do, they may invite you back and so you will be repaid. But when you give a banquet,

> invite the poor, the crippled, the lame, the blind, and you will be blessed. Although they cannot repay you, you will be repaid at the resurrection of the righteous.
>
> Luke 14:12-14

The joy one experiences during a Kairos weekend is of the kingdom of heaven. It can't be bought with monetary means. It can only be obtained by giving oneself in service to others. Philip Yancey describes the joy of the kingdom of heaven embodied in the Beatitudes in his book *The Jesus I Never Knew:*

> In the Beatitudes, strange sayings that at first glance seem absurd, Jesus offers a paradoxical key to abundant life. The kingdom of heaven, he said elsewhere, is like a treasure of such value that any shrewd investor would "in his joy" sell all he has in order to buy it. It represents value far more real and permanent than anything the world has to offer, for this treasure will pay dividends both here on earth and also in the life to come. Jesus places the emphasis not on what we give up but on what we receive. Is it not in our own self-interest to pursue such a treasure?[92]

Then there is the paradox that Jesus had to die in order to defeat death or as Philip Yancey put it: "For Jesus to save others, quite simply, he could not save himself." It is highly unusual to celebrate the life of a great man by focusing on his mode of execution or murder. The Christian symbol is the ubiquitous cross, the execution device; no other religious figure or any other great person of history is memorialized or celebrated by their execution device. J. P. Moreland discusses this central facet of Christianity in Lee Strobel's book *The Case for Christ*:

> Think about this in modern terms. If a group of people loved John F. Kennedy, they might meet regularly to remember his confrontation with Russia, his promotion of civil rights, and his charismatic

> personality. But they're not going to celebrate the fact that Lee Harvey Oswald murdered him!
>
> However, that's analogous to what these early Christians did. How do you explain that? I explain it this way: they realized that Jesus' slaying was a necessary step to a much greater victory. His murder wasn't the last word - the last word was that he had conquered death for all of us by rising from the dead. They celebrated his execution because they were convinced that they had seen him alive from the tomb.[93]

Finally the entire Bible contains the grand paradox of sin and grace. The history of humanity is sin, consequences, and ultimately God's mercy and compassion. As the apostle Paul puts it: where sin increases, grace increases all the more. The supreme manifestation of God's grace, forgiveness, compassion, and mercy is found in Christ Jesus, who reconciles us to the Father and gives us a chance for a new life. What Christ accomplished on the cross is greater than any sin. This is what is called amazing grace, something that prisoners are more keenly aware of than most other groups of people. The more sinful a person (and what group is more sinful than the men who reside in a maximum-security prison), the greater the potential for spiritual power because grace means more to them because of how far they have fallen. Prisoners are amazed by God's grace, that God loves them and forgives them in spite of what they have done.

It has been my experience that the very roughest convicts who have the most horrible records have become the most ardent exponents of the Christian faith if they accept Christ's love and forgiveness. If these tough prisoners who have committed atrocities crack, watch out. These men, when they are baptized by the Holy Spirit, become firebrands for Christ, denying themselves to champion Christ. The same characteristic that makes prisoners gang leaders, if channeled and harvested for Christ, make them effective leaders in Christianity. The same was true for the apostle Paul who described himself as the worst of sinners. Jesus saw Paul's leadership ability, sense of commitment, loyalty, discipline, integrity, and toughness and tapped him to be an apostle.

Changes in Social and Spiritual Traditions

Another compelling piece of evidence for me in my quest for the truth was the abrupt change in several key social structures 2,000 years ago. A cataclysmic event happened to split history into two segments. The demarcation of time in western civilization falls into a classification of before Christ or after Christ.

At the time of Christ, the Jews had been persecuted or conquered during a 700-year span by the Babylonians, Assyrians, Persians, Greeks, and Romans. Many Jews had been dispersed and held as captives in these other countries. However, Jews have survived despite many oppressions and horrors; they remain a vibrant ethnicity and faith. J. P. Moreland in *The Case for Christ* elaborates on this fascinating change in social structures:

> . . . .the things that made the Jews, Jews - the social structures that gave them their national identity - were unbelievably important to them. The Jews would pass these structures down to their children, celebrate them in synagogue meetings every Sabbath, and reinforce them with their rituals, because they knew if they didn't, there soon would be no Jews left. They would be assimilated into the cultures that captured them.
>
> And there's another reason why these social institutions were so important: they believed these institutions were entrusted to them by God. They believed that to abandon these institutions would be to risk their souls being damned to hell after death.
>
> Now a rabbi named Jesus appears from a lower-class region. He teaches for three years, gathers a following of lower- and middle-class people, gets in trouble with the authorities, and gets crucified along with thirty thousand other Jewish men who are executed during this time period.

But five weeks after he's crucified, over ten thousand Jews are following him and claiming that he is the initiator of a new religion. And get this: they're willing to give up or alter all five of the social institutions that they have been taught since childhood have such importance both sociologically and theologically. . . .

First, they had been taught ever since the time of Abraham and Moses that they needed to offer an animal sacrifice on a yearly basis to atone for their sins. God would transfer their sins to that animal, and their sins would be forgiven so they could be in right standing with him. But all of a sudden, after the death of this Nazarene carpenter, these Jewish people no longer offer sacrifices.

Second, Jews emphasized obeying the laws that God had entrusted to them through Moses. In their view, this is what separated them from pagan nations. Yet within a short time after Jesus' death, Jews were beginning to say that you don't become an upstanding member of their community merely by keeping Moses' laws.

Third, Jews scrupulously kept the Sabbath by not doing anything except religious devotion every Saturday. This is how they would earn right standing with God, guarantee the salvation of their family, and be in right standing with the nation. However, after the death of this Nazarene carpenter, this fifteen-hundred-year tradition is abruptly changed. These Christians worship on Sunday - why? Because that's when Jesus rose from the dead.

Fourth, they believed in monotheism - only one God [despite the reference in Genesis 1:26: Then God said, "Let *us* make man in *our* image, in *our* likeness."] While Christians teach a form of monotheism, they say that the Father, Son, and Holy Spirit are one

God. This is radically different from what the Jews believed. They would have considered it the height of heresy to say someone could be God and man at the same time. Yet Jews begin worshiping Jesus as God within the first decade of the Christian religion.

And fifth, these Christians pictured the Messiah as someone who suffered and died for the sins of the world, whereas Jews had been trained to believe that the Messiah was going to be a political leader who would destroy the Roman armies. . . .

How can you possibly explain why in a short period of time not just one Jew but an entire community of at least ten thousand Jews were willing to give up these five key practices that had served them sociologically and theologically for so many centuries? My explanation is simple: they had seen Jesus risen from the dead. . . .

Keep in mind that this is an entire community of people who are abandoning treasured beliefs that have been passed on for centuries and that they believed were from God himself. They were doing it even though they were jeopardizing their own well-being, and they also believed they were risking the damnation of their souls to hell if they were wrong.

What's more, they were not doing this because they had come upon better ideas. They were very content with the old traditions. They gave them up because they had seen miracles that they could not explain and that forced them to see the world another way. . . .

Believe me, these changes to the Jewish social structures were not just minor adjustments that were casually made - they were absolutely monumental.

> This was nothing short of a social earthquake! And earthquakes don't happen without a cause.[94]

The radical and abrupt change in five Jewish social and theological traditions that had been treasured for centuries is powerful evidence for the truth of the Resurrection.

The Emergence and Growth of the Church

It is interesting to compare God's designs at the time of the tower of Babel (Genesis 11) and Pentecost (Acts 2). The tower of Babel was built by the Hebrews as a monument to their pride. Their goal was to build this tower so that it could reach to the heavens. Their reason was to make a name for themselves (pride) and not be scattered over the earth. The whole world had one language and a common speech. But God saw their intentions and decided to thwart their plan. God confused their language so they could not understand each other. God scattered them from there over all the earth and they stopped building the city and tower.

Now contrast this action by God with what God did at Pentecost. The *Disciple Study Manual* makes some interesting observations regarding this contrast.

> Pentecost was a Jewish festival. Originally an agricultural festival, it later became a celebration of the giving of the Law on Mount Sinai. Obedient to Jesus, all the believers were waiting and praying.
>
> How do you describe a religious experience? What words can be used to explain a baptism of the Holy Spirit so strong, so vibrant, so complete that it changed the course of human history? Luke says it was *like* a violent wind and that tongues *as* of fire appeared among them (Acts 2:2). They were filled with the Holy Spirit.
>
> They began to speak in many different languages. Apparently they ran out into the streets, telling the story of faith. Jews from all over the world were gathered for the festival of Pentecost. They listened in amazement as these enthusiastic people spoke in

> the languages of the foreigners. Luke's message from Pentecost is that Christians, empowered by the Holy Spirit, will communicate the gospel in the languages of the people as Jesus had commanded, beginning "in Jerusalem, in all Judea and Samaria, and to the ends of the earth" (Acts 1:8). Pentecost launched the missionary movement of the church.
>
> Do you realize what God was doing? In the tower of Babel, people tried to do without God; they were scattered. They could not communicate. Now at Pentecost people tried to listen to God, to empty themselves in obedience. God's Spirit swept them up into a perfect unity and enabled them to speak in every language of the world. Now in Christ people understood one another. We who were scattered are brought together in him. Pentecost was God's answer to Babel.[95]

Therefore, the inescapable conclusion is that God's will for humanity is that the message of Jesus Christ is to be communicated to all people. This is evident through the Holy Spirit's conversion of languages at the time of Pentecost so that all people in attendance could hear the message of the Gospel in their native tongues. Compare the unity of Pentecost to the disunity of Babel. The unity of the Holy Spirit at Pentecost indicates that God wants Christianity to prevail for humanity.

At the time of the Roman empire, it was the most powerful in history. If you were living at that time, would you bet on the survival of the Roman empire or a handful of physically unarmed ragtag apostles from an obscure and ridiculed part of Israel whose leader was killed in his mid-30s? The result is well known. Christianity not only triumphed over a number of competing ideologies, it eventually outlasted and overhauled the Roman empire which embraced it under Constantine. As an aside, Christ accomplished victory over the Roman empire through his followers - the very thing most Jews had hoped their coming Messiah would achieve. Today, Christianity is the world's largest faith - all started with a group of a dozen apostles, largely from the lower echelon of society in terms of occupations and education, who spent a mere three to three and one-half years under the tutelage and leadership of a carpenter born in humble circumstances, raised in a remote village in a lower-class section of Israel, who never traveled more than 90 miles from his birthplace, who had no college education, no possessions, no publications, and who was executed as a criminal in his mid-30s.

Historian Philip Schaff discusses Jesus' reach and influence:

> This Jesus of Nazareth, without money and arms, conquered more millions than Alexander, Caesar, Mohammad, and Napoleon; without science and learning. He shed more light on things human and divine than all philosophers and scholars combined; without the eloquence of schools, He spoke such words of life as were never spoken before or since, and produced effects which lie beyond the reach of the orator or poet; without writing a single line, He set more pens in motion, and furnished themes for more sermons, orations, discussions, learned volumes, works of art, and songs of praise than the whole army of great men of ancient and modern times.[96]

Yale historian, Kenneth Latourette, remarks:

> It is evidence of His importance, of the effect that He has had upon history and presumably, of the baffling mystery of His being, that no other life ever lived on this planet has evoked so huge a volume of literature among so many peoples and languages, and that, far from ebbing, the flood continues to mount.[97]

Gamaliel, a Pharisee with the esteemed Sanhedrin at the time of Jesus, made a rather remarkable observation. First some background. The Sanhedrin consisted of a full assembly of the elders of Israel. They were collaborationists who tried to operate within the Roman system. One of the functions of this council, which had restricted authority, was to observe any signs of rebellion and notify the Roman authorities. It was in their best interests to prevent riots or upheavals and the harsh retribution that would be imposed.

The apostles had been arrested for preaching Christ and were released from jail by an angel who commanded them to continue preaching in the temple courts. The Jewish authorities were incensed that they had escaped and were continuing to boldly proclaim Christ. Indeed, they wanted to put the apostles to death.

> But a Pharisee named Gamaliel, a teacher of the law, who was honored by all the people, stood up in the Sanhedrin and ordered that the men be put outside for a little while. Then he addressed them: "Men of Israel, consider carefully what you intend to do to these men. Some time ago Theudas appeared, claiming to be somebody, and about four hundred men rallied to him. He was killed, all his followers were dispersed, and it all came to nothing. After him, Judas the Galilean appeared in the days of the census and led a band of people in revolt. He too was killed, and all his followers were scattered. Therefore, in the present case I advise you: Leave these men alone! Let them go! For if their purpose or activity is of human origin, it will fail. But if it is from God, you will not be able to stop these men; you will only find yourselves fighting against God."

Acts 5:34-39

Is it an accident that Christianity is the world's largest faith? Remember, there are no coincidences in life, only circumstances engineered by God. The intervals between the Old Testament prophets span only a few hundred years with several prophets' tenures overlapping with the last prophet living only a few hundred years before Christ. Yet there have been no Jewish prophets whose writings have been added to the Hebrew Bible since the last one before Christ. In other words, is it an accident that no writings of Jewish prophets have materialized in the past 2,000 years when they appeared in much shorter intervals prior to Christ? Gamaliel was a wise man. If this movement was of human origin it was destined for a quick demise into the human dustbin of history. However, if this movement was from God, it could not be stopped. Indeed, he counseled the Sanhedrin that if this movement was from God and they tried to stop it they would only find themselves fighting against God. And look at the price that has been paid in history for humanity's fight against God. Instead of unity, we have division. Instead of love, we have hate. We have endless enmity between Arabs and Jews. We have enmity between Muslims and Christians in many parts of the world. We have enmity between Muslims and Hindus in Pakistan and India. Historically, there has been considerable enmity between Christians and Jews. Clearly the quick emergence of the church and its rapid growth, in the midst of harsh adversity 2,000 years ago, into the largest faith in the world is evidence of God's handiwork. God is in the middle of Christianity, otherwise it would have died out long ago. God would not have allowed false teaching to propagate and flourish for the past 2,000 years if Christ was not the Truth. H. G. Wells states:

> More than 1,900 years later, a historian like myself, who doesn't even call himself a Christian, finds the picture centering irresistibly around the life and character of this most significant man. . . .The historian's test of an individual's greatness is "What did he leave to grow?" Did he start men to thinking along fresh lines with a vigor that persisted after him? By this test Jesus stands first."[98]

As Philip Yancey remarked in *The Jesus I Never Knew*: "You can gauge the size of a ship that has passed out of sight by the huge wake it leaves behind."[99] The enormity of Christ's impact on history, whose allegiance now holds one-third of the world's population, is unparalleled. A bomb's impact can be measured by the intensity and range of the shock waves generated by its detonation. Well, God dropped the biggest bomb on humanity 2,000 years ago with time being split into two segments. The reverberations of that cosmic bomb are still being felt today. One measure of Christ's remarkable influence 2,000 years after he lived on earth is the amazing finding of a University of Chicago scholar who estimates that more has been written about Jesus in the last twenty years than in the previous nineteen centuries.

But of all the many impressive facts that have led me to the conclusion that Christ is the Truth - the infinitesimal probability of one man fulfilling numerous prophecies, the unparalleled miracles including Christ's resurrecting people and his own resurrection, the profound paradoxes and teachings, the radical and abrupt change in Jewish social structures, the incredible change in the apostles from a band of cowering, disillusioned, depressed, discouraged, and distraught men into a courageous, bold, and tenacious platoon of miracle-producing protagonists for Christ, the radical 180-degree transformation of the apostle Paul, the rapid growth of the church into the largest faith in the world - the one fact that I can attest to that has convinced me beyond a shadow of a doubt that Christ is the Truth is witnessing first-hand the unmatched power of Jesus Christ in transforming some of the toughest, roughest, and meanest convicts, with horrible criminal backgrounds, into new creations in Christ in a 72-hour period deep inside a maximum-security prison. When you witness miracles first hand it does something to your faith. When you see Christ's handiwork, when you see His love overpowering Satan's hate, there is an incomparable joy. For me Kairos truly is God's Special Time. Kairos has been my lightning bolt on the road to Damascus, the epiphany of the two disciples on the road to Emmaus, and the apostle Thomas' hand thrust into Christ's nail prints all rolled into one. I know Christ lives because I have seen some of the least of the least transformed into new creatures; I have seen Jesus in the love in action of my Kairos brothers and sisters in the free world and in prison. J. P. Moreland echoes this theme of transformed lives in *The Case for Christ* as being the final evidence of Christ being the Truth:

> It's the ongoing encounter with the resurrected Christ that happens all over the world, in every culture, to people from all kinds of backgrounds and personalities - well educated and not, rich and poor, thinkers and feelers, men and women. They all will testify that more than any single thing in their lives, Jesus Christ has changed them. . . .To me, this provides the final evidence - not the only evidence but the final confirming proof - that the message of

> Jesus can open the door to a direct encounter with the risen Christ. . . .
>
> Use your mind calmly and weigh the evidence, and then let experience be a confirming piece of evidence. . . .if what this evidence points to is true - that is, if all these lines of evidence really do point to the resurrection of Jesus - the evidence itself begs for an experiential test. . . .
>
> The experiential test is, "He's still alive, and I can find out by relating to him." If you were on a jury and heard enough evidence to convince you of someone's guilt, it wouldn't make sense to stop short of the final step of convicting him. And for people to accept the evidence for the resurrection of Jesus and not take the final step of testing it experientially would be to miss where the evidence is ultimately pointing.[100]

Lee Strobel interjected, "So if the evidence points strongly in this direction, it's only rational and logical to follow it into the experiential realm." Moreland nodded in approval. "That's precisely right," he said. "It's the final confirmation of the evidence. In fact, I'll say this: the evidence screams out for the experiential test."[101]

Knowing the Truth is no idle or academic exercise. According to Jesus, my eternal destiny hinges on how I respond to him. Jesus said, "I am the way, the truth, and the life. No one comes to the Father except through me." [John 14:6]. Jesus also stated: "For my Father's will is that everyone who looks to the Son and believes in him shall have eternal life, and I will raise him up at the last day." [John 6:40]. These statements are indubitable and categorical; there is no ambiguity. Christ's statements demand a decision. And to make a rational decision, one must be able to think well.

11

> Going to prison was the best thing that ever happened to me. I am freer now than when I lived in the free world.
>
> Jim Huddleston
>
> If a concept is paradoxical, that in itself should suggest that it smacks of integrity and has the ring of truth.
>
> M. Scott Peck, M.D.

PARADOXES IN THE PENITENTIARY

Jim Huddleston's comment is a common one that I hear in prison. I've heard men testify that they feel free for the first time in their life deep inside a maximum-security prison. How can this be? I've heard men testify that they are blessed to be in prison. This is a profound paradox. The Greek word *para* means "by the side of, beside, alongside, past, beyond." *Doxa* means opinion. M. Scott Peck defines paradox as "a statement contrary to common belief, or one that seems contradictory, unbelievable, or absurd but may actually be true in fact."[102] The rationale for prisoners' feeling this way is the freedom that a personal relationship with Christ brings - freedom from slavery to sin, freedom from the pain of holding someone unforgiven (a big issue in prison), freedom from the guilt of past mistakes, freedom from trying to earn your way to heaven. Prisoners, with more baggage than a fully-loaded Boeing 747, testify that they unloaded more burdens during a Kairos weekend than they knew they had carried. Other men will admit that had they not been imprisoned they would most likely have been killed out on the streets and they would likely not have met Christ.

In prison, Darwin's theory prevails. It is the toughest, meanest, and strongest that yield the most power. The gang leaders reign supreme. Yet, here is another paradox. It is the "weak" and vulnerable saints in the form of mostly lay people from a Kairos team that help break down some of the roughest convicts in the prison in a 72-hour period. The environment of a prison is different from that of society: prison is hostile, volatile, dangerous. The risk of assault is ever present; freedom is constrained; food is poor; enmity prevails among gangs along racial lines and between prisoners and officers. William James contrasts the differences between the strong, aggressive elements of society and the saints of society.

> The most inimical critic of the saintly impulses whom I know is Nietzsche. He contrasts them with the worldly passions as we find these embodied in the predaceous military character, altogether to the advantage of the latter. Your born saint, it must be confessed, has something about him which often makes the gorge of a carnal man rise, so it will be worth while to consider the contrast in question more fully.
>
> Dislike of the saintly nature seems to be a negative result of the biologically useful instinct of welcoming leadership, and glorifying the chief of the tribe. The chief is the potential, if not the actual tyrant, the masterful, overpowering man of prey. We confess our inferiority and grovel before him. We quail under his glance, and are at the same time proud of owning so dangerous a lord.[103]

James' expression above is a good description of gang leaders in prison, who rise through the ranks by the ruthlessness of their deeds. Gang members willingly submit to their leaders, cowering before them, and new prisoners are pressured to join gangs for survival. Gang leaders are necessary to ensure survival for many of its weaker members.

James goes on to describe the real world, in which aggressiveness is needed in certain arenas such as military campaigns, and where saintliness is needed to reach the highest ideals of society. In an environment where all were invariably aggressive, an implosion would materialize from inner friction. Imagine a prison with no guards. Sooner or later, only the strongest gang would survive. However, in society, there are checks and balances, good versus evil. The saint is indispensable in counterbalancing so much of human nature which is bent on greed, power, and lust. The saint helps ensure some kind of order in society. James describes in the real world that the saint may be ill-adapted, according to particular circumstances. Indeed, anyone, according to James, who makes a saint out of himself does so at his peril given the aggressive elements of society. James cites Saint Paul as an example:

> From the biological point of view Saint Paul was a failure, because he was beheaded. Yet he was magnificently adapted to the larger environment of history; and so far as any saint's example is a leaven of righteousness in the world, and draws it in the direction of more prevalent habits of saintliness, he is a success, no matter what his immediate bad fortune may be.[104]

James concludes that we should strive to be saints:

> Economically, the saintly group of qualities is indispensable to the world's welfare. The great saints are immediate successes; the smaller ones are at least heralds and harbingers, and they may be leavens also, of a better mundane order. Let us be saints, then, if we can, whether or not we succeed visibly and temporally.[105]

This is a good description of a Kairos team composed largely of lay people armed with no earthly weapons voluntarily entering a maximum-security prison to share God's love with the least of the least. The strong, aggressive members of the prison often disdain and despise Christians for being weak. Steven Toscanini of the Michael Unit summed up his attitude toward Christians prior to his Kairos weekend:

> While on the Michael Unit I had many occasions to run into many Christian inmates as well as other Christian people. I hated them. I detested them. I considered them as weak people who needed a crutch

> to lean on and used Christianity as that crutch instead of facing life as it was. To me they put on a mask and hid behind it.
>
> Eventually while walking around on the yard I heard of this thing called the Kairos. So out of curiosity I began to ask what it was. So my old radical friends I hung out with told me, "Hey man, you should go up there and hang out with them Christian people for a few days because they bring in some really great home-cooked food and a million homemade cookies. You can do it for three days and you don't gotta be a Christian to go." Well, I soon forgot that idea because, as I said before, I detested all Christian people and no way was I gonna spend no three days with them no matter how good the food and cookies were.
>
> Then one day about a month later after having this conversation I was sitting out in the dorm and the mail came around. The boss hands me a slip of paper from the Chaplain's office saying, "Congratulations, you have been picked to attend the #9 Kairos Walk." Man, at that time, I got so mad I couldn't see straight. I knew that someone had put my name in to go to this Kairos thing. So soon I was walking the yard asking who the punk was who put my name in to go to this Christian meeting. I had already planned to bash his face in. Well folks, to this day I have never found that person, if that is "A PERSON," who put my name in. You know they say God works in mysterious ways. Well folks I could be living proof of that. Right or wrong? Did God see my need to attend this #9 Walk and He put my name on the list? Think about it!

It is an amazing paradox to see prisoners who, had the circumstances been right, would have killed each other before a Kairos weekend, hugging each other a few days into the Kairos weekend because of God's love flowing through such "weak" servants. Nobody hugs anybody in prison; it is a sign of weakness.

But during the course of a Kairos weekend, hugs become the normal mode of greeting and saying farewell. And this continues beyond the Kairos weekend during the weekly prayer-share meetings and monthly reunions.

Perhaps the greatest paradox in prison is our greatest weapon from the least likely source. Of all the agape that we bombard the men with, the most powerful are the letters from small children. By any objective measure, a child is helpless. A child is completely dependent upon his or her parents for food, shelter, clothing, and medical care. A child, by world standards, is weak. Yet God uses the weakest segment of our society to overpower the strongest, meanest, and roughest convicts in a maximum-security penitentiary. The children's placemats and letters, written and illustrated as only young kids can do, help break down the walls around the most hardened criminals. Jim Huddleston once told me that he could hear 15 adult testimonies and it wouldn't have the same impact as one letter from a small child. During the five sit-down Kairos meals served during a weekend are placemats lovingly illustrated by young children. Often the men will take care not to spill food or drink on them so they can take them back to their cells at night. Some of the loudest weeping during the weekend occurs during the reading of the letters, especially those from the children. Jim Huddleston told me that the first four letters he opened were from young kids. "I had to put the letters down because I couldn't read any more - the tears were too thick."

Henry Baylor, who has served more than two decades and attended Kairos #3 at the Michael Unit, eloquently describes the impact of the children's letters and placemats.

> In a contemporary country and western song it is said, "The nearest thing to heaven . . . is a child," and I'm sure everyone is familiar with the adage that says, "Nothing is ever appreciated as much as when it is gone." When I was a "pilgrim" on my Kairos weekend, I found the strength to overcome my fears of rejection in the letter of a precious little 6-year-old boy. His letter to me said, "I know you're not a bad man . . . Jesus loves you - and so do I!" God

truly works in mysterious ways, because that was the message I personally needed to hear, so my spiritual healing could continue and I could rededicate my life to following the Lord!

A few months ago, two very special people asked me to explain why the letters and artwork from children have such a powerful impact on prisoners during the Kairos weekends inside. Immediately the words "innocence lost" sprang into my mind. That inescapable tie, which binds us all to our formative years, is the memory of how easy it was for us as children to love and accept others. I've witnessed some of the biggest, toughest, meanest convicts reduced to tears just as I was, touched by the love of a child!

It's not a simple emotion which can be taken lightly because those letters and all the artwork represent everything we as prisoners wish to put back into our life again. It's not the artistic quality of the pictures and posters and placemats which touches us so deeply - it's our own memories of the joy we had as children to draw and paint and color; and, to think that a bunch of children we have never met or known, children who have no reason to give us a second thought, would spend their time and efforts happily drawing and finger-painting or composing short notes in squiggly lines and innocent bluntness to express unconditional love and acceptance of us, is very overwhelming!

. . . I've known prisoners from both extremes of the spectrum (and in between) - those condemned to die, those so violently immature and irresponsible condemned to struggle in limbo, and the ones striving to survive and prepare for the eventual return to freedom - and, the one thing we all share in common is our desire to be loved and accepted by others, in spite of our past mistakes.

The children of the Kairos Prison Ministry touch the hearts and souls of the pilgrims in a way that can never be forgotten! Their message is twofold:

1. To love and accept someone (without all the prejudices and hangups and garbage) is really something wonderful, and
2. It's easier to do than anything else in the world!

In the children of Kairos, prisoners see:

1. A reflection of themselves as we were when we were young and innocent;
2. The reflection of how we wish we can be again now, and
3. How we can imagine it will be to spend eternity in the presence of God!

So in a very real sense (for us), the song is right - the nearest thing to heaven is a child! And, it is because of the unconditional love of the Kairos children that prisoners can look forward to the love and acceptance of free-world adults, beginning with our brothers and sisters in color [as opposed to the prisoners who dress in white] who make up the inside and outside ministry teams!

We can all learn from the children's example. I believe this is the real meaning found in Luke 18:16-17 [But Jesus called the children to him and said, "Let the little children come to me, and do not hinder them, for the kingdom of God belongs to such as these. I tell you the truth, anyone who will not receive the kingdom of God like a little child will never enter it."]; we can do a lot worse than to love our God and our neighbor with the innocent love of a child! I want to thank each and every child that has been and ever will be encouraged to participate in the Kairos Prison Ministry; and I pray as adults the Kairos family will

> continue to love and accept and support each other in every way possible that the kingdom of God might be made present to all!

In early 1998, my friend Rufus Jones told me that he had kept my daughter Hope's drawings above his bed for two years. I was dumbfounded. I asked Rufus how long he was going to keep the pictures and he remarked, "I'm taking that picture out of here someday." Rufus has been in the free world since August 1998 and still has Hope's drawings; they are sacred to him.

I've been told again and again by men in maximum-security prisons that nothing breaks them down more than a picture or letter from a young child. Why? Because a young child has no angles, no quid pro quo, no agenda. The joy comes in the doing and the giving and that is reward enough. These men have told me that in their view, nothing comes closer on this earth to the purity of God's unconditional love than that of a small child. I have seen atheists, as well as many other prisoners, testify that it was the letters from small children that cracked their hearts wide open and led them to accept Jesus Christ as their Lord and Savior.

Prisoners can become free of the burden of holding people unforgiven during a Kairos weekend, especially during the burning of their "unforgiven people" list on Saturday night. People can be free of their guilt and begin a new life. Christ said that to know the truth is to set a person free.

> If you hold to my teaching, you are really my disciples. Then you will know the truth, and the truth will set you free.

John 8:31-32

When a person can work through this type of pain, the pain of guilt and holding people unforgiven, unloading baggage and wiping away the accumulated sludge and grime from years of being held prisoner by life's difficulties (and we are all prisoners in this sense), real joy and peace can be engendered in previously hardened hearts. As M. Scott Peck, in *The Road Less Traveled and Beyond*, puts it:

> Indeed, one of the mysterious and paradoxical realities is that in addition to the pain that life brings, living

> can be accompanied by an unfathomed joy once we get past the pain.[106]

These are some of the paradoxes that I have experienced in prison. And as M. Scott Peck says, where there is paradox there is often truth.

12

> Therefore, if anyone is in Christ, he is a new creation; the old has gone, the new has come!
>
> The apostle Paul [2 Corinthians 5:17]

MAIL FROM MAXIMUM-SECURITY

Over the years I have received some interesting mail from the brothers in white. One of the blessings of being in Kairos is the establishment of relationships, including correspondence that can be a real blessing. I have extracted snippets of letters I have received to offer a glimpse of the light radiating from the darkest corners of the penitentiary.

Mike Wayne

Mike wrote in December 1998:

> Our Kairos [Christmas] party was a blessing and as always the food was good. We sung a lot of Christmas songs and it was a good fellowship. Brother it was amazing to see so many people in a room together sharing God's love. I can recall when I was in society and of the world, my friends and I would have what we call a "get together." However, it was nothing like that one [the Kairos Christmas party]. The ones we would have would be full of booze, fighting and confusion, but it's so nice now that I can enjoy such a wonderful fellowship with my Kairos brothers and sisters.

In the following letter, Mike discussed a variation of the question posed by Nathanael to Philip, "Can anything good come from Nazareth?"

> If you see Rufus [Jones] tell him I did the history at the Heavenly Voyage Anniversary this year and I did a special about him and how God used him in prison.

> There was a question in my message and it was, "Can anything good come out of prison?" When you read the Bible you will see that many good men came out of prison; even our Lord and Savior Jesus Christ came out of prison. Rufus is a living testimony that something good can come out of prison.

Jorge Garcia

Jorge sat at my table (Table of St. John) during Kairos #8. He comments on some of his feelings following his Kairos weekend, and alludes to the very real risk of leaving gangs for Christ.

> I feel the Lord is really preparing me for the outside. It was great to see some brothers reveal their true feelings and come to the Lord. Some have made some real serious changes, from being gang members to giving their life to Christ! Because in here it is no joke or game when you make changes like that.
>
> I love Jesus with all my heart, and now I have come to the understanding of things that have happened in my past. What I'm saying is I know why I didn't "die" to the ways of the world. Everyday He shows me that He wants me to get ready for what he has for me when I get out. I'm ready to be baptized with water and live for Jesus the rest of my life! And that comes from my heart. I wish I could have realized all this sooner but had I never come to prison, I would never have found salvation.

Peter Smith

Peter and I were on Kairos #8 together but not at the same table. You get to know the men at your table the best during a Kairos weekend since you spend so much time together. Conversely, you have less time to get to know the other pilgrims. Nevertheless, I got to know Peter because during introductions on Thursday evening he mentioned he hailed from my home state - Oregon. I asked myself what are the odds of meeting someone from Oregon in an East Texas prison.

> I thank God I'm not the child of my youth or the person I was six years ago when I got locked up. I'm 28 now and I still have a lot of room for growth but I am growing. I realize I have to let time run its course for people to see the new me, but I don't associate with those people or people like them. The people I most love and associate myself with are those Christians who love me the way I am, are strong enough to offer correction and patient enough to work with me as I struggle to yield and change. I'm in a maximum-security prison surrounded by corruption, sin, and perverse people. It's tough but the fact I am willing to give my life to Christ and fight the good fight of faith, and struggle against the evil, I hope says something about me. While others are planning their next crime or committing it in here, I've gotten my associates degree.

Peter is now in the free world, attending a major four-year university.

Oscar Sanchez

Oscar is a very spiritual man.

> We must take heart, for while most people look back on the past, their thoughts are tinged with remorse and disappointment. And as we look at the photos that have been embedded in our minds we relive the mistakes of the past - mistakes involving people, events, circumstances, and decisions. But these photos should not discourage us. As we look at ourselves today, we should be encouraged that we are different people than we were back then. We've changed. We've grown. We've learned from our mistakes - haven't we! Many of us, however, don't look at life that way. We groan and moan over what we've wasted, over this done or not done, over things said or unsaid. But before the pity party goes too far,

> remember this: Unending remorse and shame never made anyone better or brought anyone to maturity.

Mario Rodriguez

Mario hails from Corpus Christi, Texas. He is another of my family members from the Table of St. John during the Kairos #8 weekend.

> It was so good to see you this weekend, and it helps me a lot to be around a lot of brothers in the Lord. Every time we all get together I feel like I grow that much closer to the Lord . . . I am just like a newborn baby. I have to learn how to walk all over again in my new life with Jesus Christ. He is who I have to serve now, not man. He is the one who is going to open these prison gates for me. I feel He has put me here for a reason and that is to show me where my life was really headed. Now that I have found a new life with Jesus I feel so much happier and freer than I ever have before I went through Kairos.
>
> Now my promise is to go out and do the will of God, and show other people what God has done in my life, and through me what He can do in other people's lives. I love the Lord Jesus because He has showed me a new life and how I should live for Him and do His will and not mine.

Bob Williamson

Bob attended the first Kairos at the Michael Unit in the autumn of 1992. He was a member of the Ku Klux Klan and a gang member prior to his Kairos weekend. He told me that many gang leaders were at the first Kairos weekend. Bob said the atmosphere was very tense during Thursday's opening session and all day Friday. He said everybody was on full stand-by alert status, waiting for somebody to make the first move. A gang fight could have erupted like spontaneous combustion. Then something remarkable happened during Saturday, with the letters playing a big role in melting the tension. Bob reported that men, who a few days earlier had the circumstances been right would have killed each other, were hugging one another. Bob said his racism evaporated that weekend as God's love overcame Satan's hate in his heart.

> Tell the children I said thank you very much for their drawings. They put a smile on my face and everyone here likes them! Well they are very good and represent very good parts of life that we seem to forget! You are right, kids don't see colors or race or any of that stuff. All they see are kids who want to play on the playgrounds. We, as God's kids, need to remember that too! You are right about that, there are a lot of people who need to experience what we did on our [Kairos] weekend.
>
> Please tell your kids thank you for the get-well cards, my brother. They both put a big smile on my face. I showed them to some guys here and they thought it was great because your kids would do that for someone they do not know. I have told them about this and about the Kairos program too.

Scotty Finigan

Scotty, prior to his Kairos weekend, was a volatile man, slow to love and quick to anger, a self-described "head-bashing" man. His reputation was such that if you looked at him the wrong way you could get brutally assaulted. Scotty was truly a new creation in Christ following his Kairos #7 weekend at the Michael Unit, characterized by love, warmth, peace, and patience.

> Kairos was the big turning point in my life and I will always be a part of Kairos and I want to do all I can for Kairos!
>
> I praise God who has delivered me from the drugs, delivered me from the booze, delivered me from the tobacco, delivered me from the fast, wicked life, and most of all, delivered me from that hate factory which I was, eating me like cancer.

Johnny Hernandez

Johnny is a young man who began hanging around his "wild" cousins when he was young, his first brush with the law was at age 14 when he served time in a juvenile facility for assault with a weapon. He stayed clean until age 19 when he was incarcerated for a felony. Johnny is typical of many young people who in the brashness of youth, make impulsive, poor choices without thinking of their ramifications. Johnny attended Kairos #11 at the Michael Unit.

> I was just a kid, and bullheaded at that. If I could go back in time and make things different, I would. There's no other alternative but to accept what happened, ask God for forgiveness, and make the best of my future . . . My goal is to educate myself as much as possible while I'm here. Once I'm out I want to talk to the youth and tell them to put their guns down, and get an education. I believe I'll have a greater impact on them, because we can relate to one another.

Paul Hoffer

Paul hails from New Jersey and kind of reminds me of Rodney Dangerfield with his northeastern accent and great sense of humor. He sat at my table during Kairos #11 and underwent a complete overhaul.

> I'm still in awe of the power the Lord has. Here come the tears again. I feel truly blessed for entering Kairos. Just like a porch to the house of the Lord, and Kairos was the welcome mat as well. As I said, ten lifetimes couldn't do what you [read Christ Jesus] did for me in three days, allowing me to forgive <u>all</u> my enemies and showing me how to replace hate with love.

On Christmas night 1997, my brother-in-law, Brian Irwin, and myself were reposing in the living room after a huge dinner, feeling like beached whales and listening to Christmas music, when my six-year-old daughter Hope appeared, holding up a picture she had drawn of herself smiling with two brightly colored Christmas trees, sun, clouds, blue sky, and grass. I said, "Hope, did you make that for Uncle Brian?" Hope said, "No." I asked, "Did you make it for Daddy?" Hope responded, "No, Daddy, I want one of the prisoners to have this picture." Tears welled up in my eyes as I contemplated her act of love. Do you know what a blessing it is to have a little girl, with no prompting [except from the Holy Spirit], on Christmas night draw a picture for a Christian brother behind bars and write the following message: "Dear Paul, I hope you're having a Merry Christmas. Love, Hope." Paul Hoffer received that picture and told me a month later when I visited him that he shed tears over her picture and message.

Paul, in another letter, expresses his new-found faith.

> It was my Kairos roots that has helped me to branch out in my faith, and to shed my old bark for a new one. And I look to the Lord as a tree looks to the sun, and I continue to grow ever stronger. I hope that one day my leaves of faith will gently fall on those who have not yet seen the Light of the Lord.

A Warrior in Christ

The following letter was dated March 25, 1994 and simply signed, "A Warrior in Christ." It is a testimony to the power of Kairos.

> When I was a child, my mother told me, many times, that God has angels that He sends down to earth, just to watch over His children. I never disbelieved her; I just had a problem with the concept.
>
> I now know and understand what my mother was trying to tell me: that God's ministries, especially Kairos, are comprised of people, sent by God, doing the work of angels. I could not have imagined there were people like you, who are anointed by God to bring love, peace, and joy to prisoners of society; prisoners, who for the most part, have never experienced the love of Christ.

We participants at the Michael Unit have many things in common: rejection, hate, bitterness, strife, greed, deceit, perversion, rebelliousness, terror; and the most common denominator is that we are at the bottom of the heap in society [the least of the least].

Many of us have never known our parents, brothers, sisters, or in many cases, even known who our parents were. All of our lives, we have been misfits, never-do-wells, and rejects of society. Society did themselves and us a favor by warehousing us in these units and trying to forget about us.

Then comes Kairos! Our entire world has changed! We have learned that God forgives us, that God still loves us, and that He has a plan for us; and that the most beautiful Christian people in the world love and encourage us, and call us brother!

We were denied the opportunity to properly thank you all for the outpouring of love that we received during our four-day walk so I would like to do so now, on behalf of all the participants at the Michael Unit.

We have all been touched by the Lord during the four days and I would like to point out some of the things I personally witnessed when we got back to the wings Sunday evening. I saw posters torn off of cell walls, porno magazines torn up and thrown in the trash, cigarettes and matches, and tobacco destroyed or thrown away. I saw new brothers and older brothers hugging and crying; I saw prayer groups form everywhere and all the brothers giving thanks and hugging each other while other brothers were scrambling around trying to come up with enough Bibles to cover the new brothers' needs. The power of the Holy Spirit was absolutely palpable!

> Anyone not believing in miracles, should have been present here at the Michael Unit this past weekend. I saw convicted murderers, robbers, thieves, etc. crying like babies while reading letters from little children asking them to "be nice to God because we love God." We each now have a personal relationship with Jesus Christ and a new sense of worth. If God loves us, and you all love us, then we must be worthy of being loved.

Steven Toscanini

Steven is one of the most interesting people I've ever met and he has become a close friend. He certainly is a new creation in Christ following his Kairos #9 weekend at the Michael Unit. Steven used to despise Christians, viewing them as weak and in need of a crutch to get through life. Steven was a former mechanic (hit man or professional assassin) for the Sicilian Mafia and was a cold, heartless person. The following testimony reveals a completely transformed character.

> Then about a month ago something really weird happened to me. Here is the story. Well we had a mass murderer come to the unit and he is 66 years old, been in prison for 40 years. You may even remember some of it. His name is Kenneth Martain and he was convicted in Dallas for killing his whole family: Mom, step Dad and brothers and sisters. The man was sent to Rusk State Hospital for the criminally insane and stayed there for about 14 years. Then he was sent to death row and stayed there for another 15 years. Then the governor commuted his sentence to life without parole and he has been in and out of mental hospitals for another few years. So eventually he got well enough to be put into general population. But by this time he was getting pretty senile; he couldn't hardly remember much. He would forget to take a shower, go eat, not shave and a lot of other things. Well he was put on my wing and I noticed

> this and started looking after him somewhat. I would talk to him where others would avoid him because of his reputation. Some even started saying bad things to him about the crime he committed. Well I asked them to stop and they did. Then I noticed Kenneth talked to other people when no one was there. I remembered he was a mental patient and began praying for him, asking God to work in his life.
>
> Well soon the administration got wind of my taking care of the old guy and questioned me about why I was doing this for such a horrible person. In their eyes he was just waiting for death to creep up on him. Well my response was that I am a Christian and it is my duty to try and help others in anyway I can. So they said, OK, you do what you can for him and if you have any problems out of anyone tell them to come see us. Yes, he was talking about other officers. Well for awhile I did have some problems but that all got ironed out and now I am responsible for taking care of the old guy. I take him down to take a shower, make sure he eats properly, shaves, gets a hair cut and so on and so forth. Now I do all this outside my regular work duties. Recently I was called down to the chaplain's office and was asked why I took care of this old guy, so I explained it to them. So God went to work and now the chaplain's office is trying to get him transferred to a medical unit.

The following excerpt is another example of Steven's commitment to Christ.

> I have a good report for you today. Since I came here to the Beto Unit [from the Michael Unit], I have worked with a guy named Billy Jones. This guy was a really hardened con and was involved in just about everything. Well about two weeks ago he came over to me and asked, "Steven, you are an ex-gangster, right?" I said, "Yes, why do you ask?" He

> said, "Because I want to know how a person like you just turned about in one day and became a Christian; doesn't your conscience bother you about your past life?" I said, "Yes, very much, but God forgave me, Billy, and that's all I need." So Billy asked me, "Do you think God can forgive me?" I said, "Yes, Billy, all you need to do is confess your sins and invite Him into your heart."
>
> So then a few days later Billy was speaking to another inmate and told him that he had started to read the Bible. Well I didn't say anything until he came over to me again and told me he was going to start going to church. Well Steve he did and is now a Christian. Is this good news or what? Now at work we daily talk about how to live as a Christian. I got him a brand new Bible today.

After residing at the Michael Unit for a few years, Steven was transferred to the Beto Unit where he lived in the toughest part of the prison - the north side. As a result of good behavior Steven was given the opportunity to move to the much safer south side but he deliberately chose to stay on the north side to witness to young gang members, often men filled with the most rage that even veteran prisoners fear because of their total lack of conscience. Steven denied himself, putting himself at much greater risk by his decision.

> Well we are off the lockdown on the north side of the Beto Unit. The south side came off lockdown nine days before we did. Yes, we went through pure hell here on the north side; my Christian life was tested and tried and I came through with flying colors. Nothing, no matter what, will make me turn my back on Christ. Just before the lockdown I went up for re-class, this meaning my custody level could be upgraded from a medium-custody to a minimum-custody level. Well God granted me my minimum-custody level. At the re-class, the warden said, "I will send you down to the south side now." I replied, "Sir,

> with all due respect, I want to stay on the north side." He looked at me rather surprised and asked, "Why Toscanini?" I said, "Well, sir, I have been talking to some really young kids down here on the north side and they have agreed to go to church with me and if I'm not there to talk to them daily they may go back to wanting to be in a gang." The warden remarked, "Well Toscanini, it really is true isn't it?" I said, "What?" The warden responded, "The once Mafia killer is a Christian." I said, "Yes, you should try it yourself sometime." He just dismissed me then. So I stay here on the north side with Christ at my side.

In another letter Steven amplifies his decision to remain on the notorious north side of the Beto Unit.

> Daily I see many young men faced with the opportunity to be in a gang and I try my level best to show them a different way by asking them to attend church with me; some take me up on my request and some don't. But in my eyes if I can just get one to attend church then the devil has been defeated. What I love to see is the looks on their faces when they realize God loves them; I guess they feel the whole world has turned against them when they came to prison. Then when they walk up to the alter and invite Christ into their lives, and they walk away with that look of content on their precious faces, it is such a joyful blessing. I guess now I understand why the angels in heaven rejoice when a person is saved. It doesn't stop because when I see them in the hall they are still smiling where once they frowned, and that is an inspiration for me to go out there and find other young men who need Christ in their lives. They are always saying thank you for showing them the way to church, but I remind them I was not the one who saved them - Christ is the one who deserves all the thanks. But, all in all, Steve, it is such a wonderful

blessing to see young men walking with a light on their faces and Christ living in their hearts.

Yes, Steve, I gave up the chance to live an easier life on the south side of this unit. But look what I would have given up, that being the joy of seeing a precious smile on a young man's face who I led to church and his subsequent acceptance of Christ in his heart. No amount of luxury could offer me more than a smile on a young Christian's face. Yes, Steve, the living conditions are surely a lot better than here on the north side; there are more privileges that go with living on the south side. However, the devil is stronger here and it is my job to fight against him, so how could I do it if I lived on the south side? So it is my decision to stay here and fight the devil. Look at what the devil offered Jesus if He would worship him. And look at the price Jesus paid to not worship him. Well if Jesus gave up all this so that I may have life then it is but a small price I am paying for staying on the north side. Don't you agree? I would literally give up my life if I knew I could save one person from living a sinful life.

Steve, just look at my organized crime life, look at all the lives I destroyed, the lives I took, the misery I caused. Then you will see I just, *just* simply must give something back and the church is my only opportunity to do it. I pray daily to my Savior if a man in this prison is going to die, to spare them and take me in their place. No one on the earth knows the daily sorrow I feel for what I have done and I just hope someday I very well may be able to give something back to them.

The following heartwarming story from Steven brought tears to our eyes when I read it to my family.

I had a rather unique experience last weekend and I thought I'd share it with you today to show how our Lord and Savior Jesus Christ does His wonderful work in an inmate's life.

It all started a couple of weeks ago when a good Christian brother of mine came by my cell and told me he would soon be transferred to the Amarillo Unit to finish a vocational trade class. He asked me if I would keep a large bag of his legal books and other legal materials until he could arrange for his sister to pick them up. I told him it was against the rules for me to store his legal materials and, unless he could get it approved through the Unit Administration, I couldn't do it. A few days later he came by and showed me a piece of paper where the Unit Administration had approved it for me to store his things. He was transferred a few days later.

This past weekend, on Sunday morning, an officer I am familiar with came to my cell and asked me if I had a large plastic bag full of legal materials that belonged to another inmate and I said, "Yes." He asked me if I was going to work or anything else and I said, "No." He asked me if I would mind carrying the bag out to the visiting room because a lady had come by to pick it up. I told him I didn't mind at all so we headed to the visiting room.

When we got to the shakedown area where you have to completely undress before going into the visiting room there were two other officers I am familiar with and they told me to go ahead and undress. The officer escorting me told the other officers that I was with him and only carrying the plastic bag for him. They said, "Yes, we both know him and work in the same area he works in constantly but he still needs to follow the rules and undress." So I did.

The officer escorting me said, "O.K. let's take the bag up front." So we walked through the visiting area up to where the soda machines are. The officer instructed me to stay there until he finds the lady who had come to pick up the bag. As I was standing there, I noticed that I had not tied my boot strings, so I bent down on one knee to tie the laces.

All of a sudden there was a small hand on my shoulder. As I looked up there stood a little boy, about six or seven years old, holding two crutches, the kind that wrap around your forearm. About the time I started to get up and say something, the little boy kind of pushed down on my shoulder like he was trying to keep his balance. Out of fear of making him fall, I just stayed kneeled down on one knee. As I started to ask him if he was O.K., he said, "Are you one of the bad men who live here?" So not really knowing what to say to this little boy, I blurted out, "Well I used to be up until a few years ago when I became a Christian and I am not mean anymore."

Now about this time I noticed a lady looking at us very intently, getting a soda out of the machine behind her. She must have spotted me looking at her and she said, "Please excuse my son, sir, but he always asks a ton of questions when he meets someone he doesn't know." Then turning to her son, she remarked, "Come on son, it's time to go." He looks at his mother and responds, "O.K. mom but can I ask him another question first?" So she looks at me and kind of asks with her eyes if I would mind. So I told the little fellow he could ask me anything he wanted to.

Before he could ask me his question, the officer and lady, who had come up to retrieve her brother's belongings, walked up. I thought they would sort of interrupt but they just stood there.

So the little boy said, "Have you ever had trouble walking? I have these dumb old crutches to help me walk."

I responded, "Yes, little boy, I did have trouble walking, but not like you."

He then said, "I don't understand. Can you explain it to me?"

I said, "Well, little boy, all my life I walked around in a life full of sin and had plenty of troubles daily, but since I became a Christian I can now walk real good and don't have trouble anymore."

He said, "But I have to use my crutches to walk with or I lose my balance and fall down."

So I jumped right in and said, "Well sometimes when you're a Christian you might have a little trouble walking as a Christian and when you do you have to use Jesus as your crutches. Even if you fall down, He is always there to pick you up just as I know your mom has had to do that with you sometimes." Then, all of a sudden, I remembered the story about how Jesus healed the crippled man and I shared the story with the little fellow. The little boy smiled and said, "Where is it in the Bible so I can read it when I get home?"

Then all of a sudden I remembered: John 5:1-9. Now how I remembered the location of that Scripture is a mystery because I normally have to look up all verses when I speak of them. But, as I said, it just jumped right into my mind. Then the little boy said, "Do you think that Jesus will ever heal my legs so I can walk like all the other kids I go to school with?"

I said, "Little boy, someday Jesus is going to heal your legs and you're gonna walk real good, your gonna throw away those old crutches and never use them again. All you gotta do is to go to Sunday School and church, pray and have faith in Jesus and you'll do just fine. I know this because you see I was like the blind man in the Bible story."

Then the little boy said, "Mom can he tell me the story?" She said, "Yes, I guess so." So I looked up at the officer and the lady standing there and they just kind of nodded their heads in affirmation. So I told the little boy the story of John 9:1-7, how Jesus healed the blind man and after the blind man's eyes were opened, he could see all the wonderful and beautiful things God had made but he had never been able to see. And all it took was a little faith in God. Then I told him I was like the blind man and couldn't see all the beautiful things God had made until I became a Christian. And again I don't know how I remembered the verse. And then I noticed his mother was writing down the verses.

So about this time the little fellow dropped one of his crutches; I reached around to pick it up, but he said, "Wait! I can't hug you if I have to hold the crutch." So then the little boy put his arm around me and hugged my neck real tight and said, "You really aren't a bad man no more, are you? I'll never forget you 'good man' and I think I gotta get my mom to take me to Sunday School so I can be able to walk and see real good like you." His mother spoke up at that time and said to her son, "After what I heard you two talk about for the last few minutes, I think it's time for us to go to Sunday School and church."

As they walked away, but before they were out of sight, I noticed the little boy's fingers on the crutch and they were waving good-bye, and he was smiling. I have to admit that tears welled up in my eyes.

> The officer and lady said it was time for them to go to church too after what I and the little boy talked about. Then the lady said, “Thank you.” I responded, “You don’t need to thank me for keeping your brother’s things.”
>
> She said, “I am not thanking you for that, but instead for opening my own eyes so I could see the beauty of a Christian even though he is an inmate.” Then the officer said, “And that goes for me too.”

Steven was transferred to the Terrell Unit [changed to the Polunsky Unit in July 2001] in Livingston from the Beto Unit in Tennessee Colony in late 2000. His cell had an interesting view of Texas’ death row.

> The new death row is here on this unit. Now when I look out my cell door there is a window and I can see the death row building. So at night I can make out a man walking around in that cell when he turns on his light. Now you may ask yourself why is this so interesting. Well, Steve, each time I look out that window at him walking around I tell myself, “Steven, that could be you walking around in that cell if they had caught you doing some of the things you did when you were involved in organized crime.” So Steve, I think God put me in this cell to show me what I could have faced and I also think He put me here to pray for that man walking around in it. And each time I look out that window I thank God for the Kairos Prison Ministry which showed me the way to a Christian life. Now Steve, can you see how important it is what you are doing? If it had not been for folks like you I would have never been here to see this picture. I am not on death row; I have life, and that life is going to be spent being a servant to others.

Steven’s 2000 Christmas letter was a wonderful gift for us.

> If you’ll only take a moment and look at me then you’ll see I am a personal witness to the unselfish

and gracious work you do for our Lord and Savior Jesus Christ because over four years ago I met you and since then my life has not been the same. And I say this because you introduced me to a man named "Jesus Christ." When I trusted you, I invited Him into my heart, my life had light in it, and the darkness disappeared. So you see, without your presence in my life I wouldn't have known the man named Jesus Christ, would I? So please, just for a second, look into this new heart you have given me by reading these words I am writing to you today, and you can see that a once cold and unfeeling heart made of stone is now gone, and I have a heart full of love, feeling, and emotions!

You took a Sicilian Mafia Mechanic's stone-cold heart and melted it. So can't you just please see how much I care for you? And you know I only wish at this moment in time you could see this face with a stream of tears running down my cheeks as I write you this letter, then you could see how much I care for you. You took the frown off this old face made of stone and replaced it with a smile. So please see all the things I now have by your presence in my life.

So this year, when you're putting Christmas presents under the tree, please remember the present you gave me over four years ago. You gave me a heart. So what better Christmas present could you give a person? Thank you for my heart transplant because that is exactly what you gave me. You took all of the hatred and bitterness out of my heart and transplanted love into it. So this year when I think of everyone out there opening up all those beautiful Christmas presents, I will be here with mine already open - an open heart full of love. Thank you for this wonderful, living Christmas present.

> So in closing this Christmas letter to you please know I would love to be able to give you a Christmas present, but I can't although I can send you a whole bunch of love from the heart you gave me. So please know I love you and you shall be on my mind and in my heart during this Christmas season.

Robert Black

Robert attended the Kairos #12 weekend at the Michael Unit.

> There was more love shown during my Kairos weekend than I received at or outside church. I would give anything in the world to experience that loving feeling again. I have to admit everything that happened to me those four days was truly a blessing. I want to give thanks to God for being a loving God.

Gilberto Fernandez

Gilberto, *pistolero* for a Mexican gang, who played such a stirring role during my first Kairos weekend at the Michael Unit (see chapter 3), laments his transfer to another unit without a weekly Kairos presence.

> Kairos here doesn't have weekly meetings, only monthly . . . I'm having trouble dealing with this unit with the petty little rules and regulations that other units don't have to put up with. We are currently on lockdown over nothing. The Christians on this unit are sort of like robots who have been programmed. They seem to be afraid to open up to one another. They won't hold hands or exchange hugs. They won't sing.
>
> I really miss you guys. What I miss most is the unity that was there at the Michael Unit. There in no unity here.

Tom Jenkins

Tom served time in and out of prison for a span of four decades, wandering in the wilderness. He was paroled in the late 1990s, graduated from a Christian program sponsored by Calvary Commission in Lindale, Texas and is now happily married. One of his missionary trips, while Tom was at Calvary Commission, was to Reynosa, Mexico to an orphanage during Easter 2000.

> We are all excited about the upcoming Mexico Easter Outreach in Reynosa during April 19-23. I have been invited to participate. This is a great opportunity for me, as there will be witnessing and sharing Jesus in dramas and song, as well as distributing the toys and candy to the children . . . I feel that this will be a great step in my cross-cultural experience and Resurrection message of HOPE this Easter. Some things, I have found, are just more enjoyable when there is nothing received in return!

Tom told me subsequently that the trip was a big success, with him holding tiny babies in his big arms. He mentioned that God has a sense of humor. Two decades earlier, Tom was in Reynosa smuggling crack cocaine and now he was smuggling rice and beans to an orphanage.

Louis MacDonald

Louis is a Kairos brother from the Michael Unit who subsequently transferred to Eastham, one of the oldest prisons in Texas.

> I am thankful that after being on death row for three years that my sentence was overturned and I ended up with a life sentence. But, I am also thankful that before I went to trial back in 1978, God delivered me from spiritual death row where sin had held me in bondage for years. I got saved while in the county jail and I know my life has been full of blessings ever since! God is worthy to be praised! I know I couldn't have made it so far and so long without His presence in my life.

Larry James

Larry writes:

> My emotional and spiritual condition was on empty. I was walking around dead. The system had taken all hope out of me . . . Today I am a new creature. I am not alone. I have a family that cares about me . . . Kairos saved my life . . . My weekend was the best weekend of my life.

Fred Thompson

Fred is a tall, lanky person, a gentle giant filled with a quick laugh and warm smile with eyes that sparkle. He always seems to be in a good mood.

> I joined Kairos out of selfishness because I couldn't resist the temptation offered by all the things I had heard about how great Kairos was. The Lord really had a surprise in store for me. Since joining, I have given my whole tired life to God . . . Words cannot explain how truly wonderful and beneficial the Kairos program really is.

Miguel Garza

Miguel used to hate white people so much he didn't even like sitting next to one. His hatred was a function of past discrimination that he had suffered for years. Kairos softened his heart.

> I am no longer depressed or filled with anger and hatred toward all white people. The ministry gave me hope for a future I thought I had lost. I have found peace of mind that I never thought possible. It is not easy being a Christian, but it is fulfilling.

Jose Lopez

Jose attended Kairos #16 weekend at the Michael Unit and talks about the spirituality of Kairos.

> The spirituality of God is awesome. I was standing in the center of 7 Gym [the gym at the Michael Unit

> where regular Sunday morning worship services, Kairos weekly prayer-share meetings, and Kairos monthly reunions are held] one day and I felt chills all through my body. Good feelings. I don't like to say religious feelings because religion has rules, do's and don'ts. Spirituality, like our Kairos weekend and Kairos meetings, are nothing but love - no rules, just God's pure love.

Richard Williams

Richard was a pilgrim on Kairos #16 and he wrote about his experience.

> I just can't believe what's happened to me. Let me say this, Steve, I've been locked up 22 years and I've never seen or been around so much love and caring in my life. I don't have any family or any one. I just didn't know so many people cared. I've always been the hard person. I didn't care about anybody or any thing. If you knew my life story you would know what I mean. You know, Steve, I haven't cried in 20 years but I sure did during those three days and still am. But you know what, Steve? Those are not sad tears but tears of joy. . . .
>
> I just can't believe what has happened to me after my walk. Every thing in my life has changed and for the first time for the good. . . .I just have never felt or been around anything like this; it sure has changed me, something I never believed could happen. But it has, thank God and Kairos for a new start before it was too late. . . .
>
> Steve, I just don't know how to explain what is going on in my life, but I do know this: it's all for the glory of God. . . .I want to grow in Christ, Steve. I lived my old life for 48 years and see what it got me? Now that I have a new life, thank Jesus, I want to live it the right way.

Dean Clark

Dean was one of the toughest cases I've seen when I saw him during Thursday introductions at Kairos #16 at the Michael Unit. He had an impassive face with a toothpick dangling from his lips and his comments were terse. He spent the entire first day (Friday) and Saturday morning with arms folded, uninvolved in table discussions, not making any contact. It wasn't until the letters Saturday afternoon that his heart began to thaw.

> You see, church, God, and religion are all things that were never discussed in my family as a child. Yes, we would say grace before meals during the holidays but never discussed it at any other time . . .
>
> My whole life has changed since my [Kairos] walk. There is not one part of my life that has not improved. My heart is softer; my outlook is totally different. The way I look at myself and others is so different that I can't even start to tell you how that has changed. Nothing is the same as it was before my walk. I do not believe that it is possible for anyone, not even the hardest soul, to go through a weekend and not change. Not the hardest soul!

Ronald Bench

Ronald attended Kairos #17 which was aborted Friday at noon due to a statewide lockdown. He was able to attend Kairos #18 six months later.

> I really appreciate your letter of encouragement, and the love and concern you and the Kairos brothers have shown me in the short time I've known you. I want you to know, Steve, I have never experienced the kind of love you guys showed and shared with me since I have been incarcerated.

Ed White

Ed also attended Kairos #17 and #18 at the Michael Unit.

> I'm very glad to be the first to say that your letter is very special to me. It touched me deeply due to the fact that I can't ever recall any other white male brother in the Lord ever taking the time to write me as their brother in Christ, or in any other name.

These are just some of the examples of letters I have received from transformed Christians. Each man, in his own way, is a miracle of the unmatched power of Jesus Christ to transform a human life.

13

> I've read and heard that witnessing the birth of a baby is a miracle. Let me assure you another miracle is witnessing the birth of a Christian in a 72-hour period, especially the transformation of some of the toughest, roughest, and meanest convicts in a maximum-security prison. There is nothing more fulfilling than bringing someone to Christ and nothing more thrilling on the face of this earth than witnessing the unmatched power of Jesus Christ's love overpowering Satan's hate in arguably the most hardened human beings in the harshest of environments.
>
> Steve Kincheloe

MIRACLES IN MAXIMUM-SECURITY

Christ told the disciples that they would go on and do greater things than He did after Jesus ascended into heaven. I've often wondered what Christ meant by that statement. How could regular human beings top or even match any of the amazing miracles that Jesus performed in three short years? During my time with Kairos Prison Ministry it began to dawn on me that perhaps Christ meant that we would reach far more people for Him than He did while He was with us 2,000 years ago. Jesus promised and delivered the Holy Spirit that we might be used as His hands and feet in reaching new people for Christ, far more people than Jesus could reach directly during his earthly ministry. Christ has blessed us by allowing us to be co-workers with him in participating in the Christian birthing process. In this chapter I will describe some miraculous transformations I have witnessed or have knowledge of through interviews with my teammates.

Jim Huddleston

When Jim was arrested he was half way between his house and vehicle without any weapons, one of the few times during the preceding several years that he did not have any weapons on his person. Jim had some guns in his vehicle and 17 assault rifles and 23 handguns in his house with 57,000 rounds of ammunition. Huddleston, a 9-year Army veteran, was very proficient in the use of guns, being able to take out a target the size of a silver dollar 75 yards away in a heartbeat. Huddleston reported that four officers approached him from the front and two from the rear. He indicated that had he had his usual gun or two on his person he could have killed at least two officers before probably being killed himself. It wasn't until years later in the confines of the Michael Unit that he realized it was God's providential timing that he was caught between his house and vehicle with no weapons when he was arrested, a serendipitous circumstance engineered by God.

Jim attended Kairos #7 at the Michael Unit in the autumn of 1995. He was considered one of the toughest men in the 3,300-man maximum-security institution. Prior to his incarceration, Jim cared about one thing and one thing only - himself. His only interest in dealing with other people was to manipulate them into doing things for him. His spiritual state when he arrived at Kairos was one of defiance and skepticism. He heard about Kairos' cookies and meals and figured he could put up with anything to enjoy some good food for three days. He vowed not to show any emotion, to limit his participation. Although the Kairos agape love was being showered on him beginning Thursday afternoon and evening and all day Friday, there were no chinks in the armor through Saturday morning. Then after lunch on Saturday, chapel time was held and Father Jim Norwood, an Episcopalian priest, took over. Norwood, who was in his late 60s at the time with a gentle demeanor, opened with a prayer and meditation and carefully began weaving a tale of personal tragedy that had about 100 men (including the 42 pilgrims, approximately 35 inside team members and 25 or so stewards) sitting in rapt attention. Kairos is about becoming vulnerable. First the free-world team members, who are selected to deliver talks and meditations, share some personal pain, hardship, struggle or tragedy.

By becoming vulnerable ourselves we give the prisoners permission to become vulnerable to one another in their table families.

Father Norwood, with his kind face and warm gaze, slowly shared the painful episode of a family tragedy.

> On a dreary December day, ten days before Christmas, some 12 years ago, our youngest daughter, Kimberly, then seven years of age, listened while older members of the family talked about taking some special floral decorations to the grave of her sister, Kathleen. Kimberly, who always had something to add to every conversation said, "Let's make a wreath ourselves, together, and put Kathleen's name on it. After all, it's Christmas." [Her sister, Kathleen, our 18-year-old daughter, had been tragically killed on Thanksgiving night three weeks before].
>
> Two days before Christmas we gathered all our immediate family members together and all twelve of us piled into the 12-passenger van after loading a beautiful family-made wreath, emblazoned with glitter-covered words, "Merry Christmas, Kathleen."
>
> As we stood, encircling the recently covered grave, the cold wind blistered our necks and frosted our noses. A quiet settled on the faces of all present. *We were acknowledging the reality of the sadness we were experiencing and the loss we felt.* Kathleen had been a member of the family since she was six years old when she came to us as an abandoned child. She had grown up with her brothers and little sister. Here was our daughter, barely 18, who had many serious problems in her short lifetime, who had been living successfully on her own since she left our home. She had called Thanksgiving Day and spoke with each member of the family because she was working and she made arrangements to have her thanksgiving the

> following Sunday. *Now she was dead - a victim of a hit-and-run driver.*
>
> We stood at her graveside two days before Christmas, silently and in tears, locked in our grief. Having just placed a large, home-made Christmas wreath on her grave, each person was deep in their own thoughts and prayers, each waiting for the other to speak. And Kimberly, our 7-year-old, with tears in her eyes, broke the silence, saying, "Merry Christmas, Kathleen. I know you are with Jesus and God now. And He is here with us too . . . *because this is Jesus' birthday.*" These were the words of pure faith from the heart of a child.
>
> After tears by everyone, we all began to say our good-byes to a loved one. In the beginning we were angry with the person responsible for this loss. Yes, we were angry with God also. But Kimberly's reminder, that we know that Kathleen is with God who gave her to us in the beginning, helped our grief. Kathleen brought to us all that she had. And knowing that she is with the Father and Jesus, His Son, changed some of our grief and sadness into joy. Kathleen had received God's sanctifying grace and has received His promise to be with Him. It was through the prayerful loving presence of many of God's people that supported us during this difficult time.

When Father Norwood finished, there wasn't a dry eye in the chapel. The men filed silently out of the room into the conference room. Jim Huddleston, deeply moved by Norwood's testimony, stopped and asked Jim what prompted him to share such a painful story. Father Norwood replied, "Because you guys are a tough nut to crack." There were indeed some real tough customers on Kairos #7 and Father Norwood deployed the heavy artillery to soften hearts.

When the men entered the conference room, the tables had been cleared of the cookies, notepads, songbooks, pencils, cups, and posters. The only items sitting on the table were large grocery bags at each pilgrim's seat and some kleenex boxes. Most of the Kairos pilgrims know about the cookies and meals; indeed, that is why many of the men sign up for Kairos. But nobody knows about the letters stuffed in those grocery bags and most of the men are puzzled why the kleenex boxes are strategically placed around the table. The team members assigned to each table briefly sit down and then excuse themselves to go back to the chapel; the only exception are team members who stay behind to assist the men who can't read English. While the men are reading their letters, the team members begin softly serenading the men with God's love songs on the other side of the tarp partitioning the conference room from the chapel. Soon the sound of letters being opened and weeping and stifled sobs fill the gym.

Jim's first four letters were from young children, colorfully illustrated as only young kids can do with simple, blunt messages of God's love. Jim said he had to quit reading after the first four children's letters because he couldn't see anymore - the tears were too thick. Later that afternoon, after being softened for the first time by Father Norwood's tragic story and melted by the children's letters, Jim Huddleston accepted Christ as his Lord and Savior. Two days later, on Monday, the day after the Kairos weekend had ended, Jim received a letter postmarked on Saturday, the day he had accepted Christ into his life. The letter was from his mother, seeking forgiveness for abandoning him for the previous 6½ years. What is amazing is that Jim had received no mail during the previous 6½ years and his mother had no idea Jim was participating in the Kairos weekend; there had been no contact between Jim and his mother or any other relative during that interval. Was this an interesting coincidence? I don't think so. It was a circumstance engineered by God with impeccable timing. Jim Huddleston still resides at the Michael Unit and he remains a transformed man, growing in the stature of Christ.

Skeeter Anderson and Raymond Garrison

It was Thursday evening during introductions on the Kairos #9 weekend at the Michael Unit in the autumn of 1996, when 30-year veteran cop Skeeter Anderson rose to introduce himself: "Sergeant, Fort Worth Police Department." A palpable gasp could be heard across the gym as the ramifications of a police officer being on the Kairos team sunk in. Police officers and prosecuting attorneys are not real popular in prisons. Some team members compared Skeeter's vulnerability to that of a large balloon being inflated on a windy day in a cactus patch.

Skeeter resisted serving on a Kairos team for some time, fearing a confrontation with any of the men he had arrested over the years. He eventually agreed to serve on the Kairos #9 weekend and felt relieved when he pored over the list of pilgrims and failed to recognize any names. However, on Friday, a teammate of Skeeter's mentioned there was an inmate who wanted to talk to him; Skeeter's heart skipped a beat at the thought of meeting someone he had arrested, his mind racing on who it might be. The team member introduced Skeeter to Raymond Garrison and Raymond reminded Skeeter that he was his arresting officer 18 years earlier. Indeed, Skeeter's arrest was the cause of Raymond's present incarceration. The atmosphere was tense initially with Raymond remembering how Skeeter was a "cowboy" cop back in those days, roughing him up pretty good when he was arrested. However, as the weekend unfolded with more and more of God's love being poured out on the men, Skeeter and Raymond reached an understanding about the circumstances that brought them together. Both men had changed since their lives intersected nearly two decades earlier. During the closing ceremony on Sunday afternoon, Raymond Garrison calmly walked to the podium. He motioned for Skeeter Anderson to join him. Skeeter made his way to the front of the gym, standing alongside Raymond. Then Raymond announced to the gym packed with about 400 people that Skeeter was his arresting officer, and that for 18 years he had hated this man, blaming him for being incarcerated. Raymond then remarked that he no longer blamed Skeeter but himself for making some poor choices which led to his arrest and subsequent imprisonment. Then Raymond turned to Skeeter and the two men embraced each other, reconciling after 18 years of hatred. The crowd erupted in cheers, rising to their feet in a prolonged, thunderous ovation at the thrilling scene of God's amazing grace melting the stone heart of Raymond Garrison.

On Kairos #10, six months later, Skeeter Anderson served on his second Kairos team, this time being assigned the *Lifelines* talk on Sunday. Skeeter shared some of the highlights of his life, both secular and spiritual, as well as his struggles and tragedies. Knowing Skeeter's occupation as a police officer, the audience was particularly riveted to his testimony. Skeeter shared about his concern coming to prison, facing his fear of spending time with men who had been on the opposite side of the law. Skeeter said he was especially apprehensive about meeting anybody he had arrested and how shocked he was when he met Raymond Garrison on Kairos #9. Then Skeeter, carefully choosing his words, concluded: "The person I arrested 18 years ago, Raymond Garrison, has been behind this curtain in the chapel praying for me while I gave this talk." There was stunned silence in the room as Skeeter departed the podium; residents looked at each other in astonishment as the power of God's reconciling love sunk in.

David Kaseman, Observing Rector slated for the rectorship of Kairos #11 in the autumn of 1997, strode to the podium. He told those in the conference room:

> There is more to this story than what you have just heard about Skeeter and Raymond. Raymond was not supposed to be here. You're new to Kairos and don't know, but the stewards who have been serving you are selected from previous Kairos participants. To be eligible you must have regularly attended all of the last six months of Kairos meetings plus not have had any major cases written against you. The list of those eligible is cut apart and each name is put in a capsule for a blind drawing. Twenty-five names were chosen out of over 50 eligible. Just before we started on Thursday one person had to drop out serving as a steward. The Chaplain had another blind drawing for one name. Whose name do you think was drawn? You are correct! Raymond Garrison was meant to be here to pray for his friend Skeeter Anderson.

Roberto Ramirez

Roberto Ramirez attended Kairos #14 in the spring of 1999 at the Michael Unit. Nothing remarkable stood out about this man until he took the podium during the closing ceremony on Sunday afternoon. Roberto dropped a bombshell when he revealed the power of the Kairos cookies in healing a fractured relationship the previous night.

On Saturday night of Kairos before the residents are dismissed, the participants are given three bags of a dozen cookies each following the last meditation on forgiveness. One bag is for themselves, another bag is for their friends, and the third bag is for their worst or one of their worst enemies in the prison. Roberto told about how he gave his bag to an intermediary to deliver to a man who lived in another part of the unit, a man who had bullied him for a considerable length of time. About an hour later, the intermediary returned with a vitriolic, vituperative and venomous note, scathing in its denunciation of Roberto and God's love, cursing Roberto and the cookies and everything they stood for. Another hour passed, and a man came to Roberto's pod, informing him that so-and-so was outside waiting for him. With a sick, nervous feeling in the pit of his stomach, Roberto prepared himself to fight the man as he headed out to the yard. When Roberto arrived, the man immediately apologized for writing the hateful note, telling Roberto that it was a mistake and that it was really a nice thing he had done for him. The men exchanged a few words and then both got down on their knees, praying together. A broken relationship transformed into a friendship - all because of a dozen homemade cookies.

Dean Clark

Since 1996 I have run two marathons for the Leukemia and Lymphoma Society's Team-in-Training program in honor of two little girls afflicted with acute lymphocytic leukemia. I shared my quest in training for and completing a marathon in 3-year-old Elizabeth Collins' honor with the men that I share God's love with. Here is the letter I sent to my Kairos brothers behind bars:

> The ultimate goal of any marathoner is to finish. But this goal pales in comparison to that of Honored Patients and their families; their goal is to finish the race with their health restored. Grateful that we train and run in their honor, they cheer our heroism. They are thankful for the financial donors who unselfishly give and the scientists and doctors who toil in the trenches to solve this mystery. They seek the finisher's glow, to persevere through the abyss from doubt and despair to hope and triumph, as we do during those seemingly interminable miles from 20 to 26.2, and somehow emerge victoriously. We have an option whether to enter the marathon and train five months in preparation. The Honored Patients and their families don't have an option. Their race arrives as an unwanted, uninvited, unexpected, unfair, and nightmarish intrusion. They have doctors and nurses but they have few coaches and no set training manual. The doctors rarely suggest a day off from training. Most of us will never truly understand the depth of their feelings. As rigorous and demanding as the marathon is, it is but a foothill compared to the Mt. Everest that Honored Patients and their families scale. We can, however, through Team In Training (TNT), share a small part of our lives with those locked in a struggle against an insidious foe. We hope and pray that the Honored Patients and their families can someday experience the light, and the peace, and the joy that will be theirs when they cross the finish line and the struggle ends.
>
> Steve Kincheloe, TNT Alumni Marathoner

Dear Friend:

Three-year-old Elizabeth Collins loves to play with her friends. She loves her gymnastics class and she is fond of watching Disney movies, especially *Tarzan.* Elizabeth's life changed in August 1999 when, at age two, she was diagnosed with acute lymphocytic leukemia. Most children when they are diagnosed with leukemia spend 4-5 days in the hospital; Elizabeth spent five weeks at Children's Medical Center in Dallas. The leukemia was found in her brain. Elizabeth endures bone-marrow aspirations and blood transfusions. She receives chemotherapy through painful spinal taps, orally, and via a four-hour drip through a needle inserted in a quarter-size port under her skin near her rib cage that goes directly into her heart muscle. She attends school when she can and loves to tell jokes. She is outgoing and loves to talk to her grandparents on the phone. During the past eight months, her favorite food has been Chik-fil-A kids meals. Whenever she takes steroids, she wants Chik-fil-A for breakfast, lunch, and dinner. She remains positive and loves the friends she has made at Children's Medical Center. *Leukemia is the number one disease killer of children, ages 1-14.* In 1960, the survival rate for the most common form of childhood leukemia, acute lymphocytic leukemia (ALL), was an appalling 4%. Today, 80% of children with ALL can be cured, and 40% of adults will achieve long-term survival. Every 10 minutes in the United States, a child or adult dies of leukemia or a related cancer: lymphoma, multiple myeloma or Hodgkin's disease. Leukemia strikes 10 times as many adults as children. More than half of all cases of leukemia occur in persons over 60. Legendary Dallas Cowboys Coach Tom Landry succumbed earlier this year to leukemia. We can be grateful for the progress during the past four decades but we can't rest until leukemia is conquered.

I have set a personal goal to raise a minimum of $3,000 for the Leukemia Society and to train, run, and complete the 25th running of the Marine Corps

Marathon (26 miles, 385 yards) on October 22, 2000 in Washington, D.C. *This marathon and all the training preceding it is dedicated to Elizabeth Collins.* She endures pain, bears hardship, and suffers from the deleterious side effects of her treatments. Yet, this courageous little girl refuses to yield to this powerful adversary. I now wear a patient-type bracelet around my right wrist with the inscription *Team In Training: In Honor of Elizabeth Collins* as a reminder of my commitment to her, to the Leukemia Society, and to all cancer patients.

In the next several months, I will mentally and physically challenge myself to run hundreds of miles in all kinds of weather conditions in preparation for this event. You can share in this celebration of human spirit, physical effort, and mental tenacity. Not everybody has the desire or ability to run a marathon, but most of us have a desire to help. Your donation, which is tax deductible, will make you a part of a very special team. Please make your check payable to the **LEUKEMIA SOCIETY of AMERICA** and return it to me in the enclosed envelope. Many employers have Matching Gift programs that can augment your contribution. Your sponsorship is greatly appreciated. *Please join me for the race of a lifetime, the race to save someone's life.* Please remember Elizabeth Collins in your prayers. Now as the poet Robert Frost wrote: *But I have promises to keep, and miles to go before I sleep . . .*

Sincerely,

Steve Kincheloe

One of the men at the Michael Unit, Dean Clark, was inspired to form a team of about ten inmates to make several gifts for Elizabeth. These gifts included a portrait of Elizabeth (there are very good artists in prison), a small wooden rocking chair with a smiling bear face, a small animal rocking chair marked "Lil Liz," a cedar book stand with a cedar-carved Bible marked 2 Corinthians 12:9 [But he said to me, *"My grace is sufficient for you, for my power is made perfect in weakness."* Therefore I will boast all the more gladly about my weaknesses so that Christ's power may rest on me], a cedar jewelry box marked "Elizabeth," a wooden cross, a wooden frog toy, a leather key chain, a leather book mark, and a beautifully illustrated card designed by one of the men and signed by several men from the Michael Unit. Another man, Roger Olson, in one of Texas' oldest prisons (Eastham) and a guy I have never met, found out about my quest from some Kairos brothers at Eastham who had been transferred from the Michael Unit. Olson was inspired to form another squad of inmates who made the following gifts for Elizabeth: leather butterfly hair clasp, wooden piggy bank, clown doll, leather purse, two necklaces, cat doll, bead-and-feather key chain, and a small wooden bear.

What is particularly remarkable is the transformation of Dean Clark. As soon as I spotted Dean at the beginning of the 16th Kairos weekend in April 2000, I knew immediately he was one of the toughest cases I had seen. He is burly with a shaved head. Dean showed no emotion with a stern face, and his trademark was a wooden toothpick dangling from his lips. Joe Adams, table leader at Dean's table, told me when Dean first sat down on Friday morning of the 4-day Kairos weekend he shoved the chairs away from his on both sides because he didn't want anyone sitting too close to him. He failed to participate in any table discussions, showed no emotion, and spent much of the time with his arms folded defiantly across his chest. This man was like a hand grenade with the pin pulled. During a Kairos weekend, as God's love is poured out on these men in so many ways, the walls come tumbling down and prisoners and free-world brothers actually begin to exchange hugs, a remarkable happening in the hostile and volatile environment of a maximum-security prison where no one shows any emotion or certainly no affection such as a hug or an arm wrapped around another's shoulders, actions that normally would instigate violence or be construed as weakness. During the last half of Friday and for much of Saturday during the singing of contemporary Christian songs, when an Hispanic prisoner on one side of Dean attempted a few times to gently put his arm around his shoulder, Dean shoved his hand away and eventually threatened the man.

Then an amazing thing happened on Saturday afternoon. Dean and the other 41 prisoners participating in the Kairos weekend received their handwritten letters. Of all the agape love that these men are bombarded with during a Kairos weekend, the letters are the most powerful, especially those from little children. After this special time, Joe Adams' table family went into the chapel to pray together. And for the first time that weekend, Dean Sterling opened up. He said: "Guys, all my life when I tried to get close to someone I got hurt badly. If I make this commitment to Christ, will you stand by me?" Of course, the men said yes and the guys at Joe's table were ecstatic. Our approximate 60-person team had prayed for Michael the night before back at our base church, hoping that the walls upon walls around his hardened heart would melt away. Joe's table family returned to the conference room and for the first time formed a complete 9-man circle during the next Kairos song, connected by arms wrapped around each other's shoulders. Joe said Dean was staring straight at the floor during the song, never looking up. This puzzled Joe, until Joe saw the tears flowing down Dean's cheeks and he knew Dean didn't want anyone seeing him crying. I was told later by a man who knew Dean prior to that weekend that he was an in-your-face type of guy, a man who was not afraid of confrontations.

Dean was released in June 2001 and he is on fire for Christ.

When my 12-year-old son, Oscar, and I delivered the gifts to Elizabeth and her family, we were the ones richly blessed. Dean and his friends toiled in obscurity and Oscar and I reaped the joy of seeing Elizabeth and her family's reaction. Elizabeth and her family were overwhelmed by the gifts. The joy on little Elizabeth's face reminded me of the joy that a small child has on Christmas morning. She even emitted a giggle when she recognized the likeness of herself in the beautiful portrait. She was more animated, excited, and talkative than I had ever seen before.

Here are excerpts from some of Dean's letters:

August 10, 2000

Steve, God is great! You are being blessed in a way that you'll never know! I can't hold back the tears as I write because of the love God has shown through these men here at the "Trustee Camp." When you see the love coming from the gifts for baby Elizabeth and her parents along with a gift from me to you, you will see the love that has been given to us in our [Kairos] weekend given back to you. I have been praying over the projects, each one by one. I pray that this will be overwhelming in spirit that will tear down a world of disbelief. I can almost see the tears in your eyes, her parents' eyes and my heart when this happens . . . I do wish it was more but . . . we also have a card made from a guy here also! We are all going to write a few words in it. I can't wait to give this stuff to you! Bob Stanton [Kairos volunteer and a volunteer chaplain at the Michael Unit] is trying to get this approved by the chaplain and warden so that's where we're at now! I'll keep you posted. Steve, this has given me a new outlook on life. It's great to give instead of take! I feel great about this!

August 19, 2000

I organized this to maybe give a small percentage of what my experience was on my Kairos weekend. Most of the guys who helped me do this are members of Kairos. I told them to close their eyes and remember their weekend. I told them to remember the feelings of agape [unconditional] love. It's funny; they were all smiling. I knew at that one special moment, I, along with God, had then committed in helping give to Elizabeth's family. It is time to give back to the world that we are all destroying . . . We are all praying for you and Baby Elizabeth!

October 31, 2000

I've written a few other letters and saved yours for last because this is very hard for me! It's hard because of the tears that will be dropping on this paper from the emotions that I can't hold back . . . You said it was like giving her an early Christmas. You don't know how many men here just received the BEST Christmas gift of all time [notwithstanding God's gift to us!]. Not only the men who helped but the men, the guards and staff that we showed your letter and pictures to. We have seen more tears in men's and women's eyes over this than you could believe!

Steve, you have let us receive such a beautiful blessing, by helping us pull this off! We gave from the heart and we received to the heart! If I never receive another blessing from God in my life, I will be happy because of this little girl and her family. I will be content. This has been the biggest blessing of blessings!

Please pass along my joy of tears to her parents. When you told us that she laughed when she saw her picture, that was the big one! Also, her talking more than usual. Please let her parents know that I thank them from the deepest part of my heart for trusting us and letting us do the work of God so freely! Isn't God beautiful!

Your brother in Christ, Dean

Steven Toscanini

Steven remains one of my favorite examples of Christ's unmatched power. He sent two letters to his Kairos brothers and sisters and published an article entitled "A Mafia Gangster v. Jesus Christ" documenting his remarkable transformation. I synthesized his letters and article and edited them below:

My name is Steven Toscanini and I am writing to express my feelings to you. It is my hope and prayer that some part of what I express to you will encourage you to continue in the Kairos Prison Ministry.

Since I attended the Kairos #9 weekend at the Michael Unit from October 31 through November 3, 1996, I have sat for many long hours contemplating how to compile a letter expressing my deep, heartfelt appreciation to all the volunteers who were in attendance on the inside team and those volunteers who were on the outside team preparing the delicious food and the fabulous homemade cookies. But in contemplating on what to share with you I soon found myself at a loss for words; simple words could never express my appreciation for all you have given me. And even if I sat for many more long hours I would still be at a loss for words. Actually, and in all reality, I don't think there are enough words in the English language or any other language to express my sincere thanks for what you have bestowed upon me. Because, you see, by all your untiring work, diligence, and dedication to the Kairos Prison Ministry, you have given me the opportunity to have another chance at life, a new beginning.

I guess one way to express my thanksgiving would be to share with you my past life; then, and only then, could you ever imagine or grasp the extent of my appreciation to you for giving me another chance at life.

Let me tell you first of all that during my life with one of the largest Sicilian Mafia organized crime families, I became one of the devil's best advocates and went on to be one of the family's best mechanics, who I may add was trusted and even feared by them. To help you better understand what led up to my involvement with organized crime, I think I should take you back to the very beginning, back to where I was born to a poverty-stricken family in Texas. Texas is where I was born but when I was two years old, my Mom, being very Italian, wanted to go back to her family in New York, so my Dad said okay and we moved.

My Mom (Giulini) was born and raised in Manhattan and after we moved, my Dad went to work in a huge furniture factory and soon we were all doing pretty good. When I was growing up I, of course, had to join one of the neighborhood gangs. Fighting meant a way of life if you live in lower Manhattan, believe me. I have a lot of scars to prove how many times I was beaten up and stabbed. So while growing up, I began to notice how all the big Cadillac-driving Italian men had plenty of money, beautiful blondes, and the best suits. Then I began to notice the rich kids had the best bikes, tennis shoes, and other things. I was envious of rich people and their fancy cars and wondered how they could have so much and my family and other families have so little. I vowed that someday I would live like the wealthy people did.

Around this time the gangster movies were the rage so people like Al Capone, Machine Gun Kelly, Baby Face Nelson, Dillinger, and Bonnie and Clyde became my heroes and I idolized them. I decided I would become a well-known gangster; I'd have all the money, pretty girls, and all the things they had.

When I was about 17 my Dad said we were moving back to Texas. I refused because I had already begun to run numbers for a crime family and was making pretty good money. I would give Mom most of the money to buy her things that she used to help the other Italian families who didn't have much. My Dad said I didn't have any choice - I had to move back to Texas.

I ran away from home and hid at my best friend's house. For five years my family had no idea where I was and I was coming up in the family my best friend worked for. Then I received a phone call from my Aunt Margaret Rosa, informing me that my Mom was sick in Texas and she needed me to come home. My Mom never made it and I helped bury her. This hurt so bad I became twice as heartless; I cared for nothing or no one, and had no type of emotions.

I grew up hard, cold, and mean as they come. I'd do anything for money. I got away with so many violent crimes that I should be in the *Guinness Book of World Records*. Soon I had the money, pretty girls and enough booze to float a battleship. In traveling around the country, I stopped in Sun City, Arizona and leased an apartment, trying to fit in with the rich people. I started doing small odd jobs for a man who belonged to the Italian Mafia. I did such a good job he told me if I didn't mess up he would get me into the Family. So I then set out to be a real-life gangster, just like in the movies. I dedicated myself - heart, mind, body, and soul. By the time I was 18 years old I was inducted into the most powerful Sicilian Mafia organized crime families in the world and took the "code of silence."

Before long I was traveling around the United States. My reputation within the Family grew to where they trusted me to do any job there was. During the over 20 years I spent with them I gained the reputation of being one of the best of an elite group of Mechanics. Now let me tell you what a Mechanic in the Mafia exactly is. Well, they are just like your car mechanics, they can fix any problem the family may have. So I was a trained hit man. Yes, I killed many people. I committed about every crime known to man, and then some, including drugs; extortion;

labor racketeering; kidnaping; prostitution; illegal gambling; counterfeiting money, stocks and bonds; insurance fraud; and countless other crimes. I even became feared by those within the Family. I have traveled to many foreign countries on assignment from the Family or affiliated families, leaving the countries with caskets being lowered into the ground.

I became a one-man piece of terror that would do any job, do it well, and return home a winner. And all the time I was doing these crimes I didn't even realize I was turning to stone. Nothing bothered me because I had forgotten how to care; no love existed in my heart. I had no feelings, just plain nothing was in my heart. I could take the life of a man and sit down at a table while he bled to death and eat dinner. I have seen whole families burn to death in their homes while I sat in a car making sure no one got out of the house. I never thought a thing about it. I would see this, go to a bar, have a drink, call the Family and tell them the job was done and go home. So as you can see I became a heartless person.

Now you may think that all Mafia bodyguards are big strong, muscle-bound guys, and yes, some are. But the one you had to watch out for was the small guy sitting over in the corner, yes me. All I had on my side was a gun, silencer, and a good strong trigger finger. That made up for the muscles. Plus I had a heart of stone and that was part of my reputation that the Family loved. So I earned their respect. I came up in the ranks of the Family. I could do practically anything and get away with it because of the Mafia's political connections and their money.

Now while building my reputation I had never done drugs. But a girl I was with for about six months turned me onto marijuana which led me to heroin and cocaine. Heroin became everything I lived for. The drugs led me to a prison term, then another one, and finally a third trip to the joint. After the political power, high-paid attorneys, and money got me out after only doing a short term, my Family called me into the main office in Sun City and informed me they no longer wanted me in the Family. I was told as long as I kept my "code of silence," I could go on living. I knew this was a fact because I was one of the enforcers of this "code of silence" and tracked down many a man who broke it and ended their lives. The Family gave me that much respect because of all the work I had done for them.

So here I was back on my own again. I went on with my life of crime. Actually I got worse. Before I had the Family reputation to uphold, now I had nothing to uphold but my own reputation. So I didn't really care anymore. I had just become a shell of a person, not much life existed in me. I was just more or less waiting on death to take me out.

So in knowing this, I thought I would go out in a blaze of glory, have a big shoot-out with the police and end up in the history books as being a ruthless criminal, just like my heroes, Bonnie and Clyde, Machine Gun Kelly, and Dillinger. Well I did go on this blow-out. All it left me with was five bullet holes in me and a life sentence in Texas. Soon I was just an everyday inmate. I still retained my heart of stone and never cared about anything or anyone.

You know for many years I had heard about the man called Jesus, the man who could change my life in the twinkling of an eye, the man who could give me a new and eternal life and that all I had to do was ask for it. And even though I heard these stories I couldn't accept them. While on the Michael Unit I had many occasions to run into many Christian inmates as well as other Christian people. I hated them. I detested them. I criticized them for trying to teach me about Christianity. I considered them as weak people who needed a crutch to lean on instead of facing life as it was. To me they put on a mask and hid behind it. I thought of them as people who had serious mental problems, who needed a psychiatrist instead of God. During these times and all of my entire life, up until recently that is, if a Christian inmate approached me and tried to discuss with me anything related to Christianity, I would instruct him to either get out of my presence or I would use violence to rearrange his way of thinking. And, yes, I readily admit that I did use violence sometimes toward the person trying to witness to me; sometimes hurting them just to prove my point and also to show other inmates how to deal with Christians. This is all very sad but true.

But inmates were not the only ones I took my hostility out on. At this prison unit we have a lot of volunteer chaplains who come into the prison to teach and witness to inmates. They come into the cell blocks and sit at tables in the day rooms. They invite inmates to come talk to them. Occasionally I would come by and a chaplain would be sitting talking to another inmate. The chaplain would glance at me and say, "Hi brother, would you like to join in our conversation?"

I would look him straight in the eye and say, "Take what you've come to offer and stuff it. Besides you got more than enough weak-minded people sitting there with you, listening to your repetitive propaganda. I have already seen and heard you try and get all these other inmates caught up in your web of deceit."

The chaplain would look at me and say, "God bless you, brother."

I'd then walk off, full of hatred for all those sitting there. But then, in the back of my mind, I noticed every time the volunteer chaplain would come back, he would always make it a point to invite me to the table. Yes, him and the other volunteer chaplains were very persistent, but then so was I in my nasty remarks to them. And even a few times, the senior chaplain, who is here daily, would come walking by and say, "Why don't you come to the chapel tonight, brother. We're going to have a very good service."

I'd just simply tell him to go straight to where he preached sinners would go if they didn't repent. He would stop, look at me, and start to say something. I'd quickly respond: "Chaplain, what you are about to say - don't! I don't care anything about you or your God." He would just walk off, shaking his head.

Eventually, while walking around on the yard, I heard of this thing called the "Kairos." So out of curiosity I began to ask questions about it. I remembered a few guys who had attended a Kairos weekend. So I would catch them off by themselves where no one would see me talking to them. I certainly didn't want my old friends seeing me talking to a Christian because I had a reputation to uphold as one who despised Christians. One Kairos guy told me, "Steven, a person like you needs to stay away from Kairos meetings. All you would do is disrupt the whole walk."

I said, "Hey, I hear the food is good, so I'll just go for that if nothing else."

The Kairos person said, "Yea, Steven, go get some food and then leave. That would be a great idea."

So I could tell this person certainly didn't want me attending the meeting. Now this kind of caught me off guard because other Christians would jump at the chance to get me to a meeting. So this definitely piqued my interest.

My old radical friends I hung out with said, "Hey man, you should go up there and hang out with them Christian people for a few days because they bring in some really great home-cooked food and a million homemade cookies. You can do it for three days and you don't gotta be a Christian to go."

Well, I soon forgot that idea because as I said before, I detested all Christian people and no way was I going to spend three days with them no matter how good the food and cookies were.

Then one day, about a month later after having this conversation, I was sitting out in the dorm when the mail came around. The boss hands me a slip of paper from the chaplain's office saying, "Congratulations you have been picked to attend the #9 Kairos Walk." Man, at the time I got so mad I couldn't see straight. I knew someone had put my name in to go to this Kairos thing. So soon I was walking the yard, asking who the punk was that put my name in to attend this Christian meeting. I had already planned to bash his face in. Well, folks, to this day I have never found that person. You know they say God works in mysterious ways. Well, folks, I could be living proof of that.

So here I was with that notice I could attend the Kairos Walk. Now what was I going to do with it? As time went by I did a lot of thinking and thought no one would think any less of me if I just went over for some good food and cookies. I told my old radical friends that all I was going over for was the food. They said, "Yea, Steven, go for it. We wish we were invited and we would go with you." So now that my rebellious radical friends knew I was going and my reputation was going to stay intact, I felt it was okay to go.

Well I got up early in the morning of the Walk and after two or three cups of coffee began questioning myself about why I had gotten it into my mind to do something this silly. And, yes, trying to come up with some ideas to talk myself out of going. I thought to myself that I would have to sit down and listen to some big-winded preacher preach a sermon on fire and brimstone, that I was bound for hell. I thought there are not enough cookies and food in the world to make me sit through something like that. But still there was that statement that Kairos inmate had said that stuck in my mind, that a Kairos Walk was no place for someone like me. This definitely stirred my curiosity and out of this curiosity, I went to the Walk.

I walked over to the gym where the Walk was being held, expecting a lot of people to be sitting around waiting for the preacher to show up. Wow! Was I surprised. When I entered the gym, everyone was smiling and looking happy, talking, and exchanging handshakes and occasional hugs. I didn't see a frown in the entire gym, except the one I was wearing of course. I started right then to back out of the door. Why? Because, hey, this was prison, not a place for all this niceness. This was a house of misery and pain, false hopes, hurt feelings, bitterness, heartbreaks, depression, certainly not what I was seeing. At that moment, a Kairos team member, smiling with a hand extended, said, "Welcome, brother." I started to tell him, "Hey, I ain't your brother," but I stopped myself. Well, folks, that was the first time ever talking to a Christian and not telling them what I thought. He was very friendly and didn't start preaching at me. So I stayed. I was still dumbfounded that this many people were smiling and happy in a prison. No way! Even the inmates were smiling. So I told myself right then and there I was going to figure out why all these people were so happy. This was sure a mystery to me. We spent the rest of the afternoon and evening getting to know one another. They didn't have any food, except cookies, that evening so I told myself I might as well come back the next day. I did take home some of those homemade cookies though. Gosh, they were good.

The next day was a surprise also. Here I found myself sitting at a table called St. Mark with five other inmates and three free-world volunteers. Now let me stop here and say that these men were definitely Christians. Never had I met people like this. I was amazed. They were friendly and were also not trying to preach at me so I thought to myself that I would stay. Soon I found myself surrounded by all types of volunteers, all from different walks of life, different religious backgrounds and denominations and lifestyles. I found this very interesting to find these different kinds of people who had volunteered, with no pay, to come here, and in some way, teach me how to be a Christian.

So during the next couple of days I began to feel differently, something inside me wanted this peace of mind these people had. On the last day of the Walk I got up early and prayed to God, something I had never done. I asked God to take control of my life and to show me how to love again, to teach me how to become a good Christian person like the people I had been around for the last couple of days. Well I expected some great happening, but nothing really happened. So I thought to myself that I had just been too bad of a person to ever just expect God to rush in and take over. Wow, was I ever surprised. Because as I was walking over to the Walk that day I noticed that it was like someone had reached over and took a heavy load off my shoulders. It was as though I was as light as a feather. The feeling I got that day is so very hard to explain. It was though I had just been set free from some terrible nightmare. I could never really explain to you the feeling I got that day. But I can tell you this much: I will never lose it, it just simply feels too great. No one can ever take away from me what God has given me. I would go to my death before I ever thought about giving up what I have now. God died for me to have life and I will die to keep that life.

On Sunday morning of the Walk, one of the volunteers said something that hit me like a ton of bricks. We were talking about taking a chance of living as a Christian, and what would a person have to lose. Well, I thought to myself, "Steven, you've done lost everything you ever had and your whole life as been lived on chance because you've gambled with your life a million times. So why not go for this Christian life." Then another volunteer says, "Could you handle it, Steven?" Well that did it, no one challenges me. So I told myself I would meet this challenge and win.

A couple of days later I knew something was eating my insides up. I was needing something in my life. I felt so alone in the world. I had nothing or no one who cared for me. Then I remembered what the volunteers said, "God loves you and so do we." So at that moment I knew I needed Christ in my life. I went and got a pass and went to the chaplain's office. There, the chaplain and I got down on our knees and I accepted Christ into my heart! And since that day I have had that peace of mind I was searching for. I now have met the challenge and won. I now have

> Christ who is the ruler of my heart. I now know that God loves and cares for me and will never let me down.
>
> And you know I owe all this to you members of the Kairos Ministry. If it had not been for you, I would still be out there in a lost world full of hatred, lust, deceit, greed, and a million other things. I would still be bound for hell this very day if it had not been for all you volunteers. So as you can see, you saved my life by coming here and volunteering your time. Now how can a person, such as myself, thank you enough? I, in all reality, owe each one of you my life. Yes, God died so that I may have life but you are the ones who showed me the way. So never doubt me when I say thank you from the bottom of this new heart you have helped me get for what you have given me. You have showed a once heartless man the way to live a Christian life. So, hey, pat yourself on the back and say to yourself, "Well done. I helped a man know God."

Steven Toscanini, as letters in other sections of this book testify, has been on fire for Christ ever since his Kairos weekend. He has denied himself, risking his own life in one prison, by deliberately staying in the most dangerous part of the unit to witness to young gang leaders. He courageously agreed to testify against a murderer in a killing he witnessed in one unit. A contract was placed on him and he suffered three severe beatings in two prisons because of his unflinching decision to testify. He has been tireless in his devotion to Christ. The same characteristics - commitment, loyalty, discipline, dedication - that propelled him to be one of the best mechanics in the Mafia are now being harvested to win souls for Christ. The incredible transformation of a mechanic in the Mafia to a champion for Christ is truly a miracle.

Kairos #19 at the Michael Unit

On November 15-18, 2001, for the first time in four years we were able to have a full Kairos weekend during the fall at the Michael

Unit. It was 1997 that we held our last full Kairos weekend due to gang fights, murders, or rumored gang hits causing lockdowns at the unit the past three years. We raised a record 5,228 dozen homemade cookies. The 42 candidates were inundated with cookies shortly after entering the gym (along with fresh fruit) on Thursday afternoon and during each of the next three days. They were given at least three bags of a dozen cookies each night before being dismissed and a fourth bag on the third night, designated as "forgiveness cookies" to be delivered to their worst enemy or one of their worst enemies in the prison. One of the participants said, "My Kairos was the most memorable and special time in my life. I know there was God's love in each and every cookie that was baked."

On Sunday, we delivered one dozen cookies to each inmate and officer in the prison. We were informed by a Muslim that we had inadvertently overlooked them because they were observing Ramadan (the month of fasting, although Muslims can eat in the evenings) in an area of the prison that we hadn't reached. The Muslims inquired if we could send them a dozen cookies each. We sent them two dozen cookies each and informed them that the cookies had been prayed over for each person to come to know Jesus. One of those Muslims who received the cookies attended the 20th Kairos weekend six months later. He came in Thursday as a Muslim and left Sunday as a Christian. James Simpson, with his Islamic name crossed out on his name tag, strode to the podium and boldly proclaimed: "Muhammad performed no miracles. Muhammad saved no one."

The deliverance of the cookies to the Muslims reminds me of a prisoner who told me when he attended his Kairos weekend that three of the six prisoners at his table were a Muslim, devil worshiper, and atheist. All three became Christians that weekend.

Two major gang leaders attended the weekend, including Gilberto, head of a Mexican gang. This is a very dangerous gang comprised only of Mexicans and this top leader was considered one of the most dangerous men in the unit at the beginning of the weekend. On Thursday afternoon about 102 men (42 pilgrims, 27 stewards - prisoners who have attended previous Kairos weekends that serve the pilgrims during the weekend - and 33 free-world team members on the inside team) in the gym introduced themselves. Gilberto, arms folded defiantly across his chest with a dark, brooding face and stone-cold heart, refused to introduce himself, simply passing the microphone to the next person. This was the first time I had ever seen this happen. Gilberto did not participate Friday, claiming that he was illiterate. However, by Friday evening he was beginning to crack, telling an Hispanic friend of mine in the prison: "I can't believe that I've held back this long." Looking at the ceiling, he then remarked: "Forgive me." On Saturday, Gilberto was turning to the correct pages in the songbook, eventually singing along. On Saturday afternoon the men were given their letters, arguably the most powerful weapon we unleash on these men. Each man received 75 handwritten letters and Gilberto melted. By the end of Saturday, Gilberto was smiling and putting his arms around the men at his table.

On Sunday afternoon at the closing ceremony he was one of the last men to stride to the podium, amid thunderous applause from the approximately 300 people in attendance. He spoke Spanish to his former gang members in the audience, asking them to join him in promoting peace in the prison. This was a startling revelation since these very same gangs were instrumental in canceling Kairos weekends for years. Indeed, Kairos #13, #15, and #17 at the Michael Unit were aborted at inception or before completion because of the actions of these gangs. Gilberto told the audience that he was walking away from his gang, throwing away his gloves, and accepting Christ. This is no light decision as you can be killed for leaving a gang in prison even if it is to become a Christian.

Gilberto showed up at our reunion two weeks later, giving everyone a hug. He informed us that he was not just a gang leader at the Michael Unit. He was the head of several gangs in various prisons, earning the title "El General." Gilberto told us how, one year earlier, one of his captains approached him and said he could no longer be in the gang because he had accepted Jesus as his savior. Several of Gilberto's captains wanted to execute this new Christian. However, Gilberto said he admired this man for his integrity and courage. Gilberto decided to spare this man's life. Gilberto told his gang leaders: "Jesus Christ has not done anything bad to us and we have nothing against this Jesus Christ. If this brother's religion is real, he will be okay. If not, he will return to us. So, leave him alone."

Over time, Gilberto saw such a transformation in his former captain that he decided to attend Kairos. As the Kairos weekend concluded, Gilberto gave his heart to Christ because he desired the transformation experienced by his former captain and the other men during the weekend. Gilberto said, "When I gave my heart to Jesus, I felt such a heavy weight leave my shoulders and mind. Now I want to have the integrity to stand in front of all my men and show them that Jesus Christ can change all of their hearts."

Another man's birthday fell on the first day in the unit and the rector announced, after our introductions, for the candidate and his free-world sponsor to go to the center of the gym. The rector announced it was Charlie Hobb's birthday and we all sang "Happy Birthday" to Charlie. He told us later that he was nervous when the rector announced it was his birthday because if they find out in prison that it is your birthday you get beat up. Charlie told us later that he almost cried during the singing of "Happy Birthday" but he saved his tears for the letters!

One man was overwhelmed with the letters since he had received only four letters in 24 years, and no letters or visits in the past nine years. Numerous inmates broke down in tears as they read their letters, experiencing God's love through total strangers. One especially moving scene involved a Spanish-speaking inmate who didn't understand English. As he held a letter, tears were streaming down his face. A bi-lingual volunteer offered assistance and discovered that the man was holding his letter upside down! He didn't understand the letter but he felt so much love that it moved him to tears.

Many men remarked that it had been years since they had eaten a lettuce and tomato salad or fried catfish. Many of the men took the placemats drawn by little children back to their tables and later to their cells at night. One man reportedly went back to his cell and threw away all his pornographic material.

One man said he swore there was tear gas in his letters. He covered his face as the tears streamed down his cheeks, only to discover that other men were crying too, tears of joy as the men began to understand that God loves them and people still care for them.

Of the 42 men in attendance, two were former cellmates that did not get along. At a follow-up Kairos meeting two weeks later, Terry Tran, a Vietnamese of mixed marriage, confessed that he had grown weary of his former cellie (cellmate), Samuel Johnson, a large African-American man, because of his zealousness for the Lord. He got tired of his preaching, reading the Bible, lecturing him, and listening to Christian radio stations. One day Samuel's radio broke down and he asked Tran if he could fix it. And Tran replied, "Sure! I can fix your radio." After Samuel left, Tran took the radio apart and poured water into the radio. To his surprise, the radio still worked and then he knew that God was with Samuel! He then rewired the transformer causing the box to get real hot. When Samuel returned, Tran told him that his radio was indeed broken and that he could not fix it.

Later on, Tran told Samuel that there was a man who was out to get him. Samuel asked Tran who it was and Tran said, "I don't know but this man wants to harm you." Samuel asked Tran what he should do and Tran responded, "Get your stuff packed and move to another building." So Samuel got permission and moved. Well, after sharing this in our small group at the follow-up meeting, Tran got up and told everyone in the gym about what he had done to Samuel and that he was sorry and wanted to ask for Samuel's forgiveness. Then, these two men embraced. Later Samuel told me he was happy because he had been praying for Tran for quite some time!

Frank Wallace shared that when he went to work at the machine shop after the Kairos weekend a man gave him a hard time, accusing him of only going to Kairos for the food and cookies. The man continued to ridicule Frank and Frank got so upset with him that he thought about hitting him over the head with a wrench but thought better of it when he contemplated what Christ would do under the same circumstances. Later Frank apologized to the man for getting mad at him, explaining to him that he got more than physical food from the Kairos weekend, but spiritual food that will last. The man apologized for giving Frank a hard time. Frank went back to his work. Out of the corner of his eye he could see the other man glancing at him periodically. Then he noticed the man walking over to him and he thought, "Oh boy this guy is up to something." But instead the man said, "Frank, what's it take to get into Kairos?"

The stories cited in this chapter are a microcosm of what happens in Kairos prisons all over the United States and several foreign countries.

As impressive as all the evidence is for Christ being the Truth, from the incredible statistical odds of him fulfilling over a hundred prophecies to the incomparable miracles he performed 2,000 years ago, the witnessing first hand of miraculous transformations of men, who, in many cases, come from broken and impoverished homes, who have been abandoned or abused in one form or another, who have committed some of the most horrible crimes, who reside in the worst pit with the hardest of hearts, is the most compelling reason why I know Christ is the Truth. Witnessing miracles does something to your faith.

APPENDIX

Several experts in criminology, prison work, former prisoners, and pastors have been moved by their own experience with Kairos. Listed below are some testimonies from men impacted by the Kairos experience.

Kairos Testimonies

- The Rt. Rev. Furman C. Stough, then Episcopal Bishop of Alabama, writes after serving on the team for that state's first Kairos weekend: *I have never seen the Gospel impact a group of people with such power and so quickly in such a short period of time. I do not think that I have ever laughed as much or cried as much or prayed as much as I did during those four days. What we saw in these 42 inmates and in ourselves as well, was the real person that God made, slowly beginning to emerge from behind all kinds of barriers erected over the years. Real human beings, your brothers and mine, beginning to once again trust God and to trust themselves to love once again.*

- The late Most Rev. Joseph G. Vath, Roman Catholic Bishop in Birmingham, writes after serving on a Kairos team: *I guess the very impressive sight of Roman Catholics, Baptists, Episcopalians, Methodists, Lutherans, and other denominations forming a team to give Christian witness to prisoners in the environment of their own prison is bound to move even those of little faith...what a transformed world this could be if everyone could share the love of Christ, the love of his fellow man, the willingness to serve community, and the deep and abiding sense of prayer in unity that this weekend brought. At the closing moments of our weekend, the inmates were allowed to express what was in their hearts and the prison chaplain, who has been with these men for the time of their incarceration, was moved to tears at the profound effect upon these men as a result of the Kairos weekend.*

- Chaplain Eldon Cornett, Supervising Chaplain of Union Correctional Institution, Raiford, Florida, where Florida's death row is and where Kairos began in 1976: *Kairos is the most effective program for prisoners ever held in this institution.*

- Thomas F. Keohane, Warden of Federal Correctional Institution, Miami, during the first three years of Kairos in that prison: *Kairos is the best and most spiritually rewarding activity I have seen in my 24 years as a prison worker.*

- Kenneth D. McKellar, Deputy Regional Administrator, South Carolina Department of Corrections: *Kairos is one of the most powerful prison ministries I have ever seen.*

- John Wright, a correctional officer in a maximum-security prison where inmates rioted: *There's no doubt about it*, says Wright, who was trapped in the prison as the riot exploded, *If it hadn't been for the influence of Kairos in this prison, I'd be a dead man now. Those guys literally saved my life.*

- William C. Nagel, author of *The New Red Barn: A Critical Look at the Modern American Prison*, writes after observing a Kairos weekend: *I've been in the church all of my life. I've worked, probably, in 600 prisons in this country. I've seen more of Christ and more of Christianity this week, in this prison, than I have seen in all of my life. The impact on those who went in that weekend, those from the free world, was something I have never observed in my nearly half a century of prison work. Those Christians who went in there were not shouting fire and brimstone, they were forgiving. They were not sitting at the head of the table but at the foot of the table. They were not being served but were serving. They were not rejecting, they were accepting. Remarkable. They were not hating, they were loving. They were friends. Believe you me, that's something of a miracle. It was especially a miracle in the setting of the penitentiary.*

- Dr. Peter P. Legins, Professor Emeritus, University of Maryland, Institute of Criminal Justice and Criminology, is considered by most people to be the dean of American criminologists. In a meeting with a group of men who were the founders of Kairos, he said: *I have known for years, as have most of the leading criminologists in this country, that the greatest hope for an inmate to avoid the revolving doors of our prisons is to undergo a religious conversion experience during his incarceration.* [Even though prison sentences in the U.S. are long in comparison with other countries, most inmates will return to society in less than three years with 96% eventually being released. For a variety of reasons, 30% to 70% of those released will return to prison again. Continuing studies being carried out in South Carolina, Texas, Colorado, and California indicate dramatic reductions in the recidivism rate among those inmates who experienced Kairos.]

- Emmett Solomon, retired Texas Department of Criminal Justice Chaplain: *Kairos Prison Ministry is now operating in 23* [now over 30] *Texas institutions* [and the state of Texas has informed Kairos that they want Kairos in all 67 medium- and maximum-security prisons in the state]. *That is such a labor-intensive volunteer program. It takes 70 new volunteers* [typically

100-110 volunteers per unit] *every year to keep that program going in each institution and you can see that would be 1,700 new volunteers every year just being phased into the Kairos program. It is a marvelous program and I applaud all who are involved in that area. You see great things are happening. God is moving.*

- One of the most famous ex-offenders in the United States, Jack "Murf the Surf" Murphy who gained notoriety as a California surfing champion then graduated to high-profile jewelry heists such as the "Star of India" from a New York museum and eventually murder and a life sentence in a Florida prison, where he was the ring leader of a prison riot, spoke to some 650 Restorative Justice Ministry volunteers at the Dallas Grand Hotel on April 17-18, 1998. Since becoming a Christian in prison and following his parole he has spoken in prisons all over the country as part of the Bill Glass Ministry. Mr. Murphy said: *Without exception it is the program Kairos that is the finest. It changes lives and it can change the whole compound, that is a Kairos prison. And if you don't know what it's all about and if you're upset because it came out of the Catholic church and has Episcopalians, Lutherans, Presbyterians, Methodists as a part of that...get over that...get over that. I went through Kairos in 1978.*

- Kenneth D. McKellar, Warden of several maximum-security prisons in South Carolina during the 1970s and 1980s and now Division Director for Security, South Carolina Department of Corrections: *During the 1986 April Fool's Day Riot at Kirkland Correctional Institution, as the Warden, I was sickened to see the institution on fire and realize that 22 of our Officers were either trapped inside or being held hostage. However, after our emergency teams regained control of the institution, I was truly grateful to learn from several of the Officers who had been freed during the riot, that, had it not been for the KAIROS inmates hiding them in their cells, they would have been seriously injured or killed by the other rebellious inmates. As Warden of our former State Penitentiary (since demolished) and as a Deputy Regional Director, I saw many hard-core convicts come to know Christ and their behavior improved dramatically. Now, as Division Director of Security for the South Carolina Department of Corrections, I have had the opportunity to visit numerous other states where KAIROS is operational. I hear good reports from Wardens and institutional staff that KAIROS is one of the most meaningful programs in their institution.*

- Freddie Engelbrecht, Area Commander of Pollsmoor prison, Cape Town, South Africa, site of the first Kairos weekend in South Africa in December 1998: *In my capacity as Area Commander of Pollsmoor prison command, I have a unique set of impressions of the value of the Kairos program in the prisons where the program is currently being applied. I am only responsible for Pollsmoor command area, but to give a complete picture, I also mention some feedback we have received from other South African prisons where the program is presently being initiated after it had commenced at Pollsmoor Medium B prison in Cape Town. The overwhelming response received from the prisons at Drakenstein (Western Cape Town area) and from the Kairos team in Krugersdorp in Gauteng is that they are extremely excited about the impact the program has on prisons. In the case of Krugersdorp, inmates belonging to different gangs have become reconciled with one another. This was previously deemed quite impossible by prison officials. In the case of Drakenstein, we have received feedback as to the impact the program has had on long-term prisoners. The area manager specifically stated that he had never before experienced a program that had such a profound effect on the inmates who attended.*

14

> The greatest difference between Jesus Christ as God and Savior and Muhammad as prophet of Allah, comes at this point. Jesus Christ shed His own blood on the cross so that people could come to God. Muhammad shed other people's blood so that his constituents could have political power throughout the Arabian Peninsula.
>
> Ergun and Emir Caner

CHRISTIANITY AND ISLAM

Numerous Muslim beliefs emanate from the Bible but the differences in Christianity and Islam are striking.

- Muslims believe in one God; Christians believe in the Trinity.
- Muslims believe in predestination; Christians believe in free will.
- Muslims believe God is the source of good and evil; Christians believe God is the source of good and Satan is the source of evil.
- Muslims consider it blasphemous to refer to Allah or God as father; Christians don't.
- Muslims believe God is strict, emotionless, and never expresses love; Christians don't.
- Muslims operate under a legalistic system and must earn their salvation through works; Christians believe salvation is from God's grace in the gift of Jesus Christ.
- Muslims don't believe Jesus is God's Son; Christians do.
- Muslims don't believe in the deity of Christ; Christians do.
- Muslims don't believe Jesus was crucified and resurrected; Christians do.
- Muslims believe man is sinful by his acts; Christians believe man is sinful by nature.
- The Qur'an has passages mandating warfare against nonbelievers; the New Testament does not.
- The Qur'an sanctions warfare to spread Islam; the New

Testament teaches love to spread Christianity.

An excellent article, entitled *Among Muslims, Jesus is a Prophet with Honor*, describes the common ground and differences between Christianity and Islam. It was written by Muzammil H. Siddiqi. Dr. Siddiqi is imam and director of the Islamic Society of Orange County, Garden Grove, California, and a former president of the Islamic Society of North America. On the National Day of Prayer and Remembrance on September 14, 2001, he was a speaker during the televised service at the National Cathedral in Washington, D.C.

> "Behold! The angels said 'O Mary! God giveth thee glad tidings of a Word from Him: his name will be Christ Jesus the son of Mary, held in honor in this world and the Hereafter and of (the company of) those nearest to God.'"

The Qur'an
Chapter 3, verse 45

> It may surprise many Americans that Muslims, like Christians, believe in Jesus. Of course, they do not believe all the same things about him, and Muslims do not celebrate Christmas. But we do respect and honor the person in whose memory this great festival is observed. We believe in all God's Prophets and Messengers, and we believe that Jesus was one of the great prophets of God.
>
> In the Qur'an he is called 'Isa. He is also known as al-Masih (the Christ) and Ibn Maryam (Son of Mary). He has many other beautiful names and titles in the Qur'an. He is a highly respected religious figure.
>
> Outside the Christian church, no religious community has given Jesus so much honor, respect, esteem and love as Muslims have. His mother is highly honored as well. Thousands of Muslim men feel proud and blessed to have the name 'Isa; thousands of Muslim

women feel honored and blessed to be called Maryam.

Unlike the Gospels and the New Testament in general, the subject matter of the Qur'an is not Jesus. The Qur'an speaks in detail about God, God's will for human beings and about many of God's Prophets and Messengers. Yet all the basic facts about Jesus' life are mentioned in the Qur'an.

The Qur'an says in several places that Mary was a pious virgin who devoted her life to prayer and divine service. The angel of God one day visited her and gave her the good news of the birth of a blessed child. This was a miraculous birth, as Mary was not a married woman. The virgin birth is clearly mentioned in the Qur'an, and no recognized authority has ever disputed this claim.

However, Muslims and Christians do interpret the birth differently. Christians see it as a sign of incarnation, the coming of earth of the Son of God. Muslims see it as a special miracle. For every prophet a particular miracle was given according to the needs and challenges of his time. Since Jesus' contemporaries used to deny the existence of spirit, they were shown the presence and the power of divine spirit by this unique birth.

Jesus performed many miracles, such as raising of the dead to life, healing the blind and lepers, speaking about the hidden things. All these miracles show that material is not the only thing; there is something beyond the material that must be recognized. The Qur'an emphasizes that Jesus performed these miracles only by the permission of God.

The message of Jesus was basically the same as the message of other prophets of God. He was sent to invite people to the worship of One God, to do righteous deeds and be kind and loving to others. He reminded his people to pay attention not only to the letter of the laws but also to the spirit of the laws.

The Qur'an says that Jesus was mistreated, denied and rejected by his people just as other prophets were also mistreated. Some of his contemporaries opposed him and tried to crucify him. Jesus, however, prayed to God to save him from them and to "remove the cup (of death)" from him. God accepted Jesus' prayer and saved him from crucifixion. He was lifted up to heaven (Al-Nisa' 4:157-158).

Jesus has yet to fulfill his Messianic role. The Messiah is not a divine figure in Islam. He is a human being who is divinely blessed and is supposed to fulfill an eschatological mission. Muslims believe that Jesus is the Messiah and that he will come back to earth before the end of time and restore peace and order, struggle against the Anti-Christ (Dajjal) or demonic forces and bring victory for truth and righteousness. The true followers of Jesus will prevail over those who deny him and reject him.

Muslims and Christians differ in their theologies (views about God) and their Christology (views about Christ), but both believe in the same God and in the same Jesus. As we both love Jesus, let us also love and care for one another. At a time when there is much misunderstanding and tension between Muslims and Christians, here and abroad, we need to discover and emphasize what we have in common.

President Bush is the first U.S. president to visit an Islamic Center in Washington, on Dec. 5, to greet Muslims on their festival after the month of fasting, Ramadan. It has been a tradition in many Muslim countries that the heads of states and local

> leaders extend their best wishes at Christmas to their Christian neighbors. Such exchanges are good and are very much needed. I wish all Christians happy Christmas and happy holidays.[107]

Muslim-to-Christian Conversions

Dr. Richard L. Dunagin, the former senior pastor at my church, told the story in one of his sermons about two graduate students - a Christian and a Muslim - at a university in Moscow, Russia who challenged each other to read each other's holy book. The Muslim became a Christian.

Another example of a Muslim converting to Christianity is found in the *Men's Devotional Bible* (NIV or New International Version) under a devotion by Mark Ritchie.

Saved by Grace

> *While working as an engineer in Afghanistan, Mark Ritchie's father had found an opportunity, despite a ban on proselytizing, to teach a new believer from the Bible.*
>
> It was strictly forbidden for any foreigner in Afghanistan to do anything to "Christianize" an Afghan. [The Muslim passenger in our car] told me how, as a student of Western civilization, he had read about the Reformation and the arguments put forward by Erasmus and Luther on the issue of justification by faith in Jesus Christ - not by the Church's system of works.
>
> "When I read it," he said, "I knew that this was the true way. Doing good works is one of the main tenets of Islam; without good works a person could never get to heaven. But anyone who has really tried to be good knows himself well enough to know he could never be good enough. So I became a believer in Jesus Christ. And I asked your father to help me understand more about it."

> I had to admit, this was a new one on me. I had never before heard of anyone being converted to Christianity by reading a history textbook. Just wait till the publishers hear about this, I thought, while our Travelall bounced through the narrow side streets of Herat. I could just see the headlines: MUSLIM READS HISTORY BOOK - CONVERTS - DIPLOMATIC SCANDAL BREWS. This could make a textbook writer's head roll.
>
> Once again I found myself surprised. The remote carpenter from Galilee had written his signature so powerfully across history that I found a Muslim in the farthest corner of the globe who came to the same conclusion about him as I had. It had taken me years of study to become convinced that the carpenter was God. Meanwhile, this man, raised in a Muslim home, saw it after one chapter in a Western civilization textbook.
>
> On reflection, I wondered why I should be so surprised. Isn't this what one might expect to find if the itinerant preacher from Nazareth was as he claimed to be, the creator of the universe?[108]

An article by Berta Delgado in the *Dallas Morning News* shares the story of brothers Ergun and Emir Caner who were raised in the Islam faith but converted to Christianity.

> Ergun Caner sits in his small Criswell College office - which is overrun by more than 6,000 books - and considers his life and the book that has put him in the national spotlight.
>
> The professor of theology and church history at the conservative Southern Baptist school near downtown Dallas teamed with his brother, who teaches at a Baptist seminary in North Carolina, to write *Unveiling Islam: An Insider's Look at Muslim Life and Beliefs.* The book, released in March [2002], is

meant to give Christians a better understanding of Islam and to provide a personal look at the trials of their conversion. The Caners, who loved their father deeply, were disowned by him when they found Jesus in a storefront church in Ohio. . . .at 16, Ergun attended Stelzer Road Baptist Church in Columbus and says he found salvation through Jesus Christ. When he told his father, Acar made him choose. Ergun lost his earthly father, by choosing his heavenly Father.

"My father thought what he was doing was an act of mercy by disowning me," he says, pointing out that his father could have sent him to Turkey to immerse him in Islam. In other places in the world, he says, people who leave the Islamic faith are to be put to death.

"This was hard for me," he says. "My father was my hero. My father was everything to me."

Ergun's two brothers would follow suit within 18 months. And just as he had done with his oldest son, Acar Caner broke ties with his young sons. Emir and another brother would go live full-time with their mother, who later converted to Christianity. The sons wouldn't see the father again until days before his death. . . .

Ergun uses this analogy to defend the purpose of their book: If a doctor tells a patient he has a disease but it can be cured, is that hateful?

"I would call a person hateful if they rejoiced in the disease," he says, the "disease" being universal sin. "A doctor who is loving will say you have a disease and there is an antidote. Jesus Christ is either who he says he is - he is either the antidote - or he is nothing.

"So I don't rejoice in the disease. I rejoice in the cure. This is not us versus them. This is us *for* them."

That is a point the brothers try to get across when they speak to groups. The Caners are in such high demand as speakers that they are booked nearly every weekend all over the country for the next few years. The book, which was in the works before the Sept. 11, 2001 attacks on America, has soared as high as No. 31 in Amazon.com's sales rank. Some 40,000 copies have been sold as it goes into its sixth printing.

"I've had the honor and privilege, and my brother has as well, to speak in some of the largest churches in this country. And every time I do it, I do it with a broken heart as opposed to wanting to spread hatred," Ergun says. "I do it because I want to reach Muslims with the gospel of Jesus Christ. I want to tell them that the love that caused Christ to go on the cross was given for them. So if they accept him, they receive grace."

Dr. Paige Patterson has known the Caner brothers for about 16 years. The Southern Baptist leader is president of Southeastern Baptist Theological Seminary in Wake Forest, N.C., where Emir teaches. Dr. Patterson says the Caner brothers are not professing hate toward Muslims.

"That would mean that they didn't like their father," says Dr. Patterson. "They loved their father very much. You'd have to look a long way to find people who love Islamic people more than they do. But to love is different from agreeing.". . . .

The Caners write that Islam has been violent throughout history. They say conclusions must be drawn from the 1,400 years of shared Muslim-

Christian history. "With the notable exception of the Crusades, Muslims have almost initiated wars, due largely to the philosophy of *jihad*."

"I know many Muslims who choose not to believe that *jihad* means military conquest, global conflict," Ergun says. "The problem is the ones that do are a significant majority around the world. I hope that the Muslims who are in the minority, who do not believe in warfare - I pray their tribe increases."

Emir says one must look at how things are played out in history to make a determination about the differences between Christianity and Islam.

"Not all Muslims are violent, but Islam purports violence," he says. "To say Islam is peaceful - only in America can we say such a thing. . . .To say that is to go against actual events played out today in the Sudan, in Pakistan, in Sri Lanka."

Dr. Akbar S. Ahmed, a professor at American University in Washington, D.C., has written the book *Discovering Islam: Making Sense of Muslim History and Society*, says Islam does appear to be violent because of what is happening in the Muslim world. But he says the tenets of Islam, the central virtues of Islam, very much advocate peace. The question, he says, is: Why is there so much violence in Muslim society?

The answer is multi-fold, he says:

Political interference from outside the Muslim world and unresolved problems of Palestine, of Kashmir, of Chechnya contribute.

Problems are caused because most political leaders of the Muslim world are military dictators, kings, sheiks or royal dynasties. The rulers and leaders tend to concentrate on wealth and money, which has created a divide in Muslim society that has led to violence.

Education, once a high priority, has collapsed in the Muslim world.

And the vast majority of Muslims are young, he says, noting it is the youngest religion in the world demographically.

"So when you have unemployment, a brutal local regime, and ongoing problems and along comes someone who says, 'I have a solution. Here is a bomb. Here is a grenade,' the young man will not say, 'What does Islam say?' He will have an emotional response to the world," Dr. Ahmed says. "You are not seeing a reasonable, rational response."

This is not a question of fundamentalism or extremism at work, he says. These are ordinary people.

Ergun Caner says he might easily have been one of those young, armed men had it not been for Jesus.

"I am saved by one who didn't call me to hatred, but to love," he says. . . .

Ergun says he is often asked what he would do if his son converted to Islam.

"If my son, raised in the church, taught to love Jesus Christ, chooses later to turn to Islam, I can't disown him," he says. "We don't see that in the Father. We don't see that with the story of the prodigal son. We see the father standing by the gate waiting.

"I would hope that I'd be a strong enough Christian to continue to pray for my son and watch for him and wait for him to return."[109]

Excerpts from the Caners' book *Unveiling Islam: An Insider's Look at Muslim Life and Beliefs*:

- When he was forty years old, he believed the angel Gabriel called him as the last and most authoritative prophet. . . .Muhammad's "call" creates difficulties. The future prophet expresses skepticism of the encounter, though he sees in his vision one of God's archangels. . . Muhammad was deathly afraid of the source of the revelation, believing at first that he was possessed by an evil spirit or *jinn.*

- The greatest difference between Jesus Christ as God and Savior and Muhammad as prophet of Allah, comes at this point. Jesus Christ shed His own blood on the cross so that people could come to God. Muhammad shed other people's blood so that his constituents could have political power throughout the Arabian Peninsula.

- Is Muhammad someone to be followed as the perfect example of obedience to God? The answer must be a resounding "No." How can we trust his revelations and visions when he expressed doubt that they were revelations and sometimes thought himself to be demon possessed?

- People in nations that had lost citizens in the terrorist attacks of September 11, 2001 and especially those in the United States, heard the voice of terror. For many, especially in the media, the tape seemed irrefutable proof that Osama bin Laden was a leading conspirator in the acts. His Islamic defenders, who had spent three months in front of cameras screaming for proof, were silenced. For those who do not know very well the Qur'an and Hadith, it was a shock. For those of us who do know these foundations of Muslim faith, it was a sad validation.

Eschatological Differences

Muslims believe Jesus has yet to fulfill His Messianic role. Jews are still waiting for the Messiah whereas Christians believe the Messiah has already come and will come again. When Christ returns he will arrive in great power and glory, unlike his first coming as a helpless infant born in a manger to poor parents from a backward town in a second-class area of Judea. Jesus himself describes his second coming in Matthew 24:27-31.

> For as lightning that comes from the east is visible even in the west, so will be the coming of the Son of Man. Wherever there is a carcass, there the vulture will gather. Immediately after the distress of those days 'the sun will be darkened, and the moon will not give its light; the stars will fall from the sky, and the heavenly bodies will be shaken.' At that time the sign of the Son of Man will appear in the sky, and all the nations of the earth will mourn. They will see the Son of Man coming on the clouds of the sky, with power and great glory. And he will send his angels with a loud trumpet call, and they will gather his elect from the four winds, from one end of the heavens to the other.

When Christ comes in such power and great glory on the clouds of the sky there is no doubt that many people will be drawn to him. Many Jews' expectations of a powerful Messiah could very well be fulfilled by Jesus at this time. As Philip Yancey's Jewish friend put it, "Wouldn't it be amazing if we found out we were all waiting for the same person."

A key phase in Christ's judgment involves the beast, the world ruler, and his false prophet who performs miraculous signs on his account. John, who wrote the Bible's last book (Revelation), describes this judgment in 19:20.

> But the beast was captured, and with him the false prophet who had performed the miraculous signs on his behalf. With these signs he had deluded those who had received the mark of the beast and worshiped his image. The two of the them were thrown into the fiery lake of burning sulphur.

The next judgment involves Satan. John writes in Revelation 20:1-3:

> And I saw an angel coming down out of heaven, having the key to the Abyss and holding in his hand a great chain. He seized the dragon, that ancient serpent, who is the devil, or Satan, and bound him for a thousand years. He threw him into the Abyss, and locked and sealed it over him, to keep him from deceiving the nations anymore until the thousand years were ended. After that, he must be set free for a short time.

John continues in 20:7-10:

> When the thousand years are over, Satan will be released from his prison and will go out to deceive the nations in the four corners of the earth - Gog and Magog - to gather them for battle. In number they are like the sand on the seashore. They marched across the breadth of the earth and surrounded the camp of God's people, the city he loves. But fire came down from heaven and devoured them. And the devil, who deceived them, was thrown into the lake of burning sulfur, where the beast and the false prophet had been thrown. They will be tormented day and night for ever and ever.

The final judgment involves wicked people who will be thrown into the lake of fire. John describes this final judgment in Revelation 20:11-15.

> Then I saw a great white throne and him who was seated on it. Earth and sky fled from his presence, and there was no place for them. And I saw the dead, great and small, standing before the throne, and books were opened. Another book was opened, which is the book of life. The dead were judged according to what they had done as recorded in the books. The sea gave up the dead that were in it, and death and Hades gave up the dead that were in them, and each person was judged according to what he had done. Then death and Hades were thrown into the lake of

> fire. The lake of fire is the second death. If anyone's name was not found written in the book of life, he was thrown into the lake of fire.

Finally, God ushers in a new kingdom. John writes in Revelation 21:1-4:

> Then I saw a new heaven and a new earth, for the first heaven and the first earth had passed away, and there was no longer any sea. I saw the Holy City, the new Jerusalem, coming down out of heaven from God, prepared as a bride beautifully dressed for her husband. And I heard a loud voice from the throne saying, "Now the dwelling of God is with men, and he will live with them. They will be his people, and God himself will be with them and be their God. He will wipe every tear from their eyes. There will be no more death or mourning or crying or pain, for the old order of things has passed away."

I am indebted to John Lamoreaux, Ph.D. and Assistant Professor of Religious Studies at Southern Methodist University for insights into Islam's interpretation of the end times. Professor Lamoreaux describes in brief the events that will occur before Judgment day in Islam.

> The Muslim community will break into a number of conflicting sects. There will be political chaos. In particular, there will arrive in the civilized world the barbarian tribes of Gog and Magog.
>
> Eventually God will send a redeemer, a descendant of Muhammad, *the Mahdi*, who will receive allegiance from the Muslims at the sanctuary of Mecca, whence he will make pilgrimage to Jerusalem, where he will reign in justice.
>
> He will rule for just a decade, however. Thereafter, the al-Masih al-Dajjal (imposter messiah) will appear in Iraq and fight against the Muslims, the last remnant making their stand on a mountain in Syria.

> In this hour of need, Jesus will descend from heaven. This will occur at the time of the afternoon prayer, in Damascus. He will appear as "a man symmetrical in stature, of reddish-white complexion, lank-haired with hair dripping with perfume." He will be wearing a greenish-yellow garment; though some say, two saffron-yellow garments.
>
> He will lead the last Muslims against al-Dajjal, slaying him at the gate of Lydda in Palestine.
>
> Then Jesus will reign in justice: exterminating all pigs and breaking the crosses of Christians; and making war on behalf of Islam, in time destroying all religions other than Islam.
>
> After 40 years, when Jesus dies, this period of justice will end and the world will be destroyed and the final judgment will take place after the resurrection of the living and the dead.

Robert Spencer, author of *Onward, Muslim Soldiers* and publisher of jihadwatch.org, wrote an article in the *Dallas Morning News* entitled "No: Novels aren't Scripture."

> I am not a Christian fundamentalist and do not believe in the theology that the "Left Behind" series (several books by Tim LaHaye and Jerry B. Junkins on end times) expresses, but in likening those novels' violent end-of-the-world scenario to extremist Islamic rhetoric, columnist Nicholas Kristof (he wrote a companion article entitled "Yes: Their Jesus wages jihad") has missed a fundamental distinction: A depiction of Jesus killing people at the Last Judgment, no matter how glorious a reader may find it, is not even remotely equivalent to an explicit repeated call for believers to wage war against unbelievers.
>
> Calls like that go out from mosques worldwide with numbing regularity. One would be hard pressed to

find a church making the same kind of call on the other side. No one who reads the “Left Behind” novels is going to kill you because of it. He might be waiting for Jesus to do it, but that is not a call to action.

Traditional Christianity and traditional Islam both believe in judgment and hell. Mr. Kristof’s analysis suggests that if you believe that those things exist, you must want to kill people. He completely ignores the fact that the two religions actually have quite developed teachings about how to behave in this world that don’t depend at all on their eschatologies (that is, their respective teachings about the end of the world).

Mr. Kristof either has no clue or doesn’t care that Christianity does not have and *never has had* a doctrine mandating warfare against non-Christians. Islam, on the other hand, has now and *has always had* a doctrine mandating warfare against non-Muslims.

See, just to cite a few references, Quran 9:29 (“Fight those who believe not in Allah nor the Last Day. . .(even if they are) of the People of the Book [Jews and Christians], until they pay the Jizya [the special tax on non-Muslims] with willing submission, and feel themselves subdued”) and hundreds of other verses; Sahih Muslim 4294 (Muhammad says: “Fight against those who disbelieve in Allah. Make a holy war”); a legal manual endorsed by the closest thing to a Vatican that Sunni Islam has, Al-Azhar University: “Umdat al-Salik o.9.8 ([“make] war upon Jews, Christians, and Zoroastrians. . .until they become Muslim or pay the non-Muslim poll tax”); plus writings of all the major Islamic jurists.

I am not saying that Christians have never behaved in a beastly manner. I am saying that they didn’t do

> it because of their ideas of what was going to happen at the end of the world - or, for that matter, because of the teachings of Jesus. Whatever you can say about the Crusades and the Inquisition, you will never find a New Testament verse commanding that Christians go out and kill people.
>
> But jihadists who kill today are doing so because of the teachings of Islam to which I referred above, and others. Muslims who do not kill don't have different teachings; they just ignore these.
>
> This is, of course, the one thing that people like Nicholas Kristof can never and will never admit, because it would explode the foggy multiculturalism and relativism that passes for a worldview in their minds. But it is simply a fact. Prove me wrong.[110]

Islam's Holy Book, the Qur'an, as noted in the article by Robert Spencer, has passages that advocate waging war against nonbelievers. Other passages condemn nonbelievers to hell. Nowhere in the Gospels (Matthew, Mark, Luke, and John) does Jesus teach violence. And nowhere in the New Testament is hell mentioned as the destination for non-Christians. I have read the Qur'an[111], as translated by M. H. Shakir, and have found some interesting verses.

> We will cast terror into the hearts of those who disbelieve, because they set up with Allah that for which He has sent down no authority, and their abode is the fire, and evil is the abode of the unjust.

Surah [Chapter] III, Verse 151

> Of those who are Jews (there are those who) alter words from their places and say: We have heard and we disobey and: Hear, may you not be made to hear! and: "Listen to us", distorting (the word) with their tongues and taunting about religion; and if they had said (instead): We have heard and we obey, and hearken, and "Look at us", it would have been better for them and more upright; but Allah has cursed them

on account of their unbelief, so they do not believe but a little.

Surah IV, Verse 46

(As for) those who disbelieve in Our communications, We shall make them enter fire; so oft as their skins are thoroughly burned, We will change them for other skins, that they may taste the chastisement; surely Allah is Mighty, Wise.

Surah IV, Verse 56

What is the matter with you, then, that you have become two parties about the hypocrites, while Allah has made them return (to unbelief) for what they have earned? Do you wish to guide him whom Allah has caused to err? And whomsoever Allah causes to err, you shall by no means find a way for him. They desire that you should disbelieve as they have disbelieved, so that you might be (all) alike; therefore take not from among them friends until they fly (their homes) in Allah's way; but if they turn back, then seize them and kill them wherever you find them, and take not from among them a friend or a helper.

Surah IV, Verses 88-89

And when you journey in the earth, there is no blame on you if you shorten the prayer, if you fear that those who disbelieve will cause you distress; surely the unbelievers are your open enemy.

Surah IV, Verse 101

And when you are among them and keep up the prayer for them, let a party of them stand up with you, and let them take their arms; then when they have prostrated themselves let them go to your rear, and let another party who have not prayed come forward and pray with you, and let them take their precautions and their arms; (for) those who disbelieve desire that you may be careless of your arms and luggage, so that they may then turn upon you with a sudden united attack; and there is no blame on you, if you are annoyed with rain or if you are sick, that you lay down your arms, and take your precautions; surely Allah has prepared a disgraceful chastisement for the unbelievers.

Surah IV, Verse 102

And whoever acts hostiley to the Apostle [Muhammad] after that guidance has become manifest to him, and follows other than the way of the believers, We will turn him to that to which he has (himself) turned and make him enter hell; and it is an evil resort.

Surah IV, Verse 115

And indeed He has revealed to you in the Book [Qur'an] that when you hear Allah's communications disbelieved in and mocked at, do not sit with them until they enter into some other discourse; surely then you would be like them; surely Allah will gather together the hypocrites and the unbelievers all in hell.

Surah IV, Verse 140

Wherefore for the iniquity of those who are Jews did We disallow to them the good things which had been made lawful for them, and for their hindering many (people) from Allah's way. And their taking usury though indeed they were forbidden it and their devouring the property of people falsely; and We have prepared for the unbelievers from among them a painful chastisement.

Surah IV, Verses 160-161

And (as for) those who disbelieve and reject our communications, these are the companions of the flame.

Surah V, Verse 10

Surely (as for) those who disbelieve, even if they had what is in the earth, all of it, and the like of it with it, that they might ransom themselves with it from the punishment of the day of resurrection, it shall not be accepted from them, and they shall have a painful chastisement. They should desire to go forth from the fire, and they shall not go forth from it, and they shall have a lasting punishment.

Surah V, Verses 36-37

O Apostle [Muhammad]! let not those grieve you who strive together in hastening to unbelief from among those who say with their mouths: We believe, and their hearts do not believe, and from among those who are Jews; they are listeners for the sake of a lie, listeners for another people who have not come to you; they alter the words from their places, saying: If you are given this, take it, and if you are not given this, be cautious; and as for him whose temptation Allah desires, you cannot control anything for him with Allah. Those are they for whom Allah does not desire that He should purify their hearts; they shall have disgrace in this world, and they shall have a grievous chastisement in the hereafter.

Surah V, Verse 41

O you who believe! do not take the Jews and the Christians for friends; they are friends of each other; and whoever amongst you takes them for a friend, then surely he is one of them; surely Allah does not guide the unjust people.

Surah V, Verse 51

O Apostle [Muhammad]! deliver what has been revealed to you from your Lord; and if you do it not, then you have not delivered His message, and Allah will protect you from the people; surely Allah will not guide the unbelieving people.

Surah V, Verse 67

Certainly they disbelieve who say: Surely Allah, He is the Messiah, son of Marium [Mary]; and the Messiah said: O Children of Israel! serve Allah, my Lord and your Lord. Surely whoever associates (others) with Allah, then Allah has forbidden to him the garden, and his abode is the fire, and there shall be no helpers for the unjust. Certainly they disbelieve who say: Surely Allah is the third (person) of the three; and there is no god but the onc God, and if they desist not from what they say, a painful chastisement shall befall those among them who disbelieve. Will they not then turn to Allah and ask His forgiveness? And Allah is Forgiving, Merciful. The Messiah, son of Marium [Mary] is but an apostle; apostles before him have indeed passed away; and his mother was a truthful woman; they both used to eat food. See how We make the communications clear to them, then behold, how they are turned away.

Surah V, Verses 72-75

And leave those who have taken their religion for a play and an idle sport, and whom this world's life has deceived, and remind (them) thereby lest a soul should be given up to destruction for what it has earned; it shall not have besides Allah any guardian nor an intercessor, and if it should seek to give every compensation, it shall not be accepted from it; these are they who shall be given up to destruction for what they earned; they shall have a drink of boiling water and a painful chastisement because they disbelieved.

Surah VI, Verse 70

And had you seen when the angels will cause to die those who disbelieve, smiting their faces and their backs, and (saying): Taste the punishment of burning.

Surah VIII, Verse 50

Surely the vilest of animals in Allah's sight are those who disbelieve, then they would not believe.

Surah VIII, Verse 55

Fight those who do not believe in Allah, nor in the latter day, nor do they prohibit what Allah and His Apostle [Muhammad] have prohibited, nor follow the religion of truth, out of those who have been given the Book [Qur'an], until they pay the tax in acknowledgment of superiority and they are in a state of subjection. And the Jews say: Uzair [Ezra] is the son of Allah; and the Christians say: The Messiah is the son of Allah; these are the words of their mouths; they imitate the saying of those who disbelieved before; may Allah destroy them; how they are turned away!

Surah IX, Verses 29-30

Allah has promised the hypocritical men and the hypocritical women and the unbelievers the fire of hell to abide therein; it is enough for them; and Allah has cursed them and they shall have lasting punishment.

Surah IX, Verse 68

O Prophet [Muhammad]! strive hard against the unbelievers and the hypocrites and be unyielding to them; and their abode is hell, and evil is the destination.

Surah IX, Verse 73

These are two adversaries who dispute about their Lord; then (as to) those who disbelieve, for them are cut out garments of fire; boiling water shall be poured over their heads. With it shall be melted what is in their bellies and (their) skins as well. And for them are whips of iron. Whenever they will desire to go forth from it, from grief, they shall be turned back into it, and taste the chastisement of burning.

Surah XXII, Verses 19-22

And (as for) those who disbelieve in and reject Our communications, these it is who shall have a disgraceful chastisement.

Surah XXII, Verse 57

(As for) those who disbelieve, they shall have a severe punishment, and (as for) those who believe and do good, they shall have forgiveness and a great reward.

Surah XXXV, Verse 7

So when you meet in battle those who disbelieve, then smite the necks until when you have overcome them, then make (them) prisoners, and afterwards either set them free as a favor or let them ransom (themselves) until the war terminates. That (shall be so); and if Allah had pleased He would certainly have exacted what is due from them, but that He may try some of you by means of others; and (as for) those who are slain in the way of Allah, He will by no means allow their deeds to perish.

Surah XLVII, Verse 4

And (as for) those who disbelieve, for them is destruction, and He has made their deeds ineffective.

Surah XLVII, Verse 8

He it is Who sent His Apostle [Muhammad] with the guidance and the true religion that He may make it prevail over all the religions; and Allah is enough for a witness.

Surah XLVIII, Verse 28

Muhammad is the Apostle of Allah, and those with him are firm of heart against the unbelievers. . .

Surah XLVIII, Verse 29

> And for those who disbelieve in their Lord is the punishment of hell, and evil is the resort.

Surah LXVII, Verse 6

> (It is) only a delivering (of communications) from Allah and His messages; and whoever disobeys Allah and His Apostle [Muhammad], surely he shall have the fire of hell to abide therein for a long time.

Surah LXXII, Verse 23

> And (as for) those who disbelieve in our communications, they are the people of the left hand. On them is fire closed over.

Surah, XC, Verses 19-20

These are just some of the verses in the Qur'an that encourage warfare against nonbelievers and consign nonbelievers to hell. Again, nowhere in the Gospels does Jesus teach warfare and nowhere in the New Testament is hell mentioned as the destination for non-Christians.

Saudi Arabia is the birthplace of Islam and Osama bin Laden. Most of the hijackers involved in the evil event of September 11, 2001 came from Saudi Arabia and all were Muslims. Since 9-11, numerous atrocities have been perpetrated by Muslims: the murdering of hundreds of Russian schoolchildren by Chechen Muslim terrorists; the killing of scores of citizens in the Spanish train bombings by Islamic terrorists; the downing of two Russian planes; the beheading of numerous people; the killing of hundreds in public places by suicide bombers; and other tragedies too numerous to mention - all committed by Islamic terrorists. The terrorists cite the Qur'an as the foundation and source of their despicable acts. The goal of the terrorists, who are all Muslims, is to forcibly impose Islamic governments or theocracies throughout the world.

> There is a sixth religious duty associated with the five pillars [The Creed (Kalima), Prayer (Salat), Almsgiving (Zakat), Fasting (Ramadan), and The Pilgrimage (Hajj)]. This is *Jihad*, the HolyWar.

> This duty requires that when the situation warrants, men are required to go to war to spread Islam or defend it against infidels. One who dies in a *Jihad* is guaranteed eternal life in Paradise (heaven).[112]

God is perfect. God is love. God gives us free will. Since God is perfect, by logical extension, His Son must be perfect otherwise God would be imperfect. Since God is love, His Son must be love. Since God offers us free will, Jesus offers us free will. A religion whose Holy Book advocates violence against nonbelievers can't be the Truth since it contradicts God's very character.

Never once in the New Testament does Jesus coerce or force anybody to follow Him. Jesus never terrorized people. He never threatened people with weapons to make them followers of Him. Indeed, Jesus became upset when his followers used violence. For example, Jesus rebuked a disciple for slashing off the ear of one of the people who came to arrest Him. The early followers of Jesus never used the threat of violence to force people to follow Christ. They mirrored the sacrificial love of Jesus to be conduits of God's love to a fractured Middle East. With the most notable exceptions of the Crusades from the 11th to 14th centuries and the Spanish Inquisition from 1478 to 1834, which Jesus never would have sanctioned, Christianity has espoused love in winning people to Christ. People who argue that the Crusades and Inquisition are evidence of Christianity not being the Truth ignore the fact that a religion should be based on its perfect founder, not imperfect humans. Therefore, a religion that is based on an imperfect human being's writings that mandate hatred, intolerance, and warfare against nonbelievers is antithetical to God's very nature. It reflects hate, not love; it reflects coercion, not free will. Therefore, I don't believe Islam is the Truth since the Qur'an mandates violence to convert nonbelievers. Fortunately, most Muslims, as Robert Spencer pointed out, ignore these teachings on hatred, intolerance, and violent jihad.

Islam, in much of the world, does not allow free will. People who are Muslims are threatened if they leave the faith. Non-Muslims are threatened if they present Christianity to Muslims. Many Islamic countries disallow or strongly discourage freedom of religion. Christianity, on the other hand, seeks to win people to

Christ through God's love and gives people free will to choose. God is love. God sanctioned free will. Therefore, God's will is for His creatures to express love, not hate; to freely choose, not be coerced.

As mentioned in Chapter 10 ("Additional Evidence"), Professor J. P. Moreland noted that Muhammad's conversion was not publicly witnessed nor did Muhammad perform any miracles to sanction anything. Moreland states:

> Let's take a look at Muhammad's conversion. No one knows anything about it. Muhammad claims he went into a cave and had a religious experience in which Allah revealed the Koran to him. There's no other eyewitness to verify this. Muhammad offered no publicly miraculous signs to certify anything.
>
> And someone easily could have had ulterior motives in following Muhammad, because in the early years Islam was spread largely by warfare. Followers of Muhammad gained political influence and power over the villages that were conquered and 'converted' to Islam by the sword.
>
> Contrast that with the claims of the early followers of Jesus [who did not use warfare to spread their faith], including Paul. They claimed to have seen public events that other people saw as well. These were things that happened outside their minds, not just in their minds.[113]

Jesus said he was God's Son and He claimed He was God. ["I and the Father are one." John 10:30]. No other prophet ever claimed to be God's Son or God Himself. The Muslims believe Jesus was a great prophet. How could a great prophet lie about His very identity, claiming He was God? Telling a lie would be a sin and the Muslims believe Jesus was a sinless prophet. Josh McDowell states in *A Ready Defense*:

> Islam does believe Jesus was a sinless prophet although not as great as Muhammad.[114]

How could an imperfect dead prophet (Muhammad) be considered a greater prophet than a sinless risen Jesus?

How can Islam be the Truth when Muhammad's conversion was not publicly witnessed whereas the early disciples of Jesus saw public events that other people witnessed as well? How can Islam be the Truth when Muhammad performed no publicly witnessed miracles to certify anything whereas Christ's and the Apostles' miracles were publicly witnessed by multitudes of people? How can Islam be the Truth when God's nature of love and gift of free will, as epitomized by Jesus Christ, are contradicted by Islam's mandatory warfare against and coercion of nonbelievers and infidels?

15

> In the end, God wins.
>
> Richard L. Dunagin

A SYNOPSIS OF THE BIBLE

I can't top the succinctness of Richard Dunagin's summarization of the Bible. However, my purpose of this chapter is to succinctly summarize my interpretation of the Bible. I encourage you to read and study the Bible for yourself. There is no substitute for it.

I'm not a theologian, having never taken a high school, college or graduate-level religion course. I'm a lay person. But since 1995 I've read the entire Bible thrice, the New Testament a half-dozen times, the Qur'an (my copy has 424 pages versus 1,405 pages in my NIV Bible), and numerous other faith-based books, many of which are footnoted in this book. I've also taken a number of Bible study classes offered by my church. Finally, I have spent much time praying, listening, and observing.

Leslie Weatherhead, a pastor in England during the darkest days of World War II, wrote a series of sermons partitioning the will of God into three components: 1) the intentional will of God, 2) the circumstantial will of God, and 3) the ultimate will of God.

> The trouble arises because we use the phrase "the will of God" to cover all three, without making any distinction between them. But when we look at the Cross of Christ, we can see, I think, the necessity of such a distinction.
>
> 1. Was it God's intention from the beginning that Jesus should go to the Cross? I think the answer to that question must be No. I don't think Jesus thought that at the beginning of his ministry. He came with the *intention* that men should follow him, not kill him. The discipleship of men, not the death of Christ, was the intentional will of God, or, if you like, God's ideal purpose - and I sometimes wish that in common

language we could keep the phrase "the will of God" for the intentional will of God.

2. But when circumstances wrought by men's evil set up such a dilemma that Christ was compelled either to die or to run away, then *in those circumstances* the Cross was the will of God, but only in those circumstances which were themselves the fruit of evil. In those circumstances any other way was unworthy and impossible, and it was in this sense that our Lord said, "Nevertheless not what I will, but what thou wilt." Because a father in the evil circumstances set up by war says to his son, "I am glad you are in the Army, John," it does not mean that from the beginning he willed the Army as John's career. The father would have much preferred, let us say, that his son should be an architect. The father wills the Army for his boy only because *in the circumstances which evil has set up* it seems to the father, and, indeed, to the boy, the most honorable, as well as inevitable, thing to do.

3. Then there is a third sense in which we use the phrase "the will of God," when we mean God's ultimate goal - the purposefulness of God which, in spite of evil and, as we shall see, even through evil, arrives, with nothing of value lost, at the same goal as would have been reached if the intentional will of God could have been carried through without frustration. I hope we shall come to see in the other sermons of the series that God cannot be finally defeated, and that is what I mean by his omnipotence - not that everything that happens is his will, but that nothing can happen which *finally* defeats his will. So, in regard to the Cross, God achieved his final goal not simply in spite of the Cross but through it. He achieved a great redemption and realized his ultimate will in as full

> a sense as he would have done if his intentional will had not been temporarily defeated.[115]

My interpretation of the Bible is as follows:

It was God's intentional will to create perfection in the Garden of Eden. Man fell. God said there are consequences for your poor choice. However, God provided a plan for redemption. Part of God's plan was to have the Hebrews sacrifice animals for the atonement of their sins. Finally, God got tired of the failure of the Israelites to turn to Him and follow His commandments. God got tired of the animal sacrifices not being adequate to atone for their sins. God got tired of all the bloodshed that is documented in the Old Testament. So God's circumstantial will was to send His Son, Jesus Christ, as the Sacrificial Lamb, consistent with the Hebrews' long tradition of sacrificing animals for the atonement of sin. God gave us over 300 prophecies about Jesus so we wouldn't mistake His circumstantial will.

God figured the animal sacrifices didn't succeed so He decided to send His Son as the perfect Sacrificial Lamb. God is perfection. Not the most ardent Muslim, devout Jew, peace-loving Hindu, ascetic Buddhist, or disciplined Christian can achieve perfection. Only God is perfect and His holiness demands perfection. We can't do it by ourselves. We are completely dependant on God's grace to rescue us from sin and provide for our salvation. And therein lies Christianity's unique embracement of grace among all the world's faiths.

God is perfect and holy. Therefore, by logical deduction, God demands a perfect Sacrificial Lamb. Only God's Son would do. God offered Jesus, His only begotten Son, to die for the forgiveness of sins for all humanity. God's circumstantial will was therefore to sacrifice His own Son.

> Yet it was the Lord's will to crush him and cause him to suffer, and though the Lord makes his life a guilt offering, he will see his offspring and prolong his days, and the will of the Lord will prosper in his hand.

Isaiah 53:10

Jesus' offspring are his followers and God's will has prospered in Jesus since there are far more Christians on this planet than any other faith's adherents.

Yet in the 2,000 years since Christ was rejected and crucified, we've continued to have immeasurable bloodshed on this earth. Why? Because too many people have failed to accept Jesus Christ as the Son of God. God tells us there are consequences for our choices. Too many people have made a poor choice regarding the stature of who Christ is. If more people on this planet accepted Christ for who He is, I guarantee you we'd have more peace.

God's ultimate will is for people to accept Jesus as the Lord and Savior of mankind. It is predicted in the book of Revelation that Jesus Christ will return and will draw many people to Him. Given God's track record of fulfilling over 700 prophecies thus far, it is a safe bet that Christ will someday return to earth. It is up to you to make a decision regarding your eternal salvation.

APPENDIX

Animal sacrifices for the atonement of sin were part of the Hebrew tradition for centuries. But they ceased when the Roman armies destroyed the Temple in Jerusalem in 70 A.D. How have Jews atoned for their sins since then? I posed that question to my close friend, Clark Gross, an Orthodox Jew. Clark responded:

> G'd forgives sin based upon prayer, repentance and acts of charity (no, you cannot pick one and ignore the other two). This applies only to sins against G'd; sins against men also require undoing the wrong (not so much of a problem for the thief to return the cow he took, but a big problem for a murderer).

16

> Thinking is difficult. Thinking is complex. And thinking is - more than anything else - a process, with a course or direction, a lapse of time, and a series of steps or stages that lead to some result. To think well is a laborious, often painstaking process until one becomes accustomed to being "thoughtful." Since it is a process, the course or direction may not always be clear-cut. Not all the steps or stages are linear, nor are they always in the same sequence. Some are circular and overlap with others. Not everyone seeks to achieve the same result. Given all this, if we are to think well, we must be on guard against simplistic thinking in our approach to analyzing crucial issues and solving the problems of life. . . .
>
> It is unquestionable that certain changes are needed in society to encourage better thinking. But at the same time, each individual is responsible for his or her own thinking and how to meet this challenge. Ultimately, if we can teach people to think well, we could heal most of the ills of individuals and most of the ills of society. In the end, however, the benefits of thinking well are worth the effort - and far better than the alternative. This is ultimately a hopeful business. Long ago I heard it said: "Once a mind is truly stretched, it never returns to its former dimensions."
>
> M. Scott Peck

THE ULTIMATE CHALLENGE

The ultimate challenge is to think well. For by thinking well your quest for the Truth will be enhanced and sharpened. The problem, as M. Scott Peck has pointed out, is that all of us are afflicted with the original sins (pride, fear, and laziness). We are too prideful to examine other faiths, thinking our faith is the Truth. We are too fearful to explore other faiths, thinking we will have to re-examine and possibly alter our position which could cause a lot of mental anguish that the psychologists call cognitive dissonance. We are too lazy to assiduously study other faiths because it is far easier to engage in leisurely pursuits than read books. It is far easier to reject what we don't know than to think about what might be.

Dr. Gary Thompson, an ordained elder in the Mississippi Conference, is the pastor of First United Methodist Church in Biloxi. He holds a Doctor of Ministry degree in Leadership Development from Princeton Theological Seminary in Princeton, New Jersey. He comments on the human tendency to reject information that does not fit into our life experiences.

> We find it very hard to make sense of information that is foreign to our personal experience. We have psychological defense mechanisms that help protect us from too much mental pain. We learn to deny truths that are too threatening. We use these mechanisms to manage anxiety, to control aggressive impulses, and to deal with disappointments and resentments. We also tend to reject information that does not "compute"; that is, we reject information that does not fit into our experiential categories or preconceived notions.[116]

My challenge to every person on the planet, bar none, is to think well. Earn the compliment that Robert Redford, as the Sundance Kid, paid Paul Newman, as Butch Cassidy, in the movie *Butch Cassidy and the Sundance Kid*, when he remarked: "Butch, you just keep thinking - that's what you're good at." Become informed so you can keep ignorance at bay. Become informed so you can make an intelligent decision on the most important question you must face - your eternal destiny.

Mother Teresa, a diminutive figure with gnarled hands and a weathered face, was the person I admired most in the 20th century. My former senior pastor, Dr. Richard L. Dunagin, once told me that Billy Graham believed, out of all the people that he was aware of, that Mother Teresa was the most Christlike. She won the Nobel Peace Prize on December 10, 1979. She posted a sign on the wall of the children's home in Calcutta that reads:

> *Take time to think*
> Take time to pray
> Take time to laugh
>
> *It is the source of power*
> It is the greatest power on earth
> It is the music of the soul
>
> Take time to play
> Take time to love and be loved
> Take time to give
>
> It is the secret of perpetual youth
> It is God's given privilege
> It is too short a day to be selfish
>
> *Take time to read*
> Take time to be friendly
> Take time to work
>
> *It is the fountain of wisdom*
> It is the road to happiness
> It is the price of success
>
> Take time to do charity
> It is the key to heaven. [italics are my emphasis][117]

Take time to think, read, research, study, probe, and analyze. Take time to pray, asking God to help you discern the Truth. If you are skeptical about Christianity, do your own research. Don't just rely on your imam's or rabbi's word. Don't just rely on my viewpoint. Pursue God's will for humanity on your own. Louis Lapides, the Jewish man who converted to Christianity as detailed in Lee Strobel's book *The Case for Christ*, put it this way:

> So here's my challenge to skeptics: don't accept my word for it, but don't accept your rabbi's either. Spend the time to research it yourself. Today nobody

> can say, "There's no information." There are plenty of books out there to help you. And one more thing: sincerely ask God to show you whether or not Jesus is the Messiah. That's what I did - and without any coaching it became clear to me who fit the fingerprint of the Messiah.[118]

One man who has made a career of studying the world's religions is Dr. Huston Smith, world-renowned scholar who has taught at Washington University, Massachusetts Institute of Technology, Syracuse University, and most recently a visiting professor at the University of California at Berkeley. He is the author of the best-selling book *The World's Religions* that noted public television personality Bill Moyers describes as "the one book on world religions I can't do without. I return to it often - and always with reward."

Kimberly Winston interviewed Smith in an article that appeared in the February 10, 2001 edition of the *Dallas Morning News*.

> Dr. Smith has spent more than 50 years looking at how the world's religions try to answer the big questions... .Upon beginning his studies in the United States at age 17, he thought he would, like one of his older brothers, become a church pastor. But he soon realized the pulpit could not support his vast curiosity and began work at the University of Chicago on a Ph.D. in naturalistic theism - a philosophical system when science doesn't have the answers.
>
> Six weeks short of earning his doctorate, he picked up a copy of *Pain, Sex and Time* by philosopher Gerald Heard. Mr. Heard's sympathetic treatment of the mystic experience was diametrically opposed to naturalistic theism. And Mr. Heard's belief that mysticism is the true experience of God was an epiphany for Dr. Smith. He finished his degree, then somewhat accidentally began seeking out the mystic path in every religion he encountered.

"It was not as though I set out with a shopping list - you know, first I'll study Buddhism and then go down the list," he said.

Throughout his life, he has always been a Christian, Dr. Smith said. But as he explored other traditions, he found "vitamin supplements" that have enhanced his faith.

He describes Hinduism - the first faith he studied - as "a tidal wave that knocked mc off my feet."

When Dr. Smith first began teaching, at Washington University, it was just after World War II. "Globalization" was the catchword in academia, and it was thought that if people understood each other better, another war could be avoided. The dean decreed that every liberal arts department would teach a course that was non-western in focus, and as low man on the department totem pole, the task of teaching a course in Hinduism fell to Dr. Smith.

"I needed help," Dr. Smith remembered, and he approached his friend Aldous Huxley for advice. Mr. Huxley, an author and philosopher, suggested that he visit a local swami, and Dr. Smith dropped in on the swami's discussion of the Hindu Upanishads.

"I was astonished," Dr. Smith said. "Astonished at how much wisdom could be compacted in so few words." He spent the next 10 years studying at the swami's feet.

Since then, Dr. Smith has never been satisfied studying world religions from the sidelines. He has whirled with ecstatic Sufi Islamic dervishes in Iran, practiced yoga with Hindu holy men in India, meditated on koans with Tibetan Buddhist monks, smoked peyote with Huichol Indian medicine men and celebrated the Jewish Sabbath with a daughter who converted

> to that faith. Today, his personal spiritual practice includes bits and pieces of almost everything he has come across - yoga, meditation, scripture reading and prayer, all built upon the foundation of his father's Christianity.
>
> "It is the tradition that formed me," he said, his voice momentarily void of the chuckle it seems to always contain. "It took. I have stayed with it because in all the other wisdom I have not encountered one I think is more profound than Christianity. It is embedded in my physiological responses. The ceremonies of other traditions, although they all mint my understanding, do not viscerally connect with me the way the religion of my upbringing does."

Despite a lifetime of immersion in other faiths, Huston Smith's original faith proved irresistible, which is true for many people. Others, like Smith's daughter, embrace different faiths after doing their own search for the Truth. The point is, everyone should embark on their own quest for the Truth. There are nuggets of gold in every faith, or as Smith puts it: "vitamin supplements" that have enhanced his faith. But, as C. S. Lewis said in *Mere Christianity*:

> If you are a Christian, you are free to think that all these religions, even the queerest ones, contain at least some hint of the truth. . . .But, of course, being a Christian does mean thinking that where Christianity differs from other religions, Christianity is right and they are wrong. As in arithmetic - there is only one right answer to a sum, and all other answers are wrong: but some of the wrong answers are much nearer being right than others.[119]

Dr. Charles Stanley addressed this same concept in a devotion entitled "Truth Demands One Way."

> A movie celebrity remarked during an interview that he had been reared in a Christian environment but he rejected Christianity as an adult. His rationale was: "There are billions of people on this earth. How can

any one group of people make a claim that their way is the only way? I just can't believe that."

He is not alone in his thinking. Multitudes reject the notion that faith in the person of Christ is the only means by which they can approach God. "Surely," they reason, "the diverse throng of tribes, cultures, and nations cannot all be expected to walk the same spiritual path. They must have their own unique staircase to the heavens."

Logically carried to its conclusion, the way to God depends on individual preference. God then is approached in millions of ways, each way right in the eyes of the seeker. Absolute truth then is nullified. God is whatever we make of Him.

What if mathematics were subject to similar logic? Would two plus two equal five in Albania, sixteen in Norway, and eight in Canada?

The Bible strikes at the heart of such nonsense. It claims Christ is the only way because He is the true way, available for all people everywhere. Truth demands one way. Jesus is the way.[120]

Jesus answered, "I am the way and the truth and the life. No onc comes to the Father except through me."

John 14:6

One thing that distinguishes Christianity from all other faiths is the concept of grace, as C. S. Lewis pointed out. Philip Yancey, in his book *What's So Amazing About Grace,* describes Lewis' insight on grace.

During a British conference on comparative religions, experts from around the world debated what, if any, belief was unique to the Christian faith. They began eliminating possibilities. Incarnation? Other

> religions had different versions of gods appearing in human form. Resurrection? Again, other religions had accounts of return from death. The debate went on for some time until C. S. Lewis wandered into the room. "What's the rumpus about?" he asked, and heard in reply that his colleagues were discussing Christianity's unique contribution among world religions. Lewis responded, "Oh, that's easy. It's grace."
>
> After some discussion, the conferees had to agree. The notion of God's love coming to us free of charge, no strings attached, seems to go against every instinct of humanity. The Buddhist eight-fold path, the Hindu doctrine of *karma*, the Jewish covenant [including 613 commandments circumscribing human behavior in the Torah], and Muslim code of law [including the Five Pillars of Islam governing their private life in dealing with God] - each of these offers a way to earn approval. Only Christianity dares to make God's love unconditional.[121]

Probably no faith has more rules than Judaism. There are 613 laws in the Torah. Philip Yancey, in his book *The Jesus I Never Knew,* describes Jesus' challenge to exceed the righteousness of the Pharisees and the teachers of the law.

> Early in the Sermon on the Mount, Jesus addressed head-on a question that worried most of his listeners: Was he a revolutionary or an authentic Jewish prophet? Here is Jesus' own description of his relationship to the Torah:
>
> Do not think that I have come to abolish the Law or the Prophets; I have not come to abolish them but to fulfill them. . . .For I tell you that unless your righteousness surpasses that of the Pharisees and the teachers of the law, you will certainly not enter the kingdom of heaven.

> That last statement surely made the crowd sit up and take notice. Pharisees and teachers of the law competed with one another in strictness. They had atomized God's law into 613 rules - 248 commands and 365 prohibitions - and bolstered these rules with 1,521 emendations. To avoid breaking the third commandment, "You shall not misuse the name of the Lord," they refused to pronounce God's name at all. To avoid sexual temptation they had a practice of lowering their heads and not even looking at women (the most scrupulous of these were known as "bleeding Pharisees" because of frequent collisions with walls and other obstacles). To avoid defiling the Sabbath they outlawed thirty-nine activities that might be construed as "work." How could an ordinary person's righteousness ever *surpass* that of such professional holy men?. . ..Using the Torah as a starting point, Jesus pushed the law in the same direction, further than any Pharisee had dared push it, further than any monk has dared live it. The Sermon on the Mount introduced a new moon in the moral universe that has exerted its own force of gravity ever since. Jesus made the law impossible for anyone to keep and then charged us to keep it.[122]

So we have Pharisees competing to see who could adhere to the most rules. Competition in this manner breeds pride, one of the original sins. Pharisees would be tempted to brag about who obeyed the most laws, who was the strictest. The apostle Paul addressed grace and works in several of his epistles, including Ephesians 2:8-9:

> For it is by grace you have been saved, through faith - and this not from yourselves, it is the gift of God - not by works, so that no one can boast.

Jesus addressed the hypocrisy of the Pharisees and teachers of the law in Mark 7:6-9 when he stated:

> Isaiah was right when he prophesied about you hypocrites; as it is written: "These people honor

> me with their lips, but their hearts are far from me. They worship me in vain; their teachings are but rules taught by men." [Isaiah 29:13]. You have let go of the commands of God and are holding on to the traditions of men. You have a fine way of setting aside the commands of God in order to observe your own traditions!

Paraphrasing lines made famous in the movie *Dirty Harry*, I can just hear one of my favorite theologians, Clint Eastwood, saying to a Pharisee:

> I know what you're thinking. Did I obey all 613 laws this past year or only 612? Well, you know in all the excitement, I kind of lost track myself. But being that God is the most powerful in the universe and perfect, you won't get into heaven unless you're perfect. The question you have to ask yourself is: "Am I as good as Jesus Christ? Well, are you. . . .punk?

The Pharisees had become blind. The Pharisees didn't realize, in the words of Oswald Chambers, that "no one can make himself pure by obeying laws." The Pharisees got so hung up on rules that they could not see the forest for the trees. They got mad at Jesus because He healed people on the Sabbath. Rigid Sabbath compliance superseded in importance miracles of healing. The Pharisees concluded that Jesus was not from God because He didn't obey the Sabbath. The Pharisees made the 613 laws and 1,521 emendations a false idol, superseding a relationship with God. The Pharisees' vision was so impaired that they were blind to the fact that a man who performed the miracles that Jesus Christ performed could only be from God. The Pharisees had forgotten how to think well. The apostle Paul described them well:

> They are darkened in their understanding and separated from the life of God because of the ignorance that is in them due to the hardening of their hearts.

Ephesians 4:18

You've heard the paradoxical statement that less is more. Jesus said the two greatest commandments were to love God with all your heart, mind, soul, and strength and to love your neighbor as yourself. If you obey these two commandments, everything else falls into line. Thus, Jesus boiled down those 613 rules and 1,521 emendations into two commandments. All of the world's religions are based on works except Christianity which is based on grace. Which faith is the Truth? It's your life and your quest.

Rev. J. Oliver Lee, one of the most impressive individuals I have ever known, addressed the troops on Saturday evening in the gym at the 11th Kairos weekend at the Michael Unit in October 1997. I must share a little of Oliver's background because it will impact the import of what he said to the 100 men in that gym. Oliver holds bachelor's and law degrees from the University of Kansas. He served in the U. S. Foreign Service from 1979 to 1982 during the Iranian hostage crisis. He served in the U. S. Justice Department from 1988 to 1994, with private practice interspersed before and after his stint at the Justice Department, where he was a prosecuting attorney in the Anti-Trust Division. From 1971 to 1984 he served in the U. S. military. For the first seven years he was in the U. S. Marine Corps, associated with Recon, an elite division within the most elite military branch. In 1973, in one national organization of karate, Oliver was ranked 7th in the heavy-weight division. For the last six years of his military career he served in Special Forces in the U. S. Army. Oliver made a life-changing decision in the mid-1990s when he felt called to pursue the Episcopal priesthood. He graduated from Harvard Divinity School in 2002 and is an ordained priest.

Oliver Lee made a bold statement that gripped the 100 men in that gym: "Gentlemen, we are not here to take sides. *We are not here to take sides*! *We're here to take over*!" Later, I asked Oliver if he had any scriptural reference for that audacious assertion. He replied, "Joshua 5:13-14." When Joshua, one of the greatest warriors in the Hebrew Bible, a man of unflinching courage and unshakable devotion to God and the successor to Moses, was near Jericho, he looked up and saw an angelic being standing in front of him with a drawn sword in his hand. Joshua approached him and asked, "Are you for us or for our enemies?"

"Neither," the angel replied, "I am here as commander of the Lord's army." Then Joshua fell facedown to the ground in reverence.

Joshua basically asked the angel whose side he was on. The angel responded by saying "I'm not on your side or your enemies' side. As commander of the Lord's army, I am on God's side." If you are on God's side, if you do God's will, you will take over. Witness what happened when, in the next few passages (Joshua 6:2-5), Joshua gets instructions from the Lord on implementing a highly unorthodox military strategy for taking over Jericho. Joshua had the troops do exactly what the Lord instructed and they took over Jericho a week later. The same principle could be applied to World War II. The Germans and Allies were praying to the same God for victory. Some people no doubt asked, "God, are you for us or for our enemies?" The real question, however, is what group - the Allies or Axis Powers - was on God's side.

> During the Civil War Abraham Lincoln cautioned that being on the Lord's side is more important than arrogantly assuming He's on our side.[123]

It is no accident that there are more Christians on this planet, accounting for approximately one-third of the world's population, than any other faiths' adherents. According to John Lamoreaux, Ph.D. and Assistant Professor of Religious Studies at Southern Methodist University, there are approximately 1.8 billion Christians, 1.0 billion Muslims, 800 million Hindus, 280 million Buddhists, and 14.5 million Jews. This corresponds pretty well with statistics presented below.

World Religions and Their Distribution	
Religion	**Population**
Christianity	1.9 billion
Roman Catholic	1.0 billion
Protestant	458 million
Eastern Orthodox	173 million
Other	195 million

World Religions and Their Distribution	
Islam	1.0 billion
Hinduism	751 million
Buddhism	334 million
Daoism	31 million
Judaism	18 million
Shintoism	3 million
Source: Peter N. Sterns, Michael Adas, Stuart B. Schwartz, and Marc J. Gilbert, *World Civilizations: The Global Experience*, Third Edition (New York, NY: Addison-Wesley Educational Publishers, Inc., 2003), 105.	

An article entitled "Religion Sweeps by Nationalism - Tidal Wive of Christianity Rolls Around the World" by William McKenzie, an associate editor of the *Dallas Morning News* editorial page, states:

> Forget politics. Think religion.
>
> That motto must guide American foreign policy-makers. And not just so they can grasp Islam's influence on nations like Yemen and Afghanistan. They also must understand the tidal wave of Christianity sweeping across the Third World. The growth of churches - and the trends within them - are crucial to appreciating the currents at play in Africa, Asia and Latin America. And those forces will land on our shores thanks to globalization and immigration.
>
> Pennsylvania State University Professor Philip Jenkins argues persuasively in *The Next Christendom: The Rise of Global Christianity* that Christianity, more than Islam, will shape the world's rapidly growing parts. Consider the data:
>
> • By 2050, the world will have three Christians for every two Muslims.
>
> • By 2025, 67 percent of Christians will live in Africa, Latin America or Asia.

- By 2050, a third of Latinos and Asians will come from Christian backgrounds.

- China soon will have more Christians than all but six nations.

- More Presbyterians worship in Ghana than in Scotland. More Anglicans worship in Nigeria than in Britain.[124]

Professor Lamoreaux also believes Christianity will be the fastest-growing religion. "Islam is almost certainly not going to be the fastest-growing religion," he remarked, "despite what the pundits say. Christianity, in the southern hemisphere and in Asia, seems almost certain to outpace it."

Why are there more current and projected Christians than any other faith? Because Christianity is on God's side. Christianity is God's will for humanity.

Is it logical that God would allow Jesus Christ to have influence for the past 2,000 years, winning billions of followers, if Christ was a fraud? Christ has won more followers by far than any other religion. *Think about it.* Would God allow a bogus sham of a facade to go on over a longer span than any of the intervals between the Hebrew prophets documented in the Hebrew Bible? The unmatched historical and projected growth of Christianity is contradictory to the presupposition of duplicity being inflicted by God on humanity through a deceitful, false, fraudulent, and spurious impostor. Such bankrupt thinking lacks integrity.

My own personal conviction matches that of Huston Smith's. I believe Christ is the Truth; He is God's will for humanity. This is my conclusion based on my own quest, borne out of my own unique circumstances and experience, prayer, research, study, and analysis. I can't tell you what your conclusion should be. It is up to you to engage in prayer, research, study, and analysis. Don't take my word for it. Don't take anybody's word for it. Inevitably, the quest for Truth is an individual proposition between you and God. You must go it alone. A person who is seeking the Truth must have an open heart and open mind; an earnest seeker after the Truth must be inquisitive and diligent. A person must be able to remove the blinders, unplug the ears, soften the heart, and clear the mind. A person must have the guts to step beyond his or her comfort zone, no matter where that leads.

Jesus demands a verdict. Your eternal life depends on it. It is the most important investment decision you'll ever make, behooving you to carefully scrutinize your options. C. S. Lewis' insights in *Mere Christianity* on this topic are illuminating.

> When they speak of being "in Christ" or of Christ being "in them," this is not simply a way of saying that they are thinking about Christ or copying Him. They mean that Christ is actually operating through them; that the whole mass of Christians are the physical organism through which Christ acts - that we are His fingers and muscles, the cells of His body. And perhaps that explains one or two things. It explains why this new life is spread not only by purely mental acts like belief, but by bodily acts like baptism and Holy Communion. It is not merely the spreading of an idea; it is more like evolution - a biological or super-biological fact. . . .
>
> Here is another thing that used to puzzle me. Is it not frightfully unfair that this new life should be confined to people who have heard of Christ and been able to believe in Him? But the truth is God has not told us what His arrangements about the other people are. We do know that no man can be saved except through Christ; we do not know that only those who know Him can be saved through Him. But in the meantime, if you are worried about the people outside, the most unreasonable thing you can do is to remain outside yourself. Christians are Christ's body, the organism through which He works. Every addition to that body enables Him to do more. If you want to help those outside you must add your own little cell to the body of Christ who alone can help

> them. Cutting off a man's fingers would be an odd way of getting him to do more work.[125]

As C. S. Lewis stated we do not know what God's provision is for the nonbeliever. Only God knows what happens to a person's soul upon death. That's why we must refrain from telling nonbelievers that they are going to hell, as some Christians are prone to do, because we simply don't know what their eternal destiny is. But C. S. Lewis also makes the unambiguous assertion: "We do know that no man can be saved except through Christ." Christ makes this inescapable conclusion reality when He states:

> I am the way and the truth and the life. No one comes to the Father except through me. If you really knew me, you would know the Father as well. From now on, you do know him and have seen him.

John 14:6-7

And then Christ goes on to provide the definition of eternal life:

> Now this is eternal life: that they may know you, the only true God, and Jesus Christ, whom you have sent.

John 17:3

The problem with much of the world's population is that we tend to be stiff-necked and hard-hearted, steeped in rigidity and intractability. Our outlook is often characterized as an "don't confuse me with the facts my mind is already made up" attitude. Most people are inflexibly entrenched in the faith of their upbringing, precluding any meaningful inquiry into the tenets of other faiths. Several nations in the Middle East are notorious for having limited or effectively no freedom of religion, including Afghanistan, Saudi Arabia, and Iran. Thus, even if people are inclined to study other religions they are strongly discouraged not to out of fear of harsh reprisals. For example, Afghans under the Taliban were subject to capital punishment if they tried to convert anybody to another faith other than Islam. Foreigners who try to convert a Muslim to another faith face imprisonment and then deportation in some Islamic countries. It is a capital crime to preach Christianity in the kingdom of the Wahhabis in Saudi Arabia. There are some countries where people who leave the Islamic faith are executed. For example, in Iran and Saudi Arabia, the law stipulates the death penalty for Muslims who convert to Christianity. The Associated Press wrote about the former Taliban rulers in Afghanistan.

> Afghanistan's Taliban rulers closed the office of a U.S.-based relief organization and arrested 24 of its workers, including eight foreigners, accusing them of propagating Christianity, a Taliban-run news agency reported Sunday.
>
> Shelter Now International is a Christian relief agency based in Oshkosh, Wis., that has been providing food, tents and blankets to impoverished Afghans for several years. Its office was sealed Sunday after a raid by enforcement officers of the Taliban's ministry for promotion of virtue and prevention of vice, witnesses said. The officers reportedly seized a Bible, two computers, Christian literature translated into the local Dari language, as well as cassettes and musical instruments.
>
> The Taliban, a religious militia that espouses a harsh brand of fundamentalist Islam, has accused Shelter Now of spreading Christianity and trying to convert Muslims, said Bakhtar News Agency.
>
> In Taliban-ruled Afghanistan, it is a crime punishable by death to propagate any religion other than Islam or convert a Muslim to another religion.[126]

Tom Robberson wrote about the tensions between Christianity and Islam in Afghanistan.

> It's not a matter for negotiation, say the evangelical aid workers in one of the world's most hostile environments for Christian activists. Their mission to introduce Afghan Muslims to Jesus comes from the highest authority, and it cannot be questioned.

> For Afghan Muslims sought out by the evangelicals, there also can be no middle ground: Conversion is out of the question, and it is punishable by death. Their duty to defend Islam is divinely mandated, they say, and it cannot be questioned. . .

Robberson continues:

> "I was told by Muslims that if a Muslim leaves his faith, you have to kill him," said George Taubmann, director of Shelter Now Germany, a Christian aid group in Kabul. "What do you call that? Good? Evil? I don't want to comment because if I say the wrong thing, I could be killed tomorrow.
>
> Mr. Taubmann understands the risks better than most. In 2001, the Taliban arrested him and seven other foreigners working for Shelter Now and accused them of proselytizing. They spent more than three months in jail before gaining freedom during the U.S.-led invasion of Afghanistan in late 2001. . .
>
> Mr. Taubmann explained that although the Taliban no longer remains in power, Afghanistan remains a devoutly Muslim nation whose people tend not to tolerate challenges to their religious beliefs.
>
> At the same time, he asserted that Afghans are questioning more and more the role that Islam may have played in their own suffering during 25 years of war.

Robberson continues:

> "The law is very strict. Anyone who converts receives three days' time to reconsider. After that he must be killed," said Muhammad Maarouf, 26, imam of the Kabul University mosque.[127]

How does this harsh, inflexible edict compare to Christianity? Christians are not mandated to kill its adherents for converting to another religion. Muslims are. Which religion is conducive to free thinking? Which religion is non-coercive? Christians are free to choose whatever religion they want to practice. Muslims are not.

Columnist Terry Eastland, publisher of *The Weekly Standard*, discusses Saudi Arabia's environment.

> Saudi Arabia is a country with no freedom of press or speech or religion, no political parties, no trade unions, no movie theaters. (The list of prohibited things is very long.). . . .So it is that Crown Prince Abdullah [the de facto ruler] and the 4,000 princes of his ruling family want to stay in power. Just how strong is their commitment to maintaining their dictatorship? The day the crown prince went to Crawford [Texas where he met with President Bush], *The New York Times* carried a front-page story in which someone close to the Saudi regime anonymously declared it was prepared to do "what is ever necessary to survive." He explained:
>
> If that means we move to the right of [Osama] bin Laden, so be it. To the left of [Libya's Moammar] Gadhafi, so be it. Or fly to Baghdad and embrace Saddam [Hussein] like a brother, so be it."[128]

In March 2003, Saudi Arabia, the birthplace of Islam, announced that it would not allow churches to be built. Defense Minister Prince Sultan reported in Saudi newspapers that foreigners could worship freely in their homes but that permitting a church in the country "would affect Islam and all Muslims." In Egypt today, indigenous Christians cannot build or repair churches without government approval, resulting in an effective ban on church activity.

Bat Ye'or, an Egyptian-born Jewish historian who was exiled from her native country in 1957, is considered by the eminent British historian Sir Martin Gilbert to be the acknowledged expert on the plight of Christians and Jews in Islamic countries. William F. Katz, an associate professor in the School of Behavioral and Brain Sciences at the University of Texas at Dallas wrote about her recently in the *Dallas Morning News.*

> *Dhimmitude* is a term coined by Bat Ye'or. The word derives from "dhimmi," the Arabic term meaning "protected," and refers to the legal and social conditions of Jews and Christians living under Islamic rule.
>
> According to the Qur'an, Jews and Christians are "people of the book" and are to be respected by Muslim conquerors. But if they refuse conversion, they must accept legally defined second-class citizenship, as mandated by Islamic law. In Bat Ye'or's usage, dhimmitude is the Islamic system, formal and informal, of governing non-Muslim populations conquered by *jihad*, or Islamic holy war. It also describes the state of mind of conquered non-Muslim peoples and their relationship between Muslims and non-Muslims at the theological, social, political, and economic levels.
>
> According to Bat Ye'or, jidad followed by dhimmitude is the process through which Islamic conquerors crushed or otherwise oppressed - and still do - indigenous non-Muslim cultures, in part through measures that deny them equal status under the law.[129]

What if many Islamic countries, that virtually prohibit other religions in their societies, embraced freedom of religion? What are these Islamic countries afraid of? If they are secure in their own religion why are they so fearful of exposing their people to other religions? The dictators, sheiks, kings, and royal dynasties are afraid of losing their grip on power and losing Muslims to the Christian faith. I am convinced that if Muslims truly examined Christianity there would be far more people converting to Christianity than vice versa. I have seen evidence of this in prison. These countries are truly weak for if they were strong they would not be afraid to stack their religion up against others. True strength is allowing people the freedom to choose what religion they want to practice. Real weakness is what the Taliban exemplified in Afghanistan and Saudi Arabia and other Islamic countries exhibit today.

A dictatorship, whether secular or religious, controls its subjects like children, like dependents who cannot make important decisions and require that their life be mapped out for them. Most of the people are indoctrinated and instructed but never become teachers or leaders. In other words, people are strongly discouraged from thinking.

There are none so blind as those who will not see. A person must be able to think well, with integrity, including coping with the pain of paradoxical thinking. It is hard work to listen to God and to think well. The big three sins of pride, fear, and laziness are constant stumbling blocks. But remember, the offspring of pride and laziness are arrogance and ignorance. Charles Stanley states:

> Ignorance is one of Satan's most potent weapons. If you dismiss him as an imaginary symbol of evil or a harmless, horned man in red tights, you have just the picture he wants you to have. You are vulnerable when your guard is down.[130]

Don't commit intellectual bigotry. Don't succumb to intellectual bankruptcy. What is more important: to blindly adhere to ancestral traditions or to seek God's will directly? Strive for the Truth and don't quit until you are satisfied. And when you have established with confidence what the Truth is then become the very best you can be in your chosen faith. At that point you can embrace Mother Teresa's philosophy:

> There is only one God and He is God to all; therefore it is important that everyone is seen as equal before God. I've always said we should help a Hindu become a better Hindu, a Muslim become a better Muslim, a Catholic become a better Catholic.[131]

I believe if we would all take the time and effort to learn about each other's faiths we would have a better chance of achieving world peace. What if we could have a Kairos weekend with 21 Catholics and 21 Protestants from Northern Ireland? Or 21 North Koreans and 21 South Koreans? Or 21 Indians and 21 Pakistanis? Or 14 Jews, 14

Muslims, and 14 Christians? Or 21 Jews and 21 Palestinians? Or 7 Hindus, 7 Buddhists, 7 Muslims, 7 Jews, 7 Christians, and 7 atheists? Or a mixture of participants from warring tribes in various African nations? It happened in South Africa when Kairos was launched in December 1998 at the Pollsmoor Medium B prison in Cape Town with candidates speaking various tribal languages and English, comprised of various races, from proponents of equal opportunity to advocates of apartheid. Ike Griffin, former Executive Director of Kairos Prison Ministry and now Executive Director of Kairos Horizon, described the inaugural Kairos weekend in South Africa that he participated in along with five other Americans.

> When Kairos crossed the ocean to land on a new shore, the local culture brings unexpected and beautiful dimensions to the weekend. The program remains the same, but the experience is heightened by meeting unforeseen challenges. This was true in Australia, England, and again in the weekend just completed in South Africa. There, the Kairos weekend unfolded not just in English, but in Afrikaans and an unknown number (maybe 12) tribal languages. Because of that country's relative stability and rich natural resources, it has become the site of huge migrations of African people, many of whom, sadly, end up in prison. . . .
>
> The weekend began when elements of the team from Cape Town, Johannesburg, Paarl and the United States [six Americans were on the team] settled into the Salvation Army's Calder's Kings Hotel at Fish Hoek, a nearby suburb on Thursday morning. South African team members displayed amazing spiritual strength and joy, as well as beautiful racial mix. Their collective vulnerability displayed unusual strength, laying bare wounds born of this promising but troubled land. Public wounds stemming from the injustice of apartheid were acknowledged. Personal wounds received in grinding social struggle and ruptured relationships were shared for the mutual

healing of all participants, prisoner and free-world team members alike.

This was a team of destiny and purpose. They knew South Africa's prisons were ready for Kairos. This group will carry Kairos with strength throughout their country and to all of Africa. . . .

Mid-way through Friday morning, we realized that we had misjudged the language capacity of the residents. Many spoke tribal languages and Afrikaans, but only limited English. Without so much as missing a beat, team speakers accepted the challenge to deliver their talks in English and Afrikaans, delivering important points first in one language and then the other. Table family discussion took place in many different languages. Only the Americans, whose secondary languages were limited to Spanish and French, did not know what was being said. Charitable team members brought the Americans along with translations. . . .We Americans who went across to help launch Kairos came away awed by the courage of the people.

There is an epidemic raging over there and it is not just HIV, although that attracts most of the public attention. Imagine the emotional impact brought by the realization that twenty-five percent of the population will be lost in the next few years to HIV! This sobering fact touches and influences every facet of life, political, economic and spiritual. It is heavy on the hearts and minds of those who run government, plan for industry, work in ministry or reside in prison. There is no escaping the awful prospect of a shrinking population over the next several years and the need to repopulate a continent.

But the real epidemic in Africa is the fire of the Holy Spirit, purifying the channel of their healing, encouraging strength out of despair, affirming and

> holding individuals in the warmth of an embrace. The Holy Spirit is palpable in the energy, commitment and pace of the volunteers who shouldered the responsibility to launch Kairos. These are people who have looked the devil in the eye and laughed! They laugh and sing in English, in Afrikaans, and a dozen tribal languages. They dance joyously in a spirit of worship and celebration, pulsing to the heartbeat rhythm of ancient spiritual songs. They encourage one another to overcome the miserable hand they have been dealt. Their sure knowledge of God's presence brings light and hope to all they touch. This is a Kairos moment.[132]

When opposing gang members with bitter enmity reconcile during a Kairos weekend, when days prior to the weekend had the circumstances been right would have killed each other, it is truly God's miracle. When such a disparate group of people, prisoners and free-world team members alike, speaking different languages and with vastly different life experiences come together in such a fractured society as South Africa, it is evidence that anything is possible. We know that with God all things are possible. Kairos, which means God's Special Time in Greek, can happen anywhere, anytime and between any groups of people. Judge Kairos not by its roots but by its fruits for the roots of the tree are invisible but the fruits are well-known. Senior Chaplain Don Lacy of the Michael Unit states:

> Kairos is a God-send. It is something that is wonderful; something that is revolutionary that changes men's [and women's] lives. I think it has a permanent and lasting effect in the lives of people. I would encourage anyone that has any doubts to come and share in it. It is much like the Walk to Emmaus; it seems to have proven results. And so therefore I wholeheartedly endorse it, I support it, and I think God is in the middle of it. And so I would like to just ask if you want to join God and experience what

> God is doing that you get involved in the Kairos movement.

Will people have the courage to give Kairos a chance? What other options do we have for world peace?

On the 19th Kairos weekend at the Michael Unit, I delivered a 20-minute talk entitled "The Church"; an excerpt is presented below:

The Church is a Team. Gentlemen, we are involved in a spiritual war. Our real enemy is Satan. St. Paul puts it this way:

> Finally, be strong in the Lord and in his mighty power. Put on the full armor of God so that you can take your stand against the devil's schemes. For our struggle is not against flesh and blood, but against the rulers, against thc authorities, against the powers of this dark world and against the spiritual forces of evil in the heavenly realms. Therefore put on the full armor of God, so that when the day of evil comes, you may be able to stand your ground, and after you have done everything, to stand. Stand firm then, with the belt of truth buckled around your waist, with the breastplate of righteousness in place, and with your feet fitted with the readiness that comes from the gospel of peace. In addition to all this, take up the shield of faith, with which you can extinguish all the flaming arrows of the evil one. Take the helmet of salvation and the sword of the Spirit, which is the word of God. And pray in the Spirit on all occasions with all kinds of prayers and requests. With this in mind, be alert and always keep on praying for all the saints.

Ephesians 6:10-18

Where there is love, peace, and unity there is God. Where there is hatred, strife, and separation there is Satan. Satan wants division, not unity. Satan wants famines, diseases, and wars. Satan wants families to divorce each other; he wants parents to abuse their children physically, sexually and/or emotionally or simply abandon their children (which is a form of abuse in itself); he wants blacks to hate whites and Hispanics to hate blacks. He wants Muslims to hate Christians and Jews, and Jews to hate Arabs. He wants Hindus to hate Muslims and vice versa. But that is not what God wants; God wants love, peace, and unity. I'm sick of Satan; I'm sick of all the hatred on our planet; I'm sick of disease, divorce, broken homes, racism, famine, and war. Satan wants us to keep fighting each other. In order to beat Satan we have to pull together, become one team, love one another.

In the military you want the strongest leaders. We are involved in a war that dwarfs World War II. Indeed all the wars since time immemorial have been caused by Satan. When you are going up against the most powerful evil force in the universe, you want the strongest leader (which is Jesus Christ in my view) at the head of your army. Since the fall of Man, Satan has been battling the world, causing diseases, famines, wars.

In order to defeat Satan you must understand him better than he understands you. General H. Norman Schwarzkopf puts it this way in his book *It Doesn't Take a Hero*:

> I *hated* what Vietnam was doing to the United States and I *hated* what it was doing to the Army. It was a nightmare that the American public had withdrawn its support: our troops in World War I and World War II had *never* had to doubt for one minute that the people on the home front were fully behind them. We in the military hadn't chosen the enemy or written the orders - our elected leaders had. Nevertheless, we were taking much of the blame. We soldiers, sailors, airmen, and Marines were literally the sons and daughters of America, and to lose public support was akin to being rejected by our own parents.
>
> Bitterly, I recalled an incident that had taken place during my first tour in 1965. My Vietnamese airborne unit had overrun a Vietcong headquarters, and among the documents we'd captured had been a directive from Ho Chi Minh. It said in effect: "I know you're facing more and more Americans right now, but don't worry.

> We're going to win the war against America the same way we won the war against the French: not on the battlefield, but in the enemy's homeland. All you have to do is hang on. The American people are not tough enough to see this war through and we are. We have fought for twenty years; we can fight another twenty years; before then, they will give up and not support their troops anymore, and we will claim victory."
>
> I'd brought it back to the Manor BOQ and we'd talked about it as a joke. "Look at this crap! Look at the propaganda these people are printing!" But Uncle Ho had known what he was talking about - he was an astute student of the western mind and understood his enemy better than we understood ourselves.[133]

An army is a team and so is a church, with every player having an important role. Take a look at this Kairos team if you want a good example of a church. We have Catholics, Baptists, Lutherans, Presbyterians, Episcopalians, Methodists, Bible Church and many different non-denominational members. We even have an Anglican from Australia. We have blacks, whites, and Hispanics. Each person on this team plays a vital role. We have 20 people 18 miles away preparing food and praying for us. We have two runners who spend all day delivering meals to us and returning with dirty dishes. We have a team of 27 stewards, brothers in white, who are here serving you. Then we have the outside people baking the cookies, preparing the posters and placemats, praying for us, and sending money to sponsor you guys this weekend. There is even a small church in Oregon that sent me six boxes of cookies and posters and placemats. We've received posters from around the world [England, Australia, South Africa, Canada, etc.] that you see on the gym walls. Every person in Kairos has a job to do and they do it. Gentlemen, if we are to defeat Satan we must love one another and become one team. A team divided will not stand [end of Kairos Church talk].

In order to achieve world peace we must quit fighting each other, unite in love and peace, and focus on the real enemy. We must strive to understand each other's religions and cultures. By loving one another we can beat Satan. The raison d'etre of Kairos is sharing the love of Christ. God's love is more powerful than Satan's hate. Mother Teresa sums it up well:

> We are all capable of good and evil. We are not born bad: everybody has something good inside. Some hide it, some neglect it, but it is there. God created us to love and to be loved, so it is our test from God to choose one path or the other. Any negligence in loving can lead someone to say Yes to evil, and when that happens we have no idea how far it can spread. That's the sad part. If someone chooses evil, then an obstacle is set up between that person and God, and the burdened person cannot see God clearly at all. That's why we have to avoid any kind of temptation that will destroy us. We gain strength to overcome this from prayer, because if we are close to God we spread joy and love to everybody around us.
>
> If evil takes possession of someone, that person, in turn, may spread evil to everybody around him. If we are in contact with such people we must try and help them and show them that God cares for them. Pray hard to help bring prayer back to them so that they may once more see God in themselves and then see Him in others. It is this which will help the person who is bad because everybody - it doesn't matter who - has been created by the same loving hand. Christ's love is always stronger than the evil in the world, so we need to love and to be loved: it's as simple as that. This shouldn't be such a struggle to achieve.
>
> Works of love are always works of peace. Whenever you share love with others, you'll notice the peace that comes to you and to them. When there is peace, there is God - that is how God touches our lives and shows His love for us by pouring peace and joy into our hearts.

Lead me from death to life
From falsehood to truth.
Lead me from despair to hope,
From fear to truth.
Lead me from hate to love,
From war to peace.
Let peace fill our hearts,
Our world our universe
Peace peace peace.[134]

Mother Teresa

Grace and peace to you in your quest for the Truth.

-ADDENDA

Appendix A

Kairos Prison Ministry

Dr. Peter P. Legins, Professor Emeritus, University of Maryland, Institute of Criminal Justice and Criminology, is considered by most people to be the dean of American criminologists. In a meeting with a group of men who were the founders of Kairos, he remarked: "I have known for years, as have most of the leading criminologists in this country, that the greatest hope for an inmate to avoid the revolving doors of our prisons is to undergo a religious conversion experience during his incarceration." Many leading authorities in academia and in the correctional system call Kairos the most effective program currently offered for altering fundamental attitudes of the imprisoned.

What if you were locked up in a maximum-security prison? How would God transform your life? How would you have access to one of the various 3-day short courses in Christianity offered in the free world since you couldn't get a weekend pass? In the mid-1970s a group of men who had been profoundly moved by God during their own 3-day short course in Christianity were inspired to apply the same type of weekend to prisoners, with some modifications for the realities of a prison environment. These men had attended a *Cursillo* weekend. Other 3-day short courses in Christianity include *The Walk to Emmaus*, *Tres Dias* and *Via de Cristo.* Kairos Prison Ministry is patterned after these weekends. Indeed, to serve on a Kairos inside or outside team, one has to have attended one of these 3-day short courses in Christianity. The result of this effort was Kairos, a world-wide, ecumenical, volunteer ministry designed to share the love of Christ with prisoners in medium- and maximum-security penitentiaries.

There are two Greek words for time: *chronos* and *kairos*. *Chronos* means linear time such as hours, days, weeks, etc. The words "chronograph" and "chronology" are derivatives of this meaning of time. New Testament Greek scholars tell us that *kairos* means a unique or special time such as "I had the time of my life!"

Thus, Kairos is described by the official Kairos Prison Ministry manual as "God's Special Time."

Kairos Prison Ministry began in February 1976 at the maximum-security Union Correctional Institution in Raiford, Florida, home of Florida's death row. Kairos weekends (Thursday afternoon through early Sunday evening) are held twice a year at every institution that has a contract with Kairos. It takes approximately 100-120 volunteers to launch Kairos in a new unit. Since 1976, Kairos has grown to over 240 prisons in 28 states and four other countries (Great Britain, Australia, South Africa, and Canada). A ministry doesn't grow this rapidly on good looks and a secret recipe. As Michael Unit Chaplain Don Lacy put it: "God is in the middle of Kairos Prison Ministry." There are now over 24,000 international volunteers but only five paid staff who work at the headquarters in Winter Park, Florida. Kairos is a lean, mean, fighting machine.

Kairos is supported by four groups of volunteers: the inside team (free-world brothers in a men's unit and free-world sisters in a women's unit), stewards (prisoners who have participated in a previous Kairos weekend as a pilgrim who now serve the new pilgrims), the outside team, and people in homes and churches around the state and world who supply the prayers and unconditional love as evidenced by homemade cookies, financial contributions, handwritten letters, posters, and placemats. Kairos is a weekend of grace bombardment designed to melt the hardened hearts of the incarcerated.

As previously discussed, Kairos is an interdenominational Christian ministry. I personally have served on teams with Methodists, Catholics, Baptists, Assembly of God members, Christian Church (Disciples of Christ), Lutherans, Presbyterians, Episcopalians, United Church of Christ members, Church of Christ members, and numerous people from non-denominational churches. Kairos is structured to be held in state and federal men's and women's penitentiaries in the United States with modifications for other nations and languages. The ministry is performed, in conjunction with the chaplains and wardens of the correctional facilities, by teams of laity and clergy who are chosen, equipped, and certified by area governing bodies of Kairos and approved by correctional facilities as citizen volunteers.

The Kairos weekend is closely monitored for quality control. Adherence to the highly structured Kairos manual is emphasized in training. The prison administration is clearly informed in advance about the logistics of the Kairos weekend.

The purpose of Kairos is to engender strong ongoing Christian communities among the residents of correctional facilities. This is done through weekly prayer-share accountability groups, monthly reunions, and semi-annual two-day retreats. Also, the Christmas party is a time of renewal and re-commitment for many of the residents.

Unlike some prison ministries, Kairos does not rely on celebrities (athletes, coaches, country western and pop singers, movie stars, etc.) and does not target directly the entire eligible population in each unit. Some prison ministries are structured using a shotgun approach with everyone who is eligible invited to attend. Kairos uses a targeted approach in which only 42 inmates (14 blacks, 14 Hispanics, and 14 whites in Texas) are invited to attend twice a year (assuming a Kairos weekend does not get canceled due to a lockdown). It is not uncommon for some inmates to have to wait several years to participate in a Kairos weekend.

The Kairos policy is to invite the leaders in the prison, both positive and negative (i.e., gang leaders involved in gambling, drugs, extortion, etc.). The philosophy is if you can reach these leaders, they in turn will have a better probability of impacting the rest of the population than anyone else, including the prison chaplain. So very often Kairos will get some of the toughest, meanest, and roughest prisoners with convictions for the most heinous crimes. Kairos volunteers are trained not to ask why the person is in prison and how much time they have left to serve. We accept them where they are just like God accepts all of us where we are. But the men who reside in a maximum-security facility, especially the leaders, often have committed all of the hall-of-shame crimes imaginable, including capital murder, rape, child molestation, robbery, burglary, car theft, drug dealing, etc. Many are multiple-time offenders. It is important not to forget the victims of these crimes. People have suffered great loss at the hands of many of these inmates.

In sum, through a structured program, the residents of correctional facilities are offered the opportunity to experience a spiritual renewal and to accept God's call to a life of Christian witness and service to one another during their duration in the unit and beyond. The Kairos strategy is to select and invite leaders from the key environments of the institution, leaders who have the greatest potential to impact others with the message of Christ's love.

Kairos has been called one of the finest examples of the early church in existence today. For the first few centuries of Christian existence, the church adhered to Christ's commands to feed the hungry, clothe the naked, look after the sick, host strangers, and visit those in prison [Matthew 25:35-36]. Today's middle-class churches typically have members from the same ethnic group and social class, where the down-and-out are rarely seen or welcomed. The Kairos church, on the other hand, embodies Christ's example of being inclusive and compassionate, embracing a wide diversity of people.

Appendix B

Additional Kairos Talks

The Kairos talks, not discussed in Chapter 1, are summarized below:

The first talk is delivered by a lay person on Friday morning entitled *Choices.* The objective of this talk is to help the participants begin to know themselves as unique human beings; to begin to see themselves as not only products of physical constraints but of past free-will choices. The goal of the talk is to get the participants to quit dwelling on themselves as being victims of circumstances but to focus on their own responsibility in influencing the direction of their lives. The fundamental objective of this talk is to get the participants to think about all choices having consequences; that their future is determined by their present choices.

The second talk Friday morning is entitled *You Are Not Alone* and is delivered by a pastor. The purpose of this talk is to let the participants know that God created us to live in community and that God is with us. The talk is designed to help the participants understand that we need not only the presence of God, which is promised to us in the Bible, but that we need the help of others. A powerful aspect of this talk is illustrating to the participants that people in the free world love them and are praying for them. Toward the conclusion of the talk, the speaker introduces a number of posters, banners or letters that have been received from various groups around the world (men's and women's prisons, Sunday School classes, Emmaus/ Cursillo/Tres Dias/Via de Cristo communities, etc.) expressing their love for the participants. These posters, banners, and letters are taped periodically around the gym walls throughout the weekend, gradually transforming a gray, drab, non-descript concrete-block gym into a colorful collage of compassion. You see men gazing intently at these posters and banners during breaks; you can see the wheels turning as they ask themselves, "Who are these people in the free world who would take the time to draw a colorful poster with a message of God's love for men like us?" The men in prison view most people in the free world as hating them, thinking of them as scumbags. So the posters, banners, and letters that eventually dominate the gym walls are a powerful piece of tangible love in breaking down the hardened hearts of the imprisoned.

The third talk Friday morning is entitled *Friendship with God* and is delivered by either clergy or a lay person. Many men in prison come from broken homes and have either been abused or abandoned by their fathers. A big challenge of a Kairos weekend is to convince the men that our Heavenly Father is a loving Father and that He desires friendship with us. As the Kairos training manual puts it, the purpose of the *Friendship with God* talk is "to convey to residents that God is not a chain-gang boss sitting behind a big control panel on the edge of heaven waiting to catch us in some infraction of the rules." This talk describes God's insatiable desire to be our friend no matter how many times we have abandoned that friendship. The men are told how God has pursued us through history and continues to pursue us. The participants are told how we are all God's children, loved and created by God.

The last talk on Friday, following *The Church* talk, is entitled *Opening The Door* and is delivered by a lay person in mid-afternoon. The objective of this talk is to alter the participants' false or negative perceptions about the Christian life. The goal is to replace those false or negative images with positive impressions in which they can envision having a viable and precious friendship with God. The Kairos training manual describes the ideal person selected to deliver this talk:

> The person chosen to give this talk should be a person who has a close personal relationship with God, a person who has been wounded and whom Jesus, our Wounded Healer, has healed, a person out of whom the Lord has made a "new creature." This speaker could be an ex-offender and must be one whose witness says, "If the Lord can allow me to establish this kind of relationship with Him, then it is available to anyone, no matter where they have been, where they are now or what they've done." Remember, most of the residents have not come from a loving community, nor are they returning to one which will welcome them with rejoicing over their new relationship with God.

Our first talk on Saturday morning is entitled *Discovery*, usually given by a lay person. The objective of this talk is to convey to the participants that the Christian life is an ongoing journey of discovery, a continuous path of learning and spiritual growth as we deepen our friendship with Jesus Christ. The talk illustrates the joy and excitement of uncovering new treasures and insights into the Person of Jesus and within ourselves as we grow into His likeness. The talk also shares with the participants some practical applications in progressing along the journey to Jesus such as study, prayer, and listening.

The second talk Saturday morning is entitled *Action*, usually delivered by a lay person. This talk lets the residents know that the only action which is for God is love. Words are not enough; deeds are required to demonstrate God's love for others. In the action of love, we not only share God's love with others but discover the presence of God in our lives affirmed and reinvigorated.

The last talk on Saturday afternoon is entitled *A Christian*, usually delivered by a lay person. The 1996 Kairos manual eloquently describes the objective of this talk.

> To convey to the residents that to be a Christian is to be a follower of Jesus. That Jesus makes it abundantly clear that being a follower of His is difficult and sometimes costly but also very rewarding. That both the costs and the rewards of being a Christian are fully contained in one word: LOVE.
>
> That to follow Jesus is an unrelenting struggle with ourselves and others and God to try to bring about truly loving relationships or to empty ourselves enough that the love of Jesus fills us and flows through us. That doing this requires some very specific intention, discipline, realism, courage, commitment, compassion, generosity, willingness to forgive others, willingness to forgive self, humility, trust, faith, and hope. All of these have their source in love and their expression is love.
>
> That to accept the challenge to travel this road is the most daring adventure life has to offer. That for those brave enough to trust God to care for them and protect them, the journey begins here and now.

ENDNOTES

[1] Inmate names have been changed to ensure confidentiality. Any inmate names herein that happen to match those in the prison system are purely coincidental.

[2] Lanny Wolfe. Copyright 1977, Lanny Wolfe Music. CCLI# 602218 [presented on page 49A of the Kairos Songbook, 1997].

[3] Lucinda Vardey, *Mother Teresa - A Simple Path* (New York, NY: Ballantine Books, a division of Random House, Inc., 1995), 85.

[4] William James, *The Varieties of Religious Experience* (New York, NY: Penguin Books, 1987), 267.

[5] George Sheehan, M.D., *Running & Being: The Total Experience* (New York, NY: Simon & Schuster, Inc., 1978), 253.

[6] Richard Gillard, *The Servant Song* (Admin. by Integrity Music, Inc., copyright 1977 Scripture in Song), CCLI# 602218 [presented on page 57A of the Kairos Songbook, 1997].

[7] M. Scott Peck, M.D., *The Road Less Traveled and Beyond: Spiritual Growth in an Age of Anxiety* (New York, NY: Simon & Schuster, Inc., 1997), 49-52.

[8] George A. Sheehan, M.D., *Running & Being: The Total Experience* (New York, NY: Simon & Schuster, Inc., 1978), 247-248.

[9] Captain Scott O'Grady with Jeff Coplon, *Return with Honor* (New York, NY: Doubleday, 1995), 202.

[10] C. S. Lewis, *The Problem of Pain* (New York, NY: Simon & Schuster Inc., 1996), 85-87.

[11] Charles Stanley, *How to Handle Adversity* (Nashville, TN: Thomas Nelson Publishers, 1989), 83-84.

[12] Philip Yancey, *The Jesus I Never Knew* (Grand Rapids, MI: Zondervan Publishing House, 1995), 105.

[13] Ibid., 69.

[14] William James, *The Varieties of Religious Experience* (New York, NY: Penguin Books, 1987), 47-48.

[15] Tony Campolo, *The Kingdom of God is a Party* (Dallas, TX: Word Publishing, 1990), 5.

[16] Ibid., 6-9.

[17] Ibid., 45-46

[18] George Sheehan, M.D., *Running and Being: The Total Experience* (New York, NY: Simon & Schuster, 1978), 246.

[19] Lee Strobel, *The Case for Christ* (Grand Rapids, MI: Zondervan Publishing House, 1998), 176.

[20] Ibid., 177.
[21] Ibid., 179.
[22] Ibid., 179-180.
[23] Ibid., 182.
[24] Ibid., 185-186.
[25] M. Scott Peck, M.D., *The Road Less Traveled and Beyond* (New York, NY: Simon & Schuster, Inc., 1998), 24.
[26] Ibid., 24-25.
[27] Ibid., 27-28.
[28] Peter W. Stoner, M.S. and Robert C. Newman, S.T.M., Ph.D., *Science Speaks* (Chicago, IL: Moody Press, 1976), 4.
[29] Josh McDowell, *A Ready Defense*, as compiled by Bill Wilson (Nashville: TN, Thomas Nelson, Inc., 1993), 210-212.
[30] Ibid., 101-102.
[31] Ibid., 102.
[32] Ibid., 102-103.
[33] Ibid., 103-104.
[34] Ibid., 104.
[35] Ibid., 104-105.
[36] Ibid., 105.
[37] Ibid., 106-107.
[38] Ibid., 112.
[39] Ibid., 182-183.
[40] Ibid., 183.
[41] Harold W. Hoehner, *Chronological Aspects of the Life of Christ* (Grand Rapids, MI: Zondervan Publishing House, 1977), 117-119.
[42] Ibid., 119-121.
[43] Ibid., 126-128.
[44] Joseph D. Wilson, *Did Daniel Write Daniel?* (New York, NY: Charles C. Cook, n.d.), 141-142.
[45] Ibid., 135-137.
[46] Ibid., 138.
[47] Ibid., 113-114.
[48] Ibid., 185.
[49] J. Barton Payne, *Encyclopedia of Biblical Prophecy* (Grand Rapids, MI: Baker Books, 1973), 256-257.
[50] John F. Walvoord, *The Prophecy Knowledge Handbook* (Wheaton, IL: Victor Books, 1990), 84.
[51] Louis Berkhof, *Principles of Biblical Interpretation* (Grand Rapids, MI: Baker, 1950), 134.
[52] J. R. Sampey, *Psalms*, ISBE, IV: 2493.

[53] Milton S. Terry, *Biblical Hermeneutics* (New York, NY: Phillips and Hunt, 1883), 399-400.
[54] Ibid., 266.
[55] Ibid., 2492.
[56] Ibid., 198.
[57] Ibid., 198-199.
[58] Philip Yancey, *The Bible Jesus Read* (Grand Rapids, MI: Zondervan, 1999), 213.
[59] Philip Yancey, *The Jesus I Never Knew* (Grand Rapids, MI: Zondervan Publishing House, 1995), 61.
[60] Robert Goralski, *World War II Almanac 1931-1945* (New York, NY: Bonanza Books, 1984), 425.
[61] *Disciple: Into the Word - Into the World Study Manual* (Genesis-Exodus Luke-Acts), (Nashville, TN: Cokesbury, 1991), 74.
[62] Ibid., 87.
[63] Philip Yancey, *The Bible Jesus Read* (Grand Rapids, MI: Zondervan, 1999), 26.
[64] Richard Brealey and Stewart Myers, *Principles of Corporate Finance*, 2nd edition (New York, NY: McGraw Hill Book Company, 1984), 87.
[65] Josh McDowell and Bill Wilson, *A Ready Defense* (Nashville, TN: Thomas Nelson Publishers, 1993), 90.
[66] Lee Strobel, *The Case for Christ* (Grand Rapids, MI: Zondervan Publishing House, 1998), 248-249.
[67] Ibid., 239.
[68] *Pre-Kairos and the Kairos Weekend Manual* (Winter Park, FL: Kairos, Inc., 1998), 246.
[69] Jon Meacham, "From Jesus to Christ", *Newsweek* (New York, NY: Newsweek, Inc., March 28, 2005), 45.
[70] Josh McDowell, *A Ready Defense* (Nashville, TN: Thomas Nelson Publishers, 1993), 230-231.
[71] Philip Yancey, *The Jesus I Never Knew* (Grand Rapids, MI: Zondervan Publishing House, 1995), 212-213.
[72] Ibid., 45.
[73] Ibid., 236.
[74] Ibid., 238.
[75] Ibid., 245.
[76] Kenneth Wyatt, *The Apostles* (Tulia, TX: Y-8 Publishing Company, 1989).
[77] Ibid., 31.
[78] Ibid., 242.

[79] Philip Yancey, *The Jesus I Never Knew* (Grand Rapids, MI: Zondervan Publishing House, 1995), 55.

[80] C. S. Lewis, *Mere Christianity* (New York, NY: Simon & Schuster, Inc., 1996), 56-57.

[81] Philip Schaff, *The Person of Christ* (New York, NY: American Tract Society, 1913), 94-95.

[82] Ibid., 243-244.

[83] Ibid., 146.

[84] Ibid., 146-147.

[85] Ibid., 148.

[86] C. S. Lewis, *Miracles* (New York, NY: Simon & Schuster, Inc., 1996), 144.

[87] M. Scott Peck, M.D., *The Road Less Traveled and Beyond* (New York, NY: Simon & Schuster, Inc., 1998), 59-60.

[88] Lloyd John Ogilvie, *Longing to Be Free* (Eugene, OR: Harvest House Publishers, 1984),153-156, 161.

[89] Ibid., 157-158.

[90] William James, *The Varieties of Religious Experience* (New York, NY: Penguin Books, 1987), 319.

[91] C. S. Lewis, *The Problem of Pain* (New York, NY: Simon & Schuster, Inc., 1996), 87.

[92] Ibid., 125.

[93] Ibid., 253.

[94] Ibid., 250-252.

[95] Ibid., 194-195.

[96] Philip Schaff, *The Person of Christ* (New York, NY: American Tract Society, 1913).

[97] Kenneth Scott Latourette, *A History of Christianity* (New York, NY: Harper & Row, 1953), 44.

[98] H. G. Wells: Quoted from *The Greatest Men in History* in Mark Link, S. J., *He is the Still Point of the Turning World* (Chicago, IL: Argus Communications, 1971), 111.

[99] Ibid., 17.

[100]Ibid., 259-260.

[101]Ibid., 260.

[102]M. Scott Peck, M.D., *The Road Less Traveled and Beyond* (New York, NY: Simon & Schuster, 1997), 59.

[103]William James, *The Varieties of Religious Experience* (New York, NY: Penguin Books, 1902), 371.

[104]Ibid., 376.

[105]Ibid., 377.

[106]M. Scott Peck, M.D., *The Road Less Traveled and Beyond* (New York, NY: Simon & Schuster, Inc., 1998), 60.

[107]*Dallas Morning News*, December 28, 2002.

[108]*Men's Devotional Bibl*e (NIV), (Grand Rapids, MI: Zondervan Publishing House, 1993), 1271.

[109]*Dallas Morning News*, September 14, 2002.

[110]*Dallas Morning News*, July 21, 2004.

[111]*The Qur'an*, 12th edition (Elmhurst, NY: Tahrike Tarsile Qur'an, Inc., 2001).

[112]Josh McDowell, *A Ready Defense* (Nashville, TN: Thomas Nelson Publishers, 1993), 310.

[113]Lee Strobel, *The Case for Christ* (Grand Rapids, MI: Zondervan Publishing House, 1998), 249.

[114]Ibid., 311.

[115]Rebecca Laird, *Leslie Weatherhead's The Will of God - A Workbook* (Nashville, TN: Abingdon Press, 1995), 12-13.

[116]Gary Thompson, *Adult Bible Studies Teacher* (Nashville, TN: Cokesbury, the United Methodist Publishing House, Winter 2004-05, Vol. 13, No. 2), 59.

[117]Compiled by Lucinda Vardey, *Mother Teresa: A Simple Path* (New York: NY, Ballantine Books, 1995), 113-114.

[118]Ibid., 185.

[119]Ibid., 43.

[120]Charles Stanley, *Enter His Gates* (Nashville, TN: Thomas Nelson Publishers, 1998), 280.

[121]Philip Yancey, *What's So Amazing About Grace?* (Grand Rapids, MI: Zondervan Publishing House, 1997), 45.

[122]Philip Yancey, *The Jesus I Never Knew* (Grand Rapids, MI: Zondervan Publishing House, 1995), 131-132.

[123]Lloyd John Ogilvie, *Falling Into Greatness* (Nashville, TN: Thomas Nelson Publishers, 1984), 85.

[124]*Dallas Morning News*, January 7, 2003.

[125]Ibid., 65.

[126]*Dallas Morning News*, August 6, 2001.

[127]*Dallas Morning News*, December 12, 2004.

[128]*Dallas Morning News*, April 29, 2002.

[129]*Dallas Morning News,* June 19, 2005.

[130]Charles Stanley, *Enter His Gates* (Nashville, TN: Thomas Nelson Publishers, 1998), 140.

[131]Compiled by Lucinda Vardey, *Mother Teresa - A Simple Path* (New York, NY: Ballantine Books, 1995), 31.

[132]Ike Griffin, *God's Special Time* (Kairos Prison Ministry newsletter; Vol. 23, No. 1, January 1999), 1-2.

[133]General H. Norman Schwarzkopf, *It Doesn't Take a Hero* (New York, NY: Bantam Books, 1992), 181-182.

[134]Compiled by Lucinda Vardey, *Mother Teresa: A Simple Path* (New York, NY: Ballantine Books, 1995), 51-52, 171.

ABOUT THE AUTHOR

Stephen C. Kincheloe is a lay minister in Kairos Prison Ministry. He is a valuation consultant in Dallas, Texas where he resides with his wife, Susan Hagemeier, and children, Oscar and Hope. He holds a B.S. degree in business administration from Oregon State University, an MBA degree in corporate finance from the Anderson School at UCLA, the CFA® (Chartered Financial Analyst) designation from the CFA Institute, and the MAI® designation from the Appraisal Institute. He has published academic articles in the *Appraisal Journal.*

Printed in the United States
39700LVS00003B/61